How to Paint it!

100 SIMPLE WATERCOLOR PAINTINGS IN SIX STEPS OR LESS

Sharone Stevens

DAVID & CHARLES
—PUBLISHING—

www.davidandcharles.com

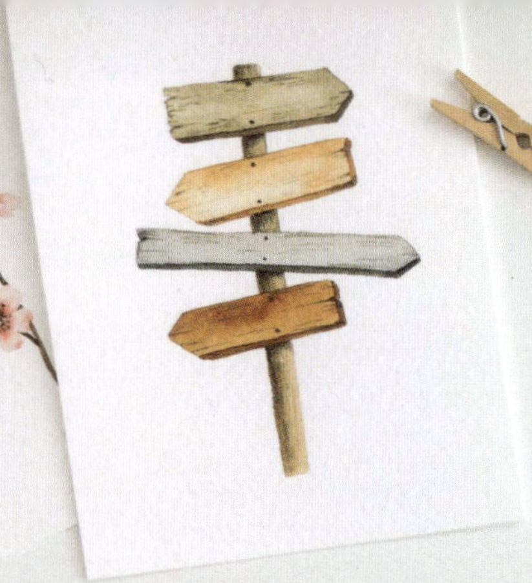

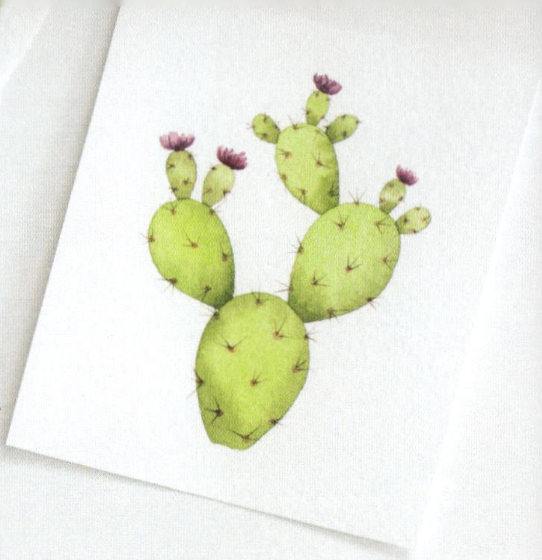

Contents

Introduction..4

Materials..6
Paper...6
Brushes...6
Paint...7
Other Supplies..7

Techniques..8
Sketching...8
Mixing Colors...8
Values..8
Methods of Applying Paint...9

Seasonal...12
Spring: Birdhouse..14
Spring: Blossom..15
Spring: Ladybird...16
Spring: Umbrella...17
Summer: Flip-Flops...18
Summer: Beach Bag..19
Summer: Sandcastle...20
Summer: Ice Cream..21
Autumn: Pumpkin..22
Autumn: Acorn..23
Autumn: Leaf...24
Autumn: Mushroom...25
Winter: Snowman..26
Winter: Robin..27
Winter: Mittens..28
Winter: Ice Skates...29

Celebrations...30
Candles..32
Graduation Cap...33
Love Letter..34
Wedding Cake...35
New Home...36
Bunting..37
Teddy Bear...38
Balloons...39
Easter Tree..40
Easter Bunny...41
Haunted House..42
Broomstick...43
Cauldron...44
Witch's Hat..45
Christmas Tree...46
Presents...47
Candy Cane...48
Christmas Pudding..49

Food & Drink...50
Coffee...52
Smoothie...53
Cocktail...54
Jar of Honey...55
Beetroot...56
Peapod...57
Pomegranate..58
Pear...59
Egg..60
Bread..61
Cookie...62
Donut..63

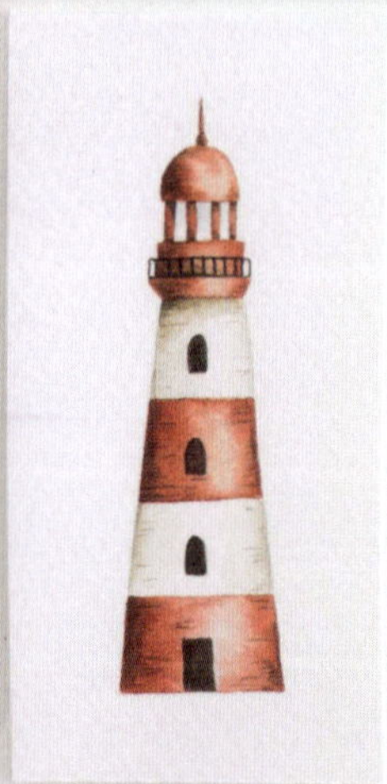

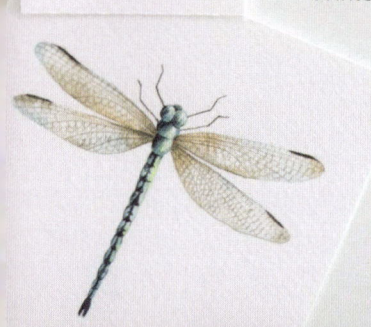

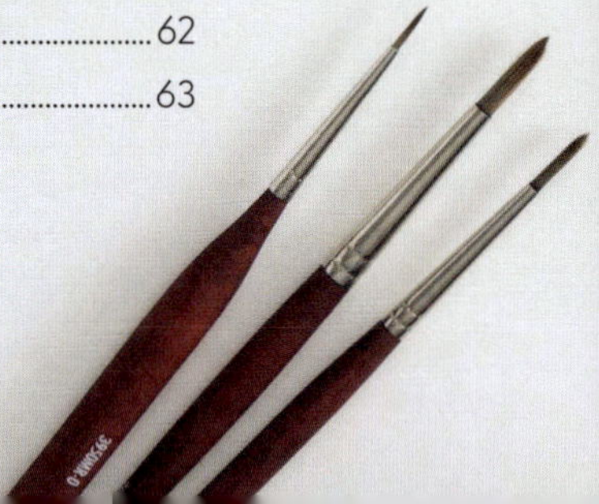

Botanical...................................64

Gingko...................................66

Monstera...................................67

Hanging Plant...................................68

Snake Plant...................................69

Eucalyptus...................................70

Tree...................................71

Cactus...................................72

Palm Tree...................................73

Forget-Me-Nots...................................74

Aster...................................75

Anemone...................................76

Lily...................................77

Berry Wreath...................................78

Floral Letter...................................79

Animals...................................80

Panda...................................82

Elephant...................................83

Deer...................................84

Chicken...................................85

Budgerigar...................................86

Owl...................................87

Dragonfly...................................88

Moth...................................89

Beetle...................................90

Snail...................................91

Crab...................................92

Seahorse...................................93

Whale...................................94

Butterfly Fish...................................95

Home & Garden...................................96

Books...................................98

Lamp...................................99

Armchair...................................100

Rug...................................101

Oven Mitt...................................102

Whisk...................................103

Thread...................................104

Buttons...................................105

Yarn...................................106

Paint Set...................................107

Garden Tools...................................108

Watering Can...................................109

Fence...................................110

Rain Boots...................................111

Around the World...................................112

Suitcase...................................114

Globe...................................115

Camera...................................116

Hot-Air Balloon...................................117

Beach Hut...................................118

Lighthouse...................................119

Windmill...................................120

Boat...................................121

Signpost...................................122

Tipi...................................123

Castle Door...................................124

Scooter...................................125

Final Words...................................126

About the Author...................................127

Acknowledgments...................................127

Introduction

I am so excited to share my second watercolor book, *How to Paint It!*, with you. If you have my first book, *Watercolor for the Soul*, or have watched any of my online classes, you will know how much I love painting with watercolor, and that I love to inspire and encourage others to build their own regular practice that is both joyful and relaxing.

I believe that painting with watercolor is a wonderful way to find peace in the rush of everyday life, and it is one of my favorite ways to relax and unwind. The way the paint moves on the paper, the array of new colors that you can mix and the ability to gradually build up detail all contribute to its unique appeal. Painting also encourages you to open your eyes more to the abundance of beauty and wonder that is all around us. Doing something as simple as taking a wander around my home, opening the fridge or going for a walk can fill me with inspiration.

So often, I hear my students say that they struggle to find ideas for what to paint and how to approach new subjects. I hope this book will show you that there is inspiration in so many areas of our lives and that it gives you the confidence to start breaking subjects down into simple, achievable steps. From a ball of yarn to a stack of books, a fallen leaf or a cup of coffee, there can often be exciting opportunities for painting in surprising places. Once you begin to notice different patterns and details, such as the markings on a leaf or the way the bubbles form on your coffee, you can start to think about how to recreate each of those elements with watercolor – which can be very exciting and quite addictive!

In this book, you will find 100 projects inspired by the world around us. I have collated these into seven categories, so you can choose what you are in the mood to paint. My goal is to provide you with inspiration for painting throughout the year, through each season and celebration, and to open your eyes to subjects that can be made even more interesting with watercolor. From simple objects around the home such as an oven mitt or spool of thread, to beautiful and unique creatures such as a seahorse or tiger moth – watercolor has the ability to transform anything into something even more captivating on paper.

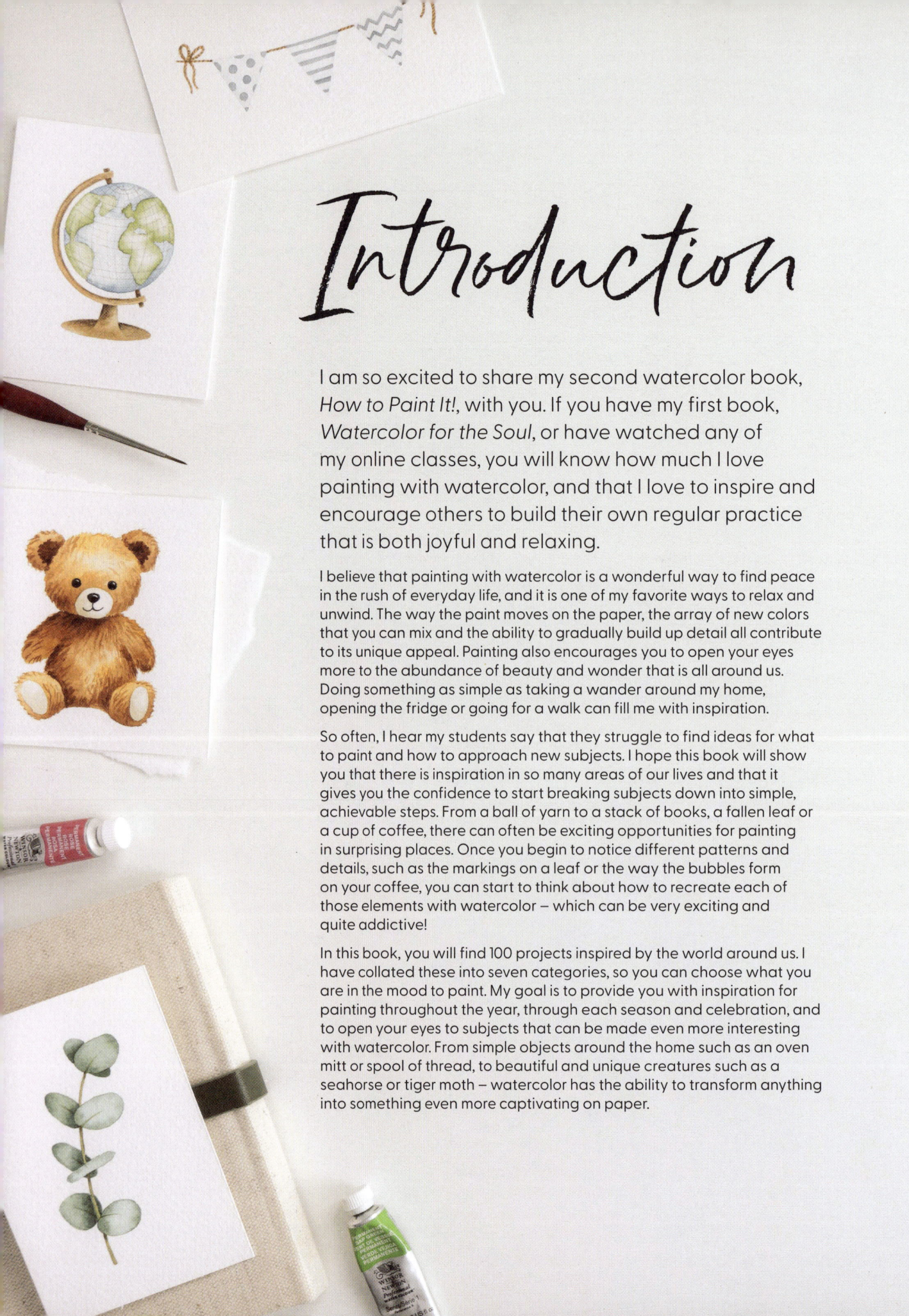

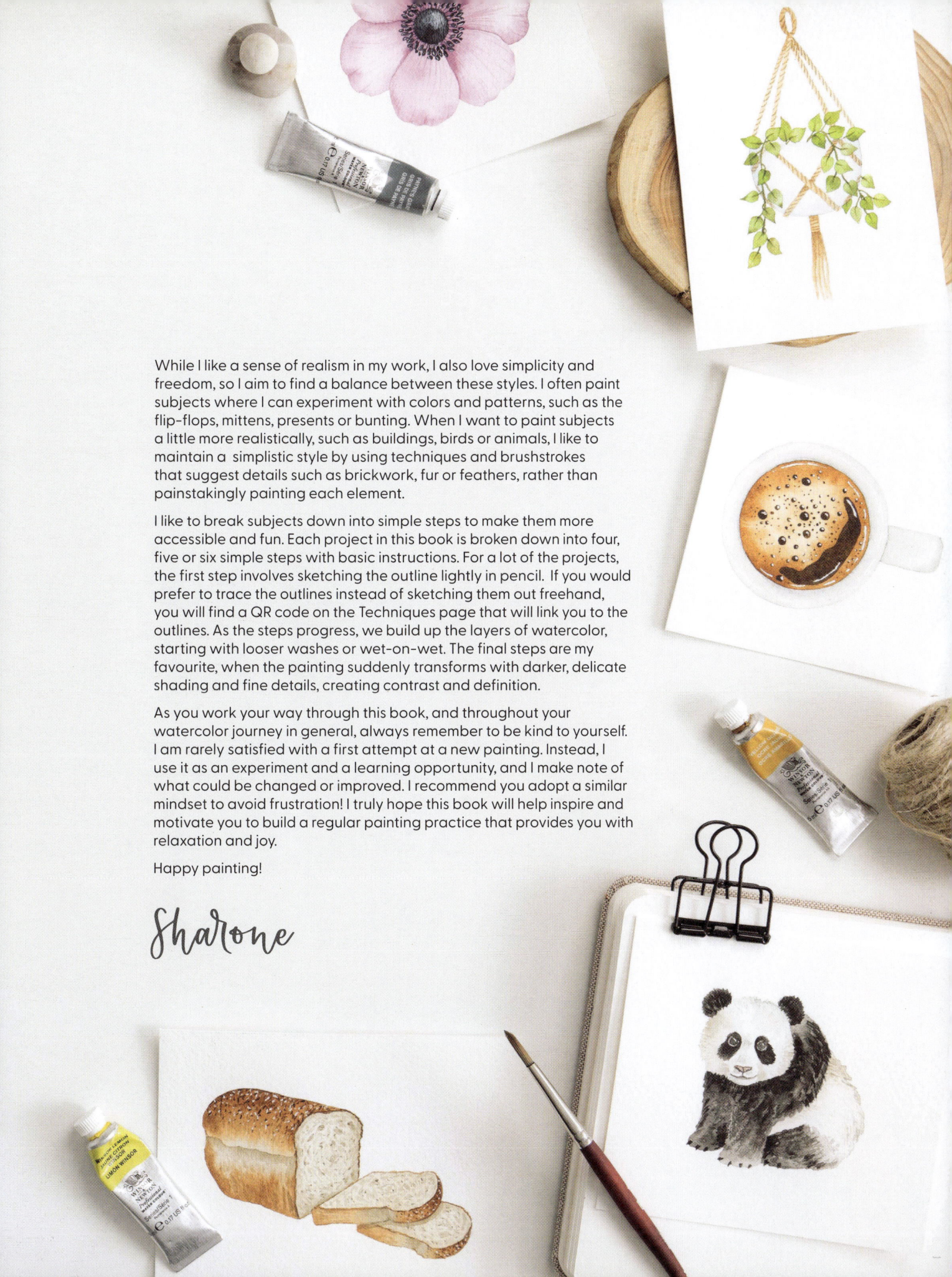

While I like a sense of realism in my work, I also love simplicity and freedom, so I aim to find a balance between these styles. I often paint subjects where I can experiment with colors and patterns, such as the flip-flops, mittens, presents or bunting. When I want to paint subjects a little more realistically, such as buildings, birds or animals, I like to maintain a simplistic style by using techniques and brushstrokes that suggest details such as brickwork, fur or feathers, rather than painstakingly painting each element.

I like to break subjects down into simple steps to make them more accessible and fun. Each project in this book is broken down into four, five or six simple steps with basic instructions. For a lot of the projects, the first step involves sketching the outline lightly in pencil. If you would prefer to trace the outlines instead of sketching them out freehand, you will find a QR code on the Techniques page that will link you to the outlines. As the steps progress, we build up the layers of watercolor, starting with looser washes or wet-on-wet. The final steps are my favourite, when the painting suddenly transforms with darker, delicate shading and fine details, creating contrast and definition.

As you work your way through this book, and throughout your watercolor journey in general, always remember to be kind to yourself. I am rarely satisfied with a first attempt at a new painting. Instead, I use it as an experiment and a learning opportunity, and I make note of what could be changed or improved. I recommend you adopt a similar mindset to avoid frustration! I truly hope this book will help inspire and motivate you to build a regular painting practice that provides you with relaxation and joy.

Happy painting!

Sharone

Materials

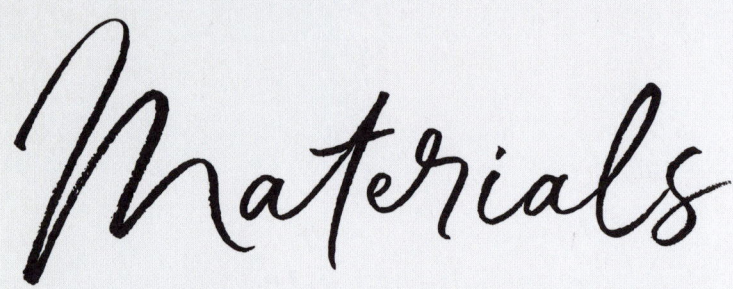

To get started with watercolor, you need paints, paper, brushes and a few extra supplies. Investing in a few good quality materials can make a big difference to the results you achieve and can also last you for years.

PAPER

Watercolor paper is one of the most important things to invest in with watercolor. It is available in different textures, weights, formats and colors. It comes in three different textures: Hot Pressed, Cold Pressed (or NOT) and Rough – I tend to use cold-pressed paper for most of my work, and this is what I recommend for beginners; it has a subtle texture and can be the easiest to work with. The weight of the paper indicates its thickness. A good, standard weight is 140lb/300gsm, and I would recommend this as a minimum to avoid your paper buckling from the water you will add. You can buy paper in a range of formats, from individual sheets and pads to blocks and hand-bound journals. Most watercolor paper will have a subtle cream tint; I like to use bright white paper, which gives your paintings more vibrancy as the white of the paper shows through the transparent washes of color.

BRUSHES

Watercolor brushes are available in many shapes and sizes. I tend to use round brushes the most. They are versatile and allow you to achieve a range of different brushstrokes by varying the pressure that you apply to the brush. With just the tip of the brush and minimal pressure, you can achieve fine lines and marks; by laying the belly of the brush flatter on the paper you will achieve much larger strokes and washes. For beginners, I would recommend starting with a few different sizes of round brushes – larger round brushes will cover a larger area of the paper, while smaller brushes are great for smaller marks and fine details. For the projects in this book, I mainly use three round brushes that are sizes 0, 2 and 4, and occasionally a size 6. In the earlier steps, I often use the larger brush to cover a larger area, then I switch to the smaller brushes for finer details. If you are painting the projects on a larger scale, you will need a larger brush.

Use a larger brush to cover large areas. Switch to a smaller brush for small areas and finer details.

PAINT

Watercolor paint most commonly comes
in pans (dried blocks of paint) or tubes (paste).
I use both, as they each have their advantages.
Pans are portable, convenient and easy to pick up
for a quick painting session. Tubes are useful when you
want to mix up larger quantities of paint. You can buy
paints individually or in sets. Good quality paints contain
more pigment than cheaper paints. They give you a more
vibrant color, mix better with other colors and will last much
longer. Popular brands like Winsor & Newton have both a student
range and a professional range of watercolors to choose from,
depending on how much you want to spend. The colors below are
the ones I use in this book. I like to work with a fairly small palette so
I can mix my own colors from these. This gives you more control and
allows you to create more harmony in your work.

My Palette (Winsor & Newton Professional Range)

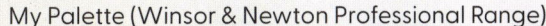  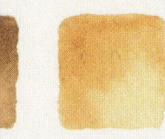 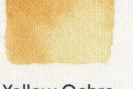  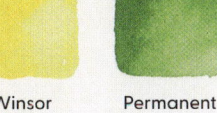 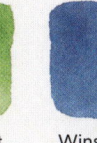 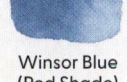  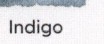  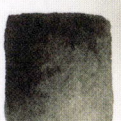

| Permanent Rose | Burnt Umber | Yellow Ochre | Winsor Lemon | Permanent Sap Green | Winsor Blue (Red Shade) | Indigo | Payne's Gray | Ivory Black |

OTHER SUPPLIES

I recommend an HB pencil and a kneaded putty eraser for your initial
sketches, and you will need a glass or two of water for adding to your
paint and cleaning your brushes. A palette or ceramic plate is great for
mixing your colors on, and a paper towel is useful for removing excess
water or paint from your brush. Occasionally, I like to add white details
to my painting; you will see this labelled in the projects as 'opaque white'.
My favourites are Dr. Ph. Martin's Bleed Proof White – a highly concentrated
opaque white watercolor – or a Uni-Ball Signo white gel pen. I also like to
use a lightbox to trace my sketches onto watercolor paper; you may wish
to use one if you are tracing the outlines from the PDFs provided (see the
Techniques page for a link to these).

Techniques

The following techniques are used for the projects in this book; take time to practice the exercises to build your understanding and confidence with watercolor.

SKETCHING

In many of the projects, the first step is to draw the outline lightly in pencil – either copy it freehand or download the outline via the QR code (right) and trace it onto your watercolor paper. A traceable outline is also available for the projects that do not have this first step, in case you would prefer to trace these shapes, too. Next, soften the pencil lines by pressing a kneaded eraser onto them before starting to paint, especially around paler areas so they will not show through the paint.

MIXING COLORS

Before starting the projects, try out some of the mixes that we use throughout the book. You will find that dominant colors are listed first in the descriptions. For example, for 'yellow orange' you start with Winsor Lemon and add a little Permanent Rose. For 'red orange' you start with Permanent Rose then add Winsor Lemon. Using different ratios of the same paints can give you very different results. Start with the dominant color and then gradually add in the second color until you get the desired result.

For some mixes like 'dark brown' or 'neutral green', we add a little complementary color (colors on the opposite side of the color wheel) to make the mix more muted or realistic. Add these complementary colors gradually and carefully to avoid the mix becoming too gray or muddy.

VALUES

You can also adjust the 'value' of each color you mix, for a darker or paler paint. Start with very little water to mix the paint at its darkest value, then gradually add more water for a lighter result. The palest values are useful for background washes or subtle colors. Most projects begin with pale mixes, then we gradually build up the colors.

EXERCISE 1: Practice mixing different values and painting swatches. First, use just enough water to activate the paint. For your darkest value, coat your brush and paint a small square 'swatch'. Now dilute the paint with slightly more water and add it to the page. Continue to add gradually lighter swatches, until they are just visible.

Access the downloadable outlines at www.bookmarkedhub.com

Winsor Lemon and a little Permanent Rose (yellow orange)

Winsor Lemon and Permanent Rose (orange)

Permanent Rose and Winsor Lemon (red orange)

 Add a little Indigo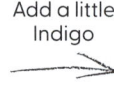

Burnt Umber

dark brown

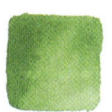 Add a little Permanent Rose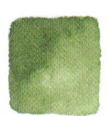

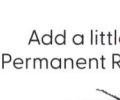

Permanent Sap Green

neutral green

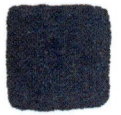  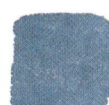 

 1 Paint a series of swatches from dark to light by gradually adding more water to your mix.

Look through the projects to see how the contrast between light and dark adds depth and dimension.

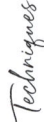

METHODS OF APPLYING PAINT

The most common methods of applying watercolor paint are wet-on-dry and wet-on-wet. The wet-on-dry technique is when you apply wet paint to dry paper (A), giving you more control and creating crisp edges. For this, it is important to leave the first layer of paint to completely dry so the new paint does not bleed and run. The wet-on-wet technique is when you apply wet paint to wet paper (B), allowing you to create soft blends and edges. When painting adjacent areas, leave the first section to dry before painting any areas that are touching it (C), otherwise the paint will bleed into the still-wet area (D). A third method is dry brushing, when you apply dry paint to dry paper (E), which creates a patchy, textured effect.

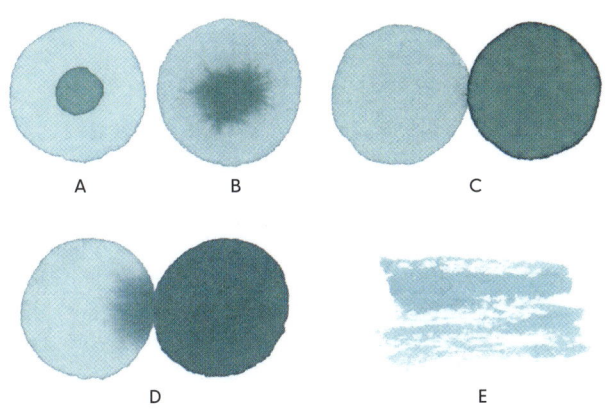

A   B   C

D   E

2

  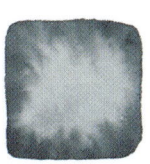

Paint a square of clear water, then add pale Payne's Gray to the edges.

Paint a square with Yellow Ochre, then add Burnt Umber to the edges.

Paint a square with pale Payne's Gray, then add darker Payne's Gray to the edges.

WET-ON-WET

This technique is regularly used throughout the early steps of the projects to add background effects and shading.

EXERCISE 2: Paint a square and add a darker color to the edges to see how it bleeds in. Try with different colors, preparing your mixes before you start.

For some projects, like the Christmas Pudding, Crab and Tree, we 'dab' paint onto wet paper. How wet the paper is will determine how the paint reacts: the wetter the paper, the more the paint will spread. The paper should not be too wet, or the paint will spread too far; if the paper is too dry, it will not spread very much. Remember, the wet paper will dilute any paint you add, so for a stronger color, start with a more concentrated paint.

EXERCISE 3: Paint a square with Yellow Ochre, then with Burnt Umber on your brush, quickly touch the square to dab in the paint a few times in different places. Repeat this using more water. Practice to see how far the paint spreads with the paper at varying levels of wetness.

3

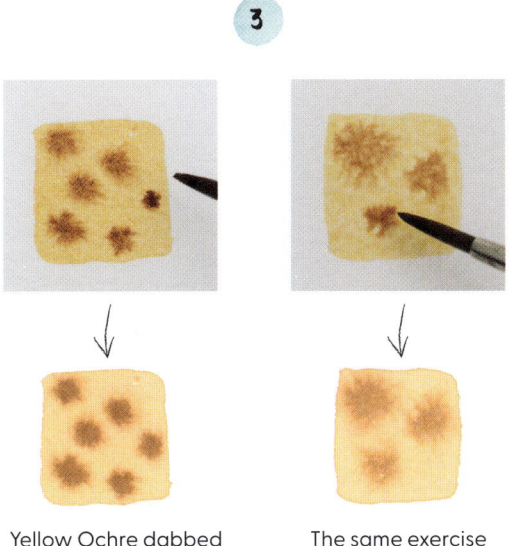

Yellow Ochre dabbed with Burnt Umber

The same exercise using more water

WET-ON-DRY

This technique is useful for solid areas of color and is regularly used throughout the later steps of the projects for more precise details. These are usually the darkest layers and can require delicate brushwork.

EXERCISE 4: A 'flat wash' is an area of evenly distributed color. Load your brush with paint and apply it to dry paper with a back-and-forth stroke. Ensure you have enough paint mixed up beforehand and use an appropriately sized brush for the size of the area that you want to cover.

EXERCISE 5: Take some time to practice a variety of the wet-on-dry marks below, using a fine brush. Remove any excess water from the brush with your paper towel before you begin, and paint on completely dry paper to get crisp edges and fine brush marks.

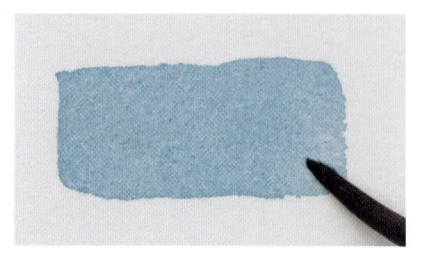

4 Practice spreading the paint evenly for a flat wash.

5

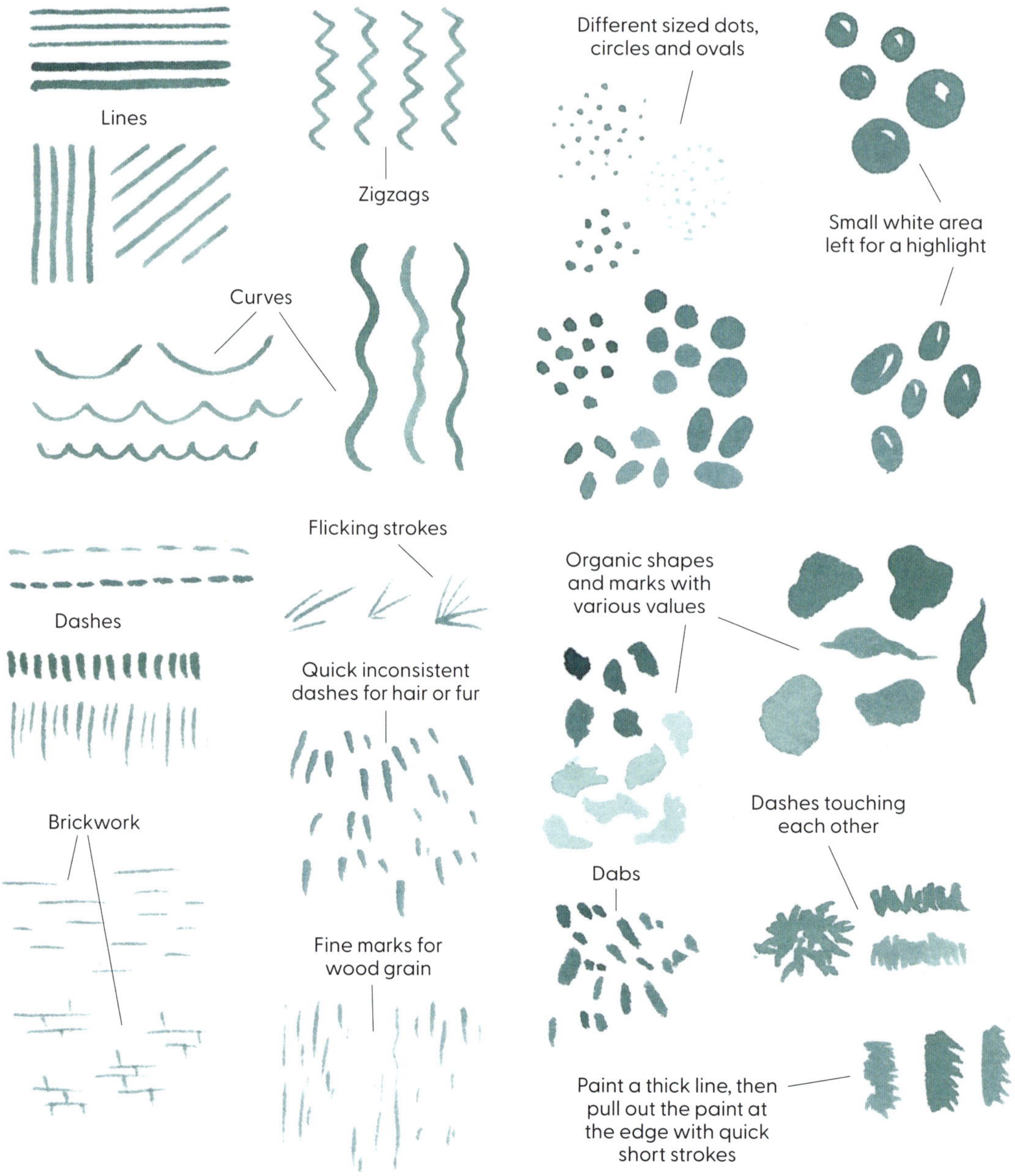

Lines

Zigzags

Curves

Different sized dots, circles and ovals

Small white area left for a highlight

Dashes

Flicking strokes

Quick inconsistent dashes for hair or fur

Organic shapes and marks with various values

Dabs

Dashes touching each other

Brickwork

Fine marks for wood grain

Paint a thick line, then pull out the paint at the edge with quick short strokes

GRADIENTS & SHADING

In many projects, we will paint a gradient where the color transitions from dark to light. You can do this by using the wet-on-wet technique that we have already practiced, or with the wet-on-dry technique, which allows you to have more control over the result. These are great for adding depth and dimension to your paintings.

EXERCISE 6: Paint a wash of color onto dry paper. Rinse the brush and remove excess water with a paper towel, then run it along the edge of the paint to soften it. Move back and forth until you are happy with the effect, rinsing and drying your brush as needed. For more contrast, add paint to the dark side or lift paint from the pale side.

EXERCISE 7: The same technique can be used to layer colors and add shading. Paint a square and leave it to dry completely. Add a bit more color at the edge and then use a damp brush to blend it out, pulling the paint outwards. You may need to rinse and dry your brush as before to repeat the process.

HIGHLIGHTS

Many of the projects require you to 'leave lighter areas for a highlight'. This is particularly useful for giving dimension to your subject. Try the exercises below to practice a few ways that you can do this.

EXERCISE 8: For a crisp, controlled highlight, leave an area free from paint.

EXERCISE 9: For a softer, less controlled highlight, use the wet-on-wet technique, avoiding the area you want the highlight to be when you add the paint.

EXERCISE 10: For a subtle, yet controlled highlight, lift some of the paint with a dried brush. Wash and dry your brush then continue to pick up more paint as many times as you need to.

EXERCISE 11: To add a highlight at the end, use an opaque white paint or pen to draw a highlight onto completely dry paint.

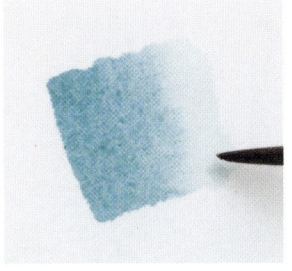

6 Avoid using too much water when softening edges as this will push the paint backwards.

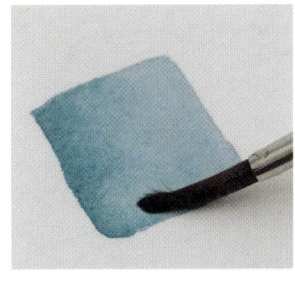

7 Avoid using too much water so you do not disturb the paint underneath.

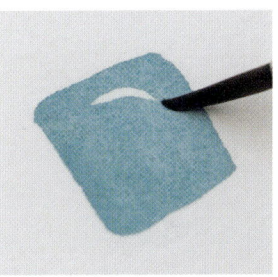

8 Paint around a highlight on dry paper.

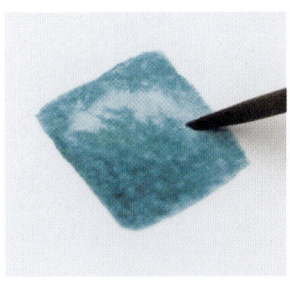

9 Paint around a highlight on wet paper.

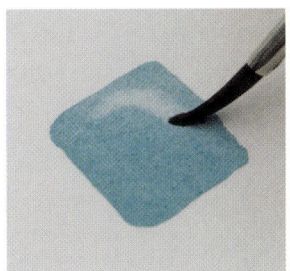

10 Lift a highlight with your brush.

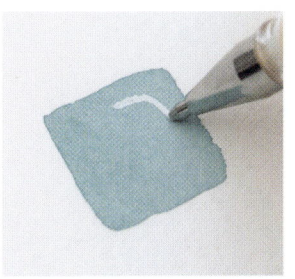

11 Use opaque white to draw a highlight.

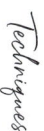

Techniques

11

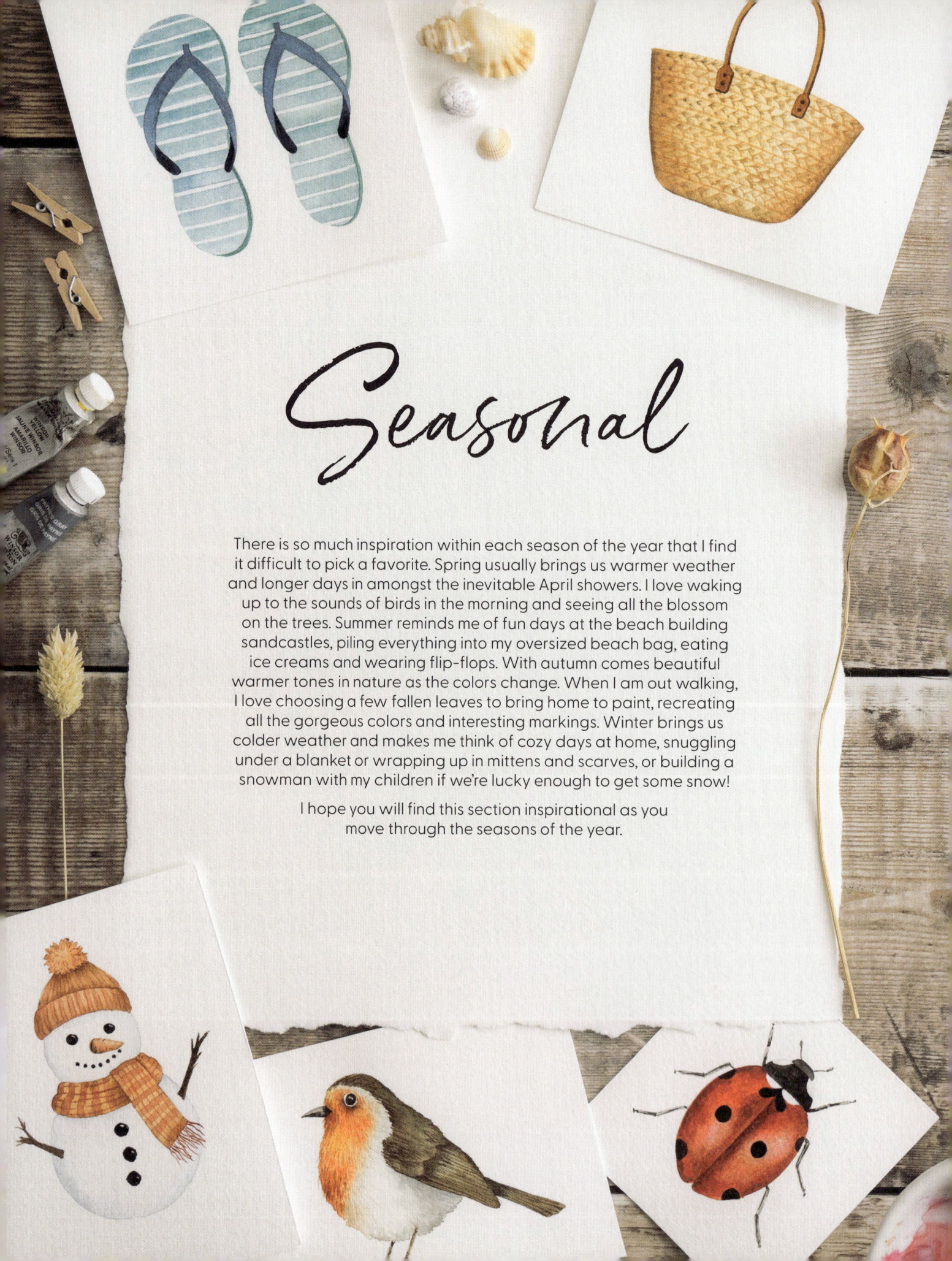

Seasonal

There is so much inspiration within each season of the year that I find it difficult to pick a favorite. Spring usually brings us warmer weather and longer days in amongst the inevitable April showers. I love waking up to the sounds of birds in the morning and seeing all the blossom on the trees. Summer reminds me of fun days at the beach building sandcastles, piling everything into my oversized beach bag, eating ice creams and wearing flip-flops. With autumn comes beautiful warmer tones in nature as the colors change. When I am out walking, I love choosing a few fallen leaves to bring home to paint, recreating all the gorgeous colors and interesting markings. Winter brings us colder weather and makes me think of cozy days at home, snuggling under a blanket or wrapping up in mittens and scarves, or building a snowman with my children if we're lucky enough to get some snow!

I hope you will find this section inspirational as you move through the seasons of the year.

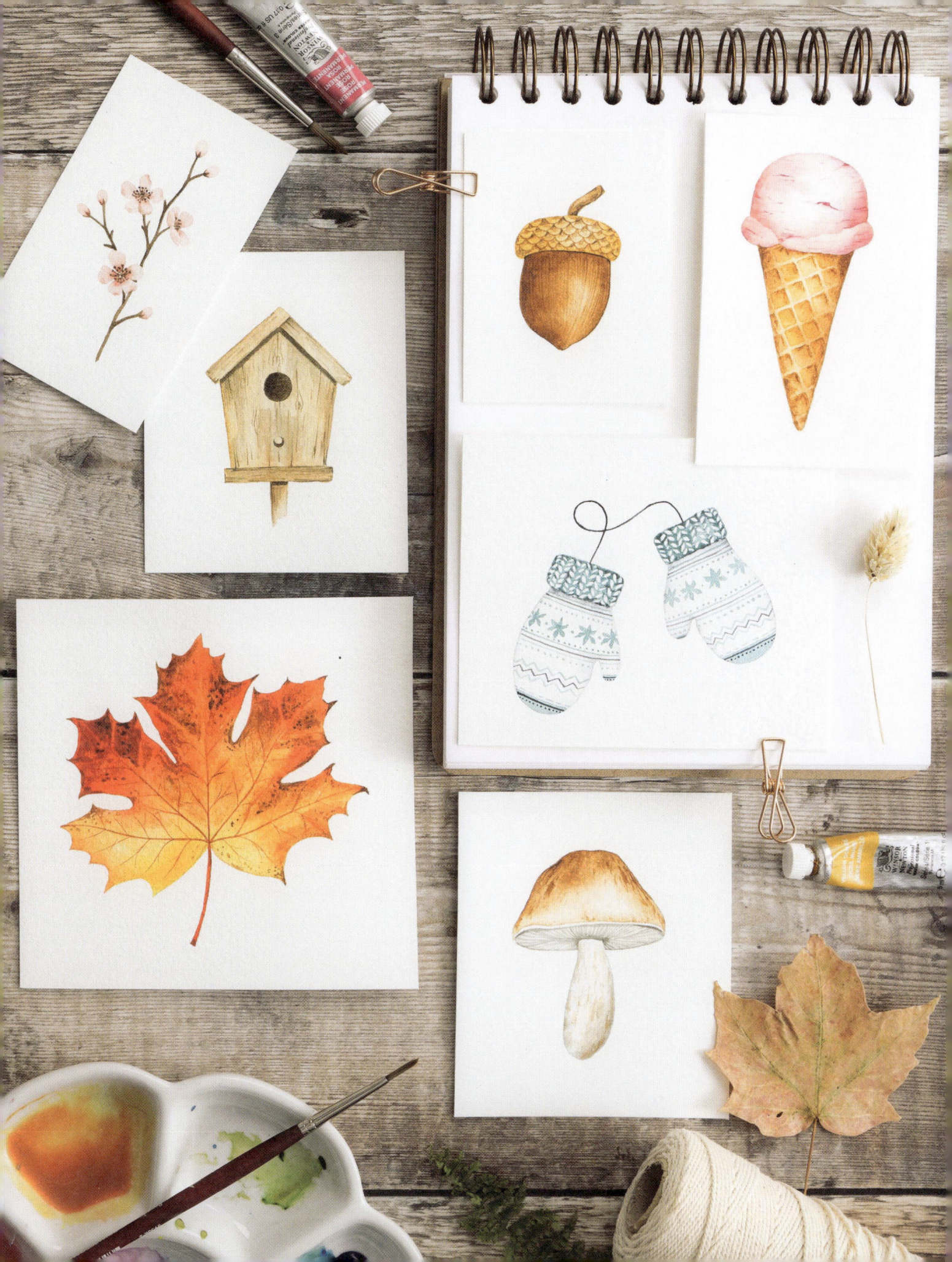

Yellow Ochre

Burnt Umber

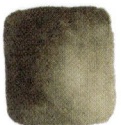

Mix 1: Burnt Umber
and a little Indigo

SPRING
Birdhouse

STEPS

1. Draw the outline lightly in pencil.

2. Paint all over with Yellow Ochre and then add in strokes of Burnt Umber while still wet.

3. Once dry, use a pale mix 1 (dark brown) and a dry brush to add patches of darker color, avoiding the perch.

4. With a darker mix 1, paint the hole and add shadows under the roof, perch and base.

5. With mix 1, add grain to the wood with lines and curves.

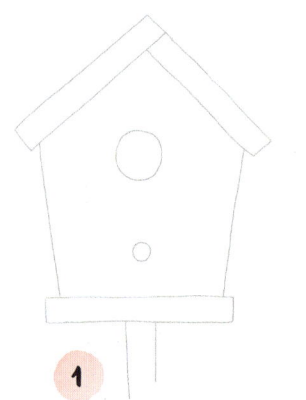

1

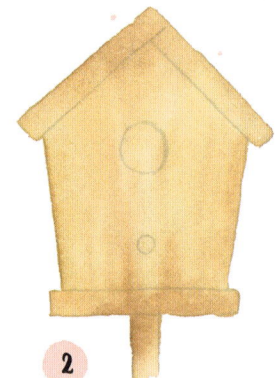

2

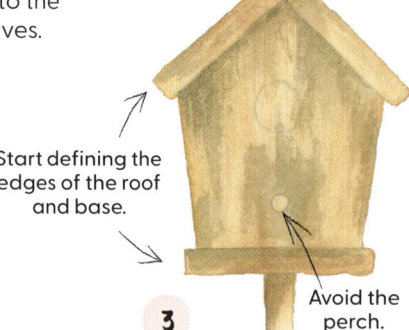

Start defining the edges of the roof and base.

Avoid the perch.

3

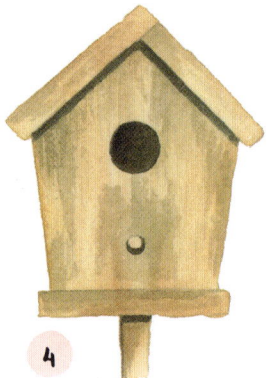

4

5

Add a splash of color with some blossom or leaves!

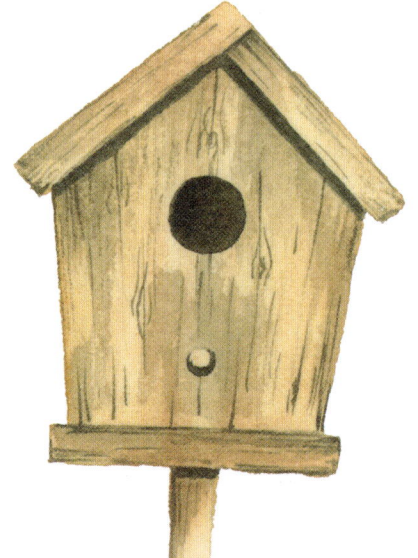

Blossom

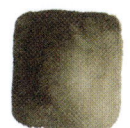

Mix 1: Permanent Rose and a little Burnt Umber

Mix 2: Burnt Umber and a little Indigo

STEPS

1. Draw a guide for the branch lightly in pencil.

2. With a pale mix 1 (pink), paint two flowers with five petals and then add a little darker mix 1 to the inside and on some outer edges. Paint two side petals for the start of a flower on its side.

3. Paint three more petals on the side-view flower. Paint some buds, adding darker paint to the bottom of each.

4. With mix 2 (dark brown), paint the branch and the base of each bud.

5. With mix 2, paint fine lines inside each flower, adding dots to the end of each line.

Side-view flower

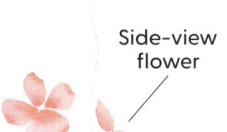

1

2

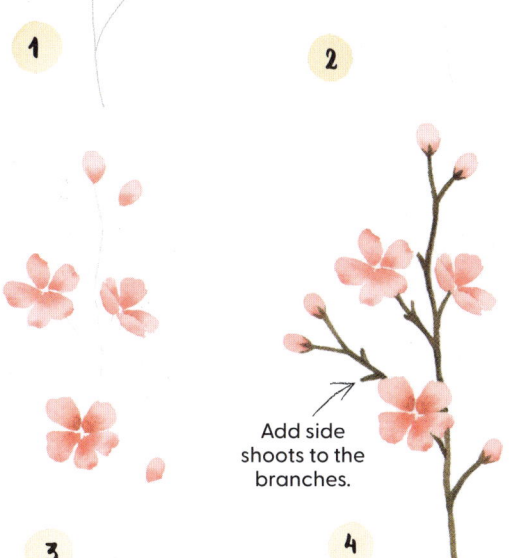

Add side shoots to the branches.

3

4

5

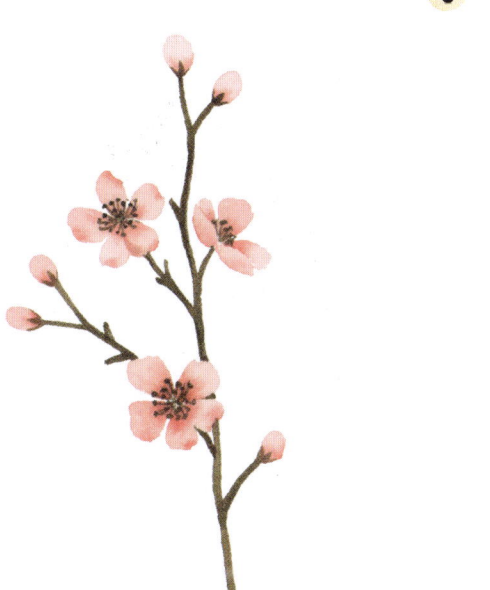

For delicate flowers like these, be careful not to use too much water.

Ivory Black

Mix 1: Permanent Rose and a little Winsor Lemon

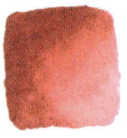

Mix 2: Permanent Rose and Burnt Umber

Ladybird

STEPS

1. Draw the outline lightly in pencil.

2. With mix 1 (red), paint the wings and lift a few highlights.

3. With pale Ivory Black, paint shadow on the white areas and paint the legs and antennae.

4. With dark Ivory Black, paint the spots, the head and add shadow to the legs and antennae.

5. Once dry, paint the front of the head with Ivory Black. With a dark mix 2 (brown red), add shading at the edges of the wings and down the center.

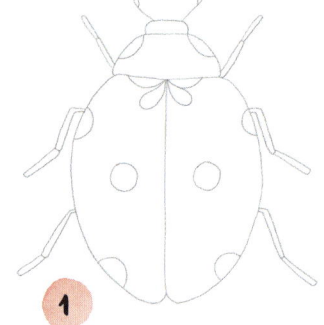

1

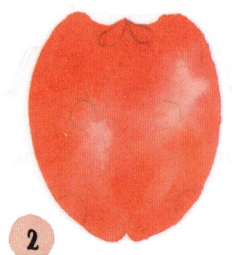

2

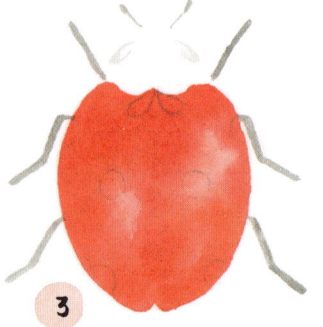

3

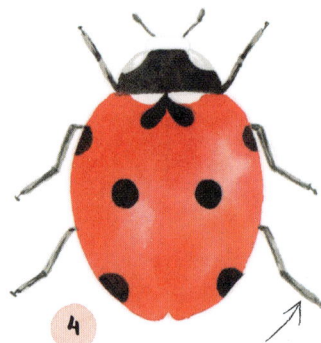

4

Leave lighter areas showing through for contrast.

For very concentrated areas like the black spots, only use a little water in your paint mix.

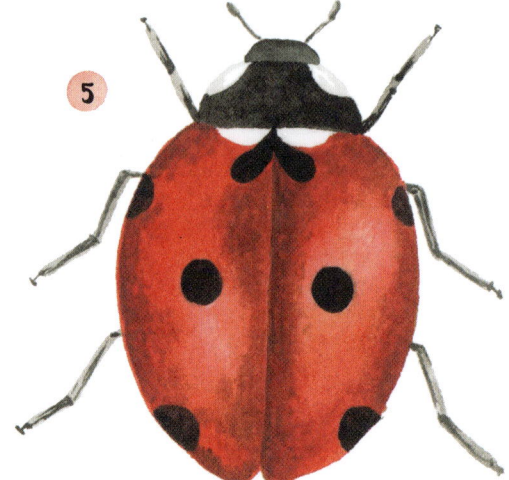

5

Umbrella

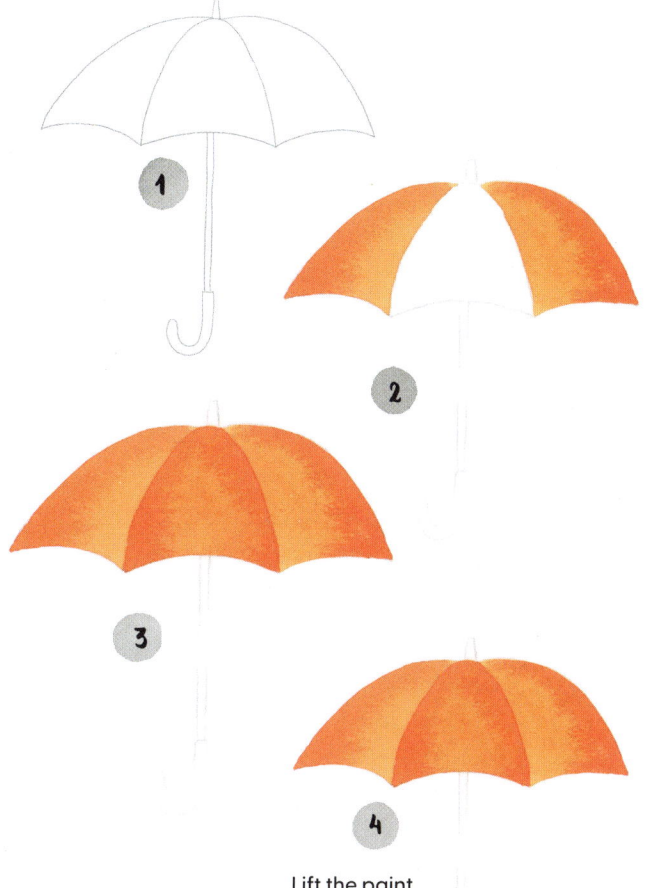

STEPS

1. Draw the outline lightly in pencil.

2. Paint the outer two sections with mix 1 (orange). While still wet, add mix 2 (red orange) to the outer edge of each.

3. Once dry, paint the middle section with mix 1, adding mix 2 to both sides.

4. Paint the handle with Burnt Umber.

5. Paint the pole, top and tips with Ivory Black.

Burnt Umber

Ivory Black

Mix 1: Winsor Lemon and Permanent Rose

Mix 2: Permanent Rose and Winsor Lemon

Lift the paint for a highlight here.

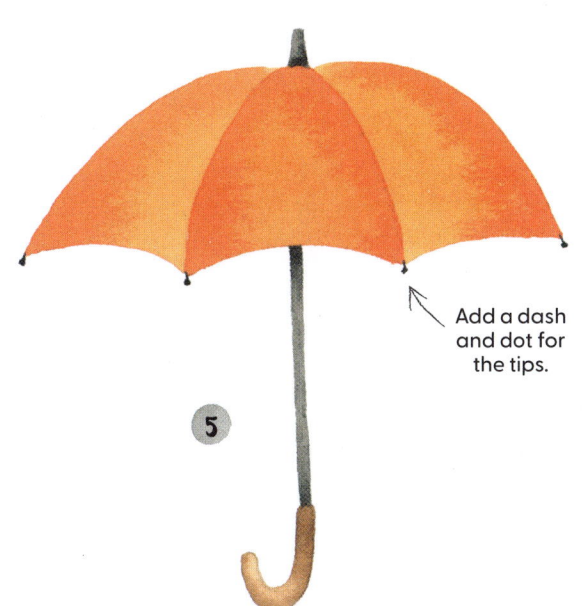

Add a dash and dot for the tips.

Once completely dry, erase any visible pencil lines from your sketches.

Payne's Gray

Indigo

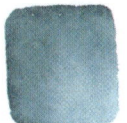

**Mix 1: Winsor Blue
(Red Shade) and a
little Winsor Lemon**

SUMMER

Flip-Flops

STEPS

1. Draw the outline lightly in pencil.

2. Paint the base in pale Payne's Gray, avoiding the straps.

3. Once dry, paint thick stripes with mix 1 (blue).

4. Paint the upper part of the straps with a mid-value Indigo.

5. With darker Indigo, paint the underside of the straps.

6. With mix 1, add an edge to the right-hand side of each flip-flop.

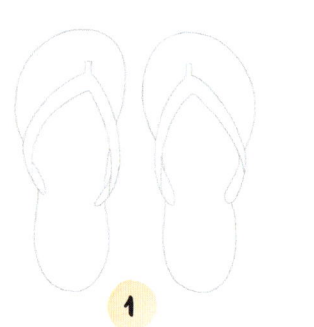

1

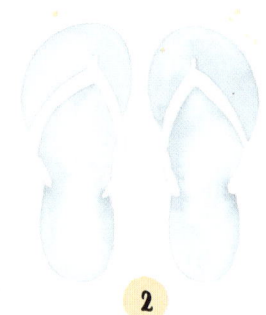

2

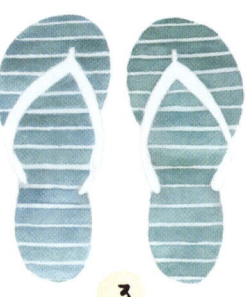

3

Don't paint the straps too dark, as we want the underside to be darker.

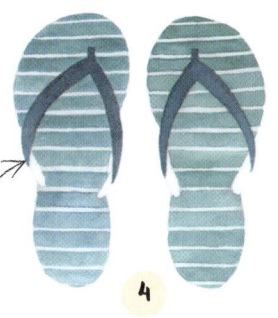

4

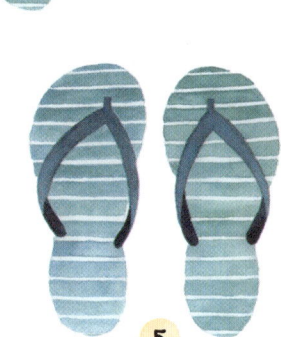

5

6

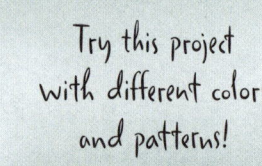

Try this project with different colors and patterns!

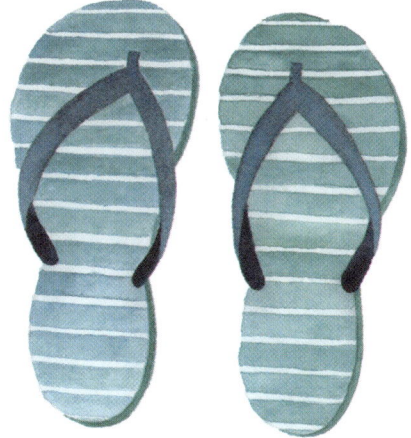

Beach Bag

Yellow Ochre

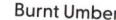

Burnt Umber

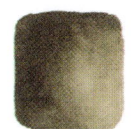

Mix 1: Burnt Umber and a little Indigo

STEPS

1. Paint the bag with Yellow Ochre, then add Burnt Umber to the side edges.

2. Once dry, paint the strap with Burnt Umber.

3. With Burnt Umber, paint slightly curved horizontal lines across the bag. Between each set of lines, paint curves, following the steps shown below (see 3a, 3b and 3c). Each new stroke is illustrated in blue.

4. With mix 1 (dark brown), paint dots for buttons and add a shadow to the right-hand side of the strap. Add shadow to each 'V' of the pattern and darken the edges of the bag.

1

2

3

Start with the horizontal lines.

3A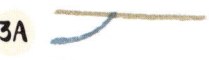

3B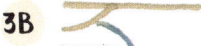

3C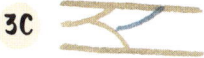

4

For the shadow, add a little paint in the 'V', then soften the edge with a damp brush.

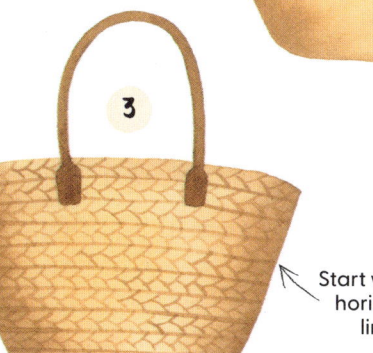

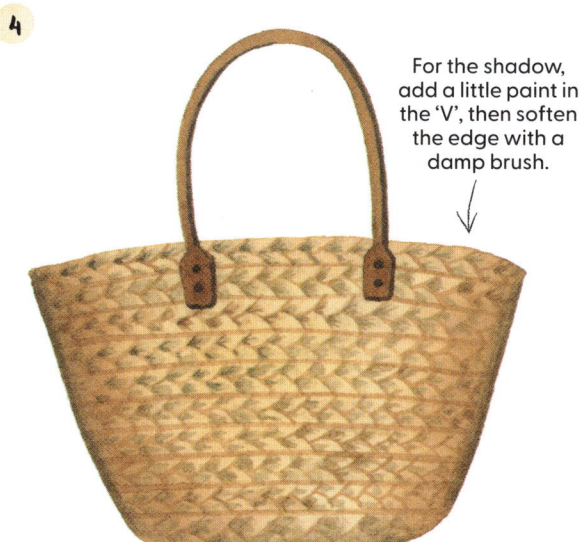

Dive straight into painting this bag or, if preferred, a traceable outline is provided in the PDF download for you.

19

Yellow Ochre

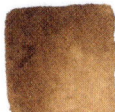

Burnt Umber

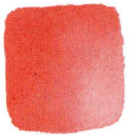

Mix 1: Permanent Rose and a little Winsor Lemon

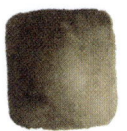

Mix 2: Burnt Umber and a little Indigo

Sandcastle

STEPS

1. Draw the outline lightly in pencil.

2. Paint alternating sections with pale Yellow Ochre, adding darker Yellow Ochre and Burnt Umber to the edges while still wet.

3. Once dry, paint the remaining sections in the same way. Then, using Yellow Ochre, paint one long stroke across the ground and blend it out roughly.

4. Once dry, paint the door and windows with Burnt Umber. Add tiny dots all over the castle for the texture of the sand.

5. Paint the flag with mix 1 (red). Once dry, paint a line for the flagpole with mix 2 (dark brown).

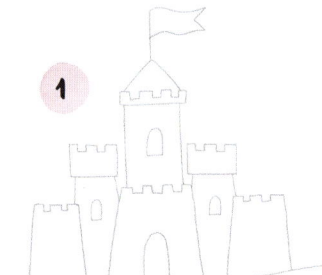

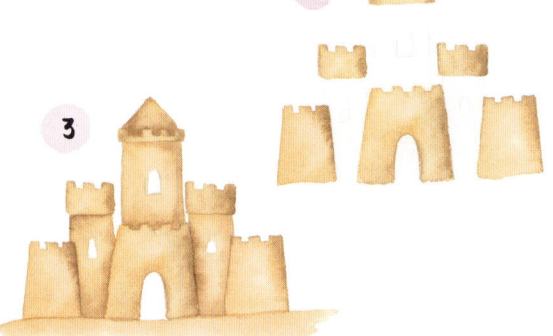

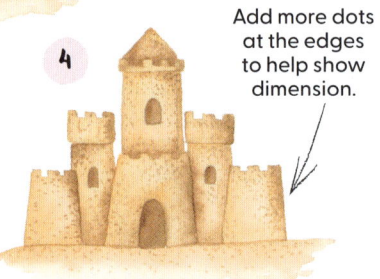

Add more dots at the edges to help show dimension.

For curved subjects like the turrets, try to keep a lighter area in the center and darken the edges.

Lift a highlight here to show the curve of the flag.

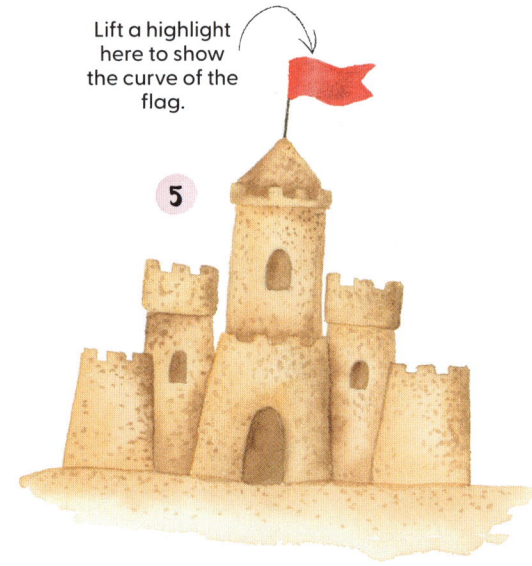

Ice Cream

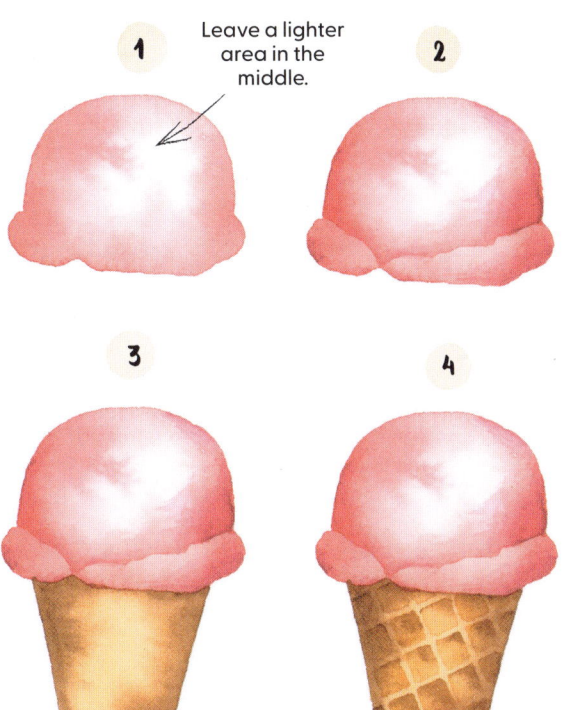

1 Leave a lighter area in the middle.

2

3 Let the Burnt Umber bleed in naturally.

4

STEPS

1. Paint the shape of the ice cream with a pale mix 1 (pink), adding darker pink at the edges. You will find a traceable outline in the PDF download if you would prefer to sketch the shape out first.

2. Once dry, build up the shadows using mix 1 and mix 2 (pink purple), defining the lower ridge.

3. Paint the cone with Yellow Ochre. While still wet, add Burnt Umber to the edges.

4. Once dry, paint squares on the cone in diagonal rows with Yellow Ochre, adding a little Burnt Umber to the top corner of each square.

5. Add extra shading to the cone with Burnt Umber and cracks and lines to the ice cream with mix 1 and mix 2.

Yellow Ochre

Burnt Umber

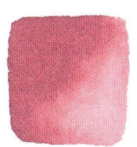

Mix 1: Permanent Rose and a little Winsor Lemon

Mix 2: Permanent Rose and a little Winsor Blue (Red Shade)

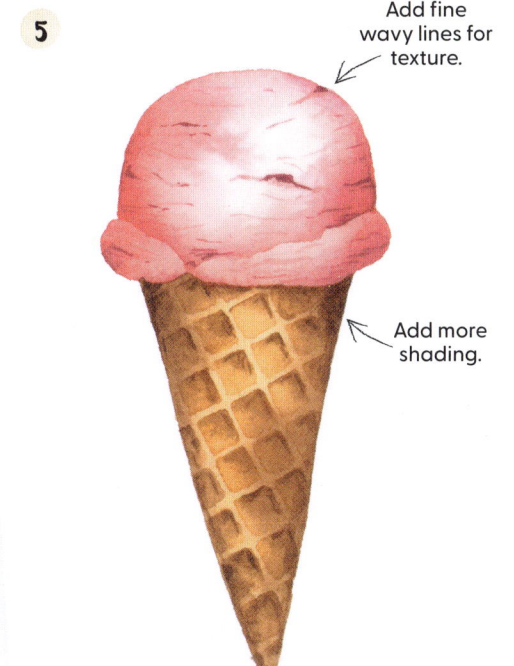

5

Add fine wavy lines for texture.

Add more shading.

For the squares in step 4, I find it easier to start with a row in the middle of the cone and then work my way up and down.

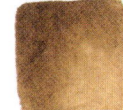
Winsor Lemon

Burnt Umber

Mix 1: Winsor Lemon and a little Permanent Rose

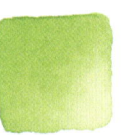
Mix 2: Winsor Lemon and Permanent Rose

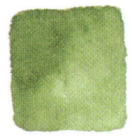
Mix 3: Permanent Sap Green and Winsor Lemon

Mix 4: Permanent Sap Green and a little Permanent Rose

Pumpkin

STEPS

1. Draw the outline lightly in pencil.

2. Paint alternate sections with Winsor Lemon in the center, blending towards the edges with mix 1 (yellow orange) and mix 2 (orange). Add Burnt Umber to darken the edges.

3. Once dry, paint the remaining sections in a similar way.

4. Once dry, paint the stalk with mix 3 (yellow green), adding mix 4 (neutral green) at the edges.

5. Build up the shading on the edges of the orange sections with mix 2 and Burnt Umber. Add lines and shadow to the stalk with a darker mix 4.

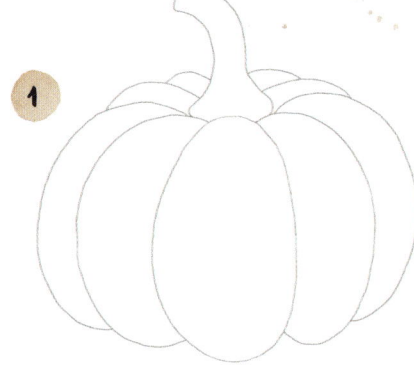

1

Leave lighter areas for highlights to help give each section dimension.

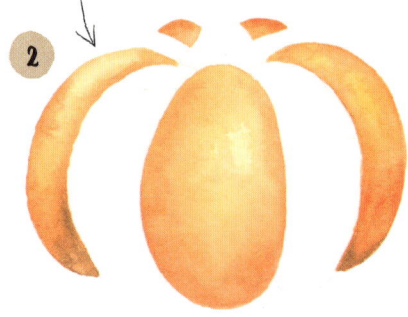

2

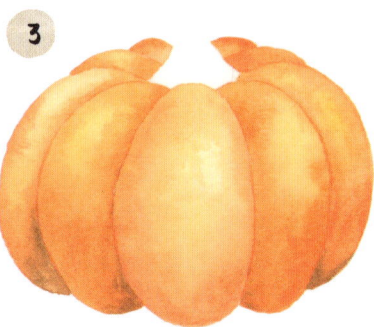

3

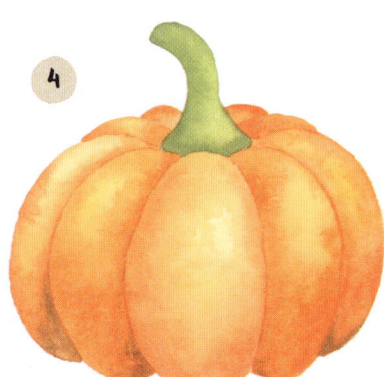

4

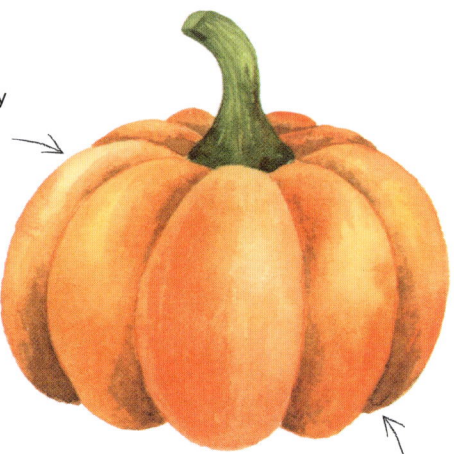

5

Leave plenty of lighter patches shining through.

For shading, add a little dark paint, then blend out with a damp brush.

Acorn

Burnt Umber

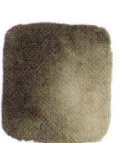

Yellow Ochre

Mix 1: Burnt Umber
and a little Indigo

STEPS

1. Draw the outline lightly in pencil.

2. Paint the nut with pale Burnt Umber, darkening the edges and lifting a highlight off-center. Paint the stalk with Burnt Umber and lift a highlight.

3. Once dry, paint the top of the acorn with Yellow Ochre, lifting a highlight off-center and darkening the edges.

4. Once dry, with Burnt Umber, paint rows of semi-circles for the scales.

5. With mix 1 (dark brown), add shading to the inverted 'V' of each scale, at the top of the nut and on the stalk. With Burnt Umber, paint fine curved lines on the nut.

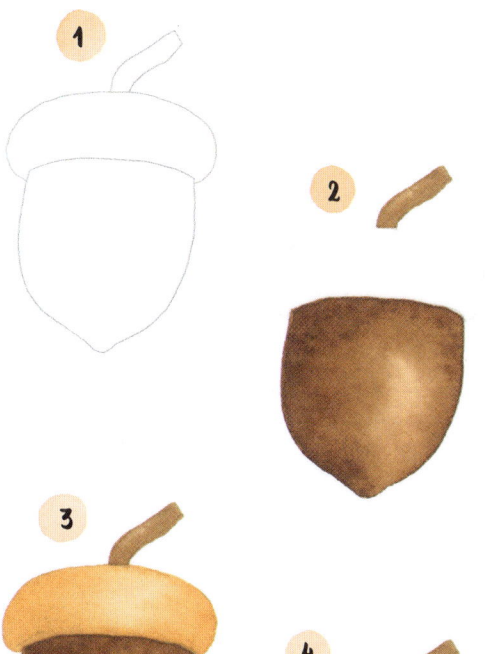

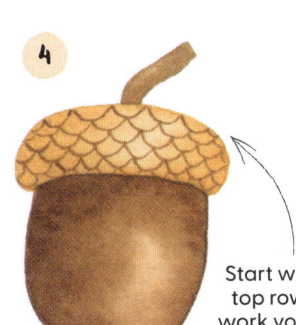

Start with the top row and work your way down.

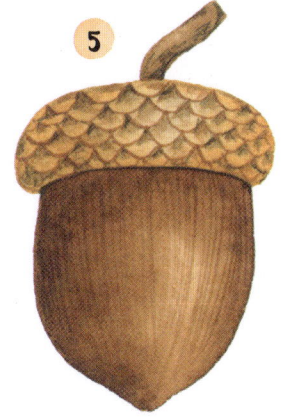

Both the highlight and the curved lines on the nut help to give this subject more dimension.

Winsor Lemon

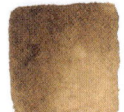
Burnt Umber

Mix 1: Winsor Lemon and a little Permanent Rose

Mix 2: Winsor Lemon and Permanent Rose

Mix 3: Permanent Rose and a little Winsor Lemon

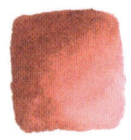
Mix 4: Permanent Rose and Burnt Umber

Mix 5: Burnt Umber and a little Indigo

Leaf

STEPS

1. Draw the outline lightly in pencil.

2. Wet the inside of the leaf. Add Winsor Lemon to the lower half and then gradually blend in mix 1 (yellow orange), mix 2 (orange) and mix 3 (red) as you move upwards. Leave to dry.

3. With Burnt Umber and mix 4 (brown red), add patches to the leaf, leaving gaps for the veins.

4. Once dry, paint the stalk and veins in mix 3 and mix 4.

5. With Burnt Umber and mix 5 (dark brown), add some final dots and markings to the leaf.

1
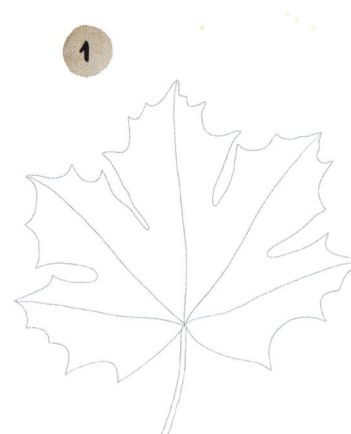

2
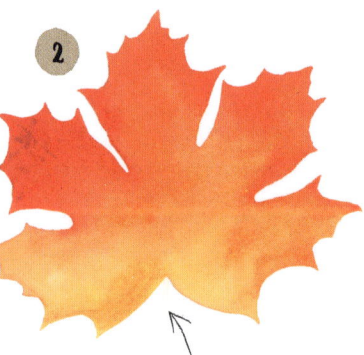

Wetting the leaf first will make it easier to blend the colors together.

For larger areas like this, use a larger brush such as a size 6.

3
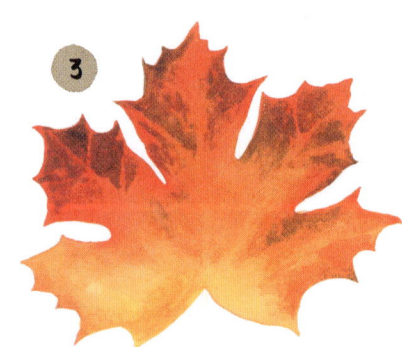

5
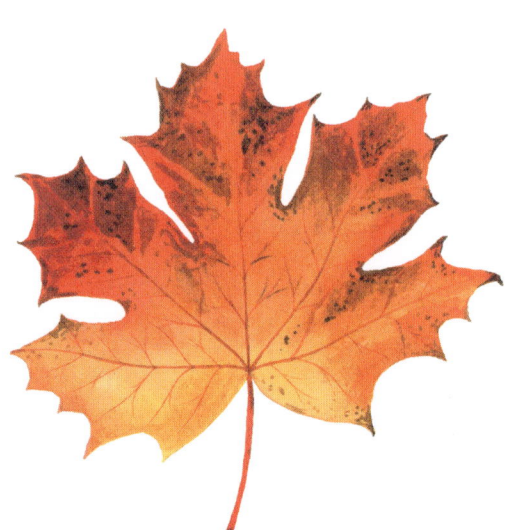

4
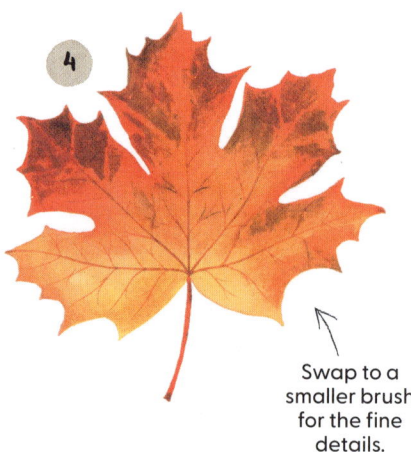

Swap to a smaller brush for the fine details.

Mushroom

Burnt Umber

Mix 1: Payne's Gray and a little Burnt Umber

STEPS

1. Draw the outline lightly in pencil.

2. Paint the underside of the cap in a pale mix 1 (gray), darkening the edges.

3. Once dry, wet the cap but keep the top dry so it will be darker, then add Burnt Umber to the top and edges. Add more paint to the top to darken. Wet the stem and add mix 1 to the edges.

4. With mix 1 and Burnt Umber, add patches and shading to the stem. With mix 1, paint fine lines fanning out from the stem on the underside. Add markings to the cap with Burnt Umber.

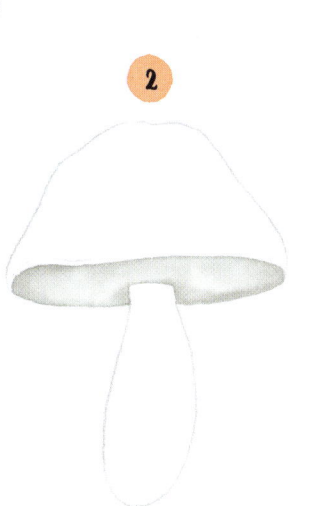

Add the Burnt Umber in at the top so it flows freely into the water for a natural bleed.

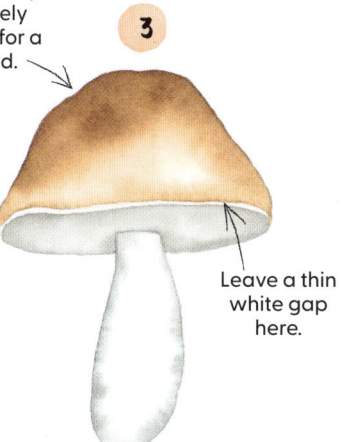

Leave a thin white gap here.

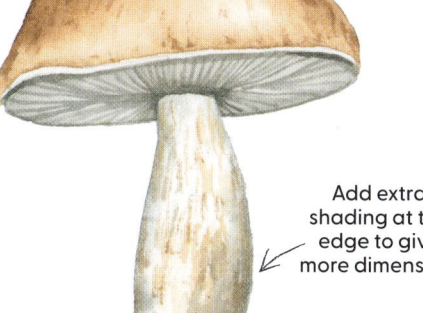

Add extra shading at the edge to give more dimension.

For the fine lines, remember to remove any excess water from your brush so the hairs form a sharp point!

Payne's Gray

Burnt Umber

Ivory Black

Mix 1: Winsor Lemon and Permanent Rose

Mix 2: Burnt Umber and a little Indigo

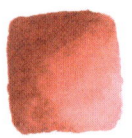

Mix 3: Permanent Rose and Burnt Umber

WINTER

Snowman

STEPS

1. Draw the outline lightly in pencil.

2. Wet the inside of the snow parts and add pale Payne's Gray to the edges. Leave to dry.

3. Paint the first sections of the hat and scarf with mix 1 (orange), adding Burnt Umber to the edges while still wet.

4. Once dry, paint the carrot and the remaining sections of the hat and scarf in the same way.

5. Using Ivory Black, paint coal for the eyes, mouth and buttons, leaving small highlights on each. With mix 2 (dark brown), paint the twigs and details on the carrot.

6. With mix 3 (brown red), add patterns and final details to the hat and scarf.

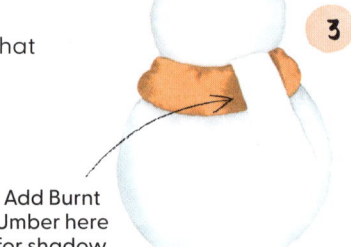

Add Burnt Umber here for shadow.

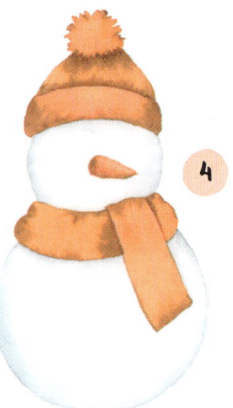

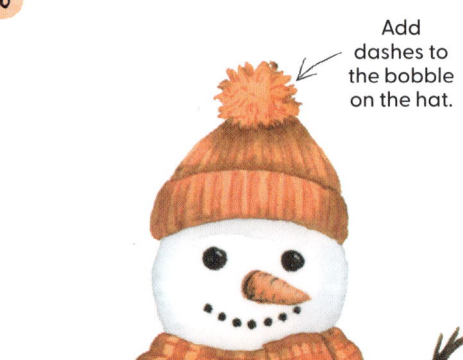

Add dashes to the bobble on the hat.

Add wavy lines for tassels at the end of the scarf.

Robin

STEPS

1. Draw the outline lightly in pencil.

2. Wet the inside of the face and body, leaving a thin gap around the eye. Add mix 1 (orange) and mix 2 (red orange) under the eye and down the chest. Add mix 3 (gray) above the eye and under the wing. Dab in a little Burnt Umber to darken under the eye.

3. Once dry, paint the wing, tail and legs with mix 4 (dark brown).

4. Once dry, add definition to the wings, tail and legs with a darker mix 4. Add a little shadow under the eye with mix 4. Paint the beak with pale Ivory Black.

5. With mixes 2 and 3 and Burnt Umber, add soft feathers to the body. With Ivory Black, paint the eye and add detail to the beak.

Burnt Umber

Ivory Black

Mix 1: Winsor Lemon and Permanent Rose

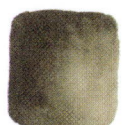

Mix 2: Permanent Rose and Winsor Lemon

Mix 3: Payne's Gray and a little Burnt Umber

Mix 4: Burnt Umber and a little Indigo

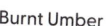
1

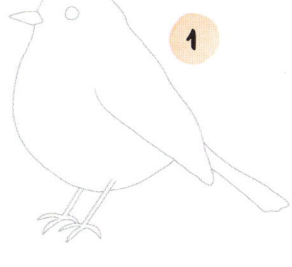

Add dashes at the edge to represent soft feathers.

2

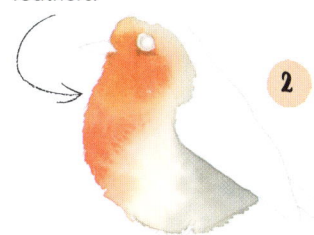

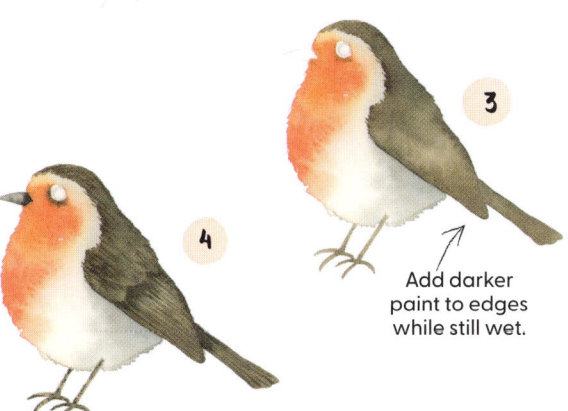

3

4

Add darker paint to edges while still wet.

5

Leave a small highlight in the eye.

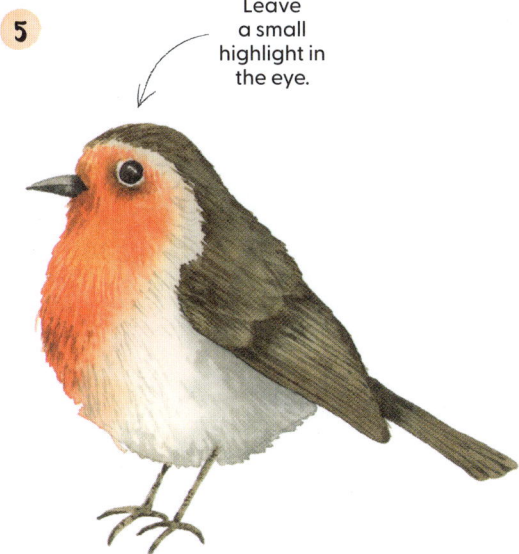

In step 2, make the edges rough to represent feathers by pulling out the paint with quick, short strokes while it is still wet.

Payne's Gray

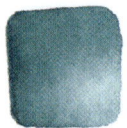

Mix 1: Winsor Blue
(Red Shade) and a
little Winsor Lemon

Mittens

STEPS

1. Draw the outline lightly in pencil.

2. Wet the inside of the top part of each mitten, then add Payne's Gray to the edges.

3. Once dry, paint the knitted pattern onto the wristbands with mix 1 (green blue) by painting the outline of diagonal leaf shapes and then filling in the gaps around them.

4. With mix 1, paint patterns on the top part of each mitten.

5. With Payne's Gray, paint the string and some extra patterns, then add shadow to the pattern on the wristbands.

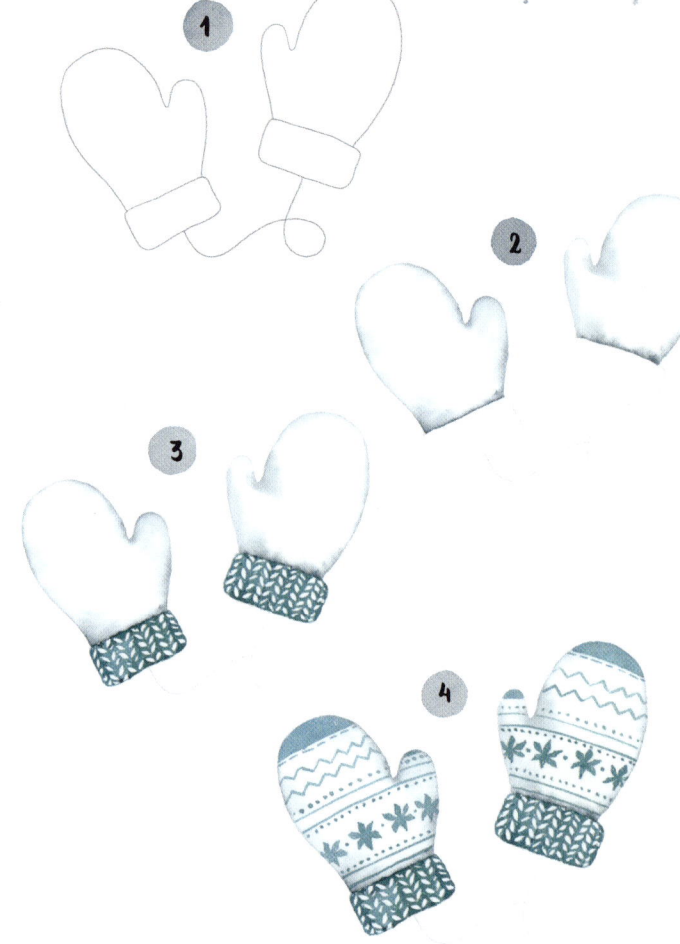

Add extra lines, zigzags and dots in the gaps.

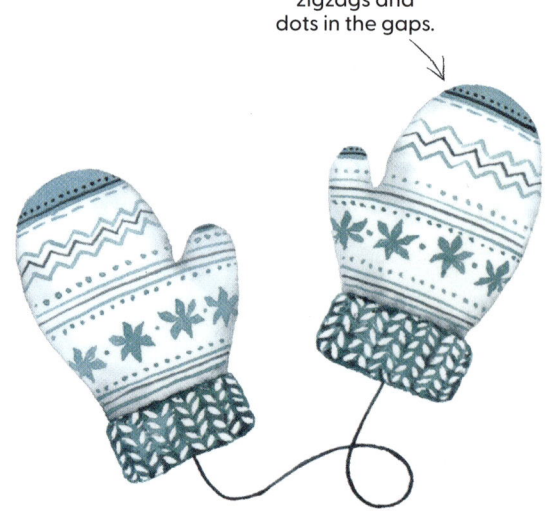

Paint a whole page of mittens with different patterns; they are great for practicing fine details!

Ice Skates

Payne's Gray

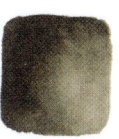

Mix 1: Payne's Gray and a little Burnt Umber

Mix 2: Burnt Umber and a little Indigo

STEPS

1. Draw the outline lightly in pencil.

2. Wet the inside of each boot then add mix 1 (gray) to the edges, leaving plenty of white area in the middle. Paint the long laces above the boot.

3. Paint the blades with pale Payne's Gray, darkening underneath the soles to add shadow.

4. Once dry, paint the soles and heels with mix 2 (dark brown), lifting a highlight on each heel.

5. With mix 1, paint a small rectangle for each lace threaded across the boots. Once dry, paint a semi-circle with mix 2 at the end of each lace for the lace holes. With mix 2, add stitching to the boots.

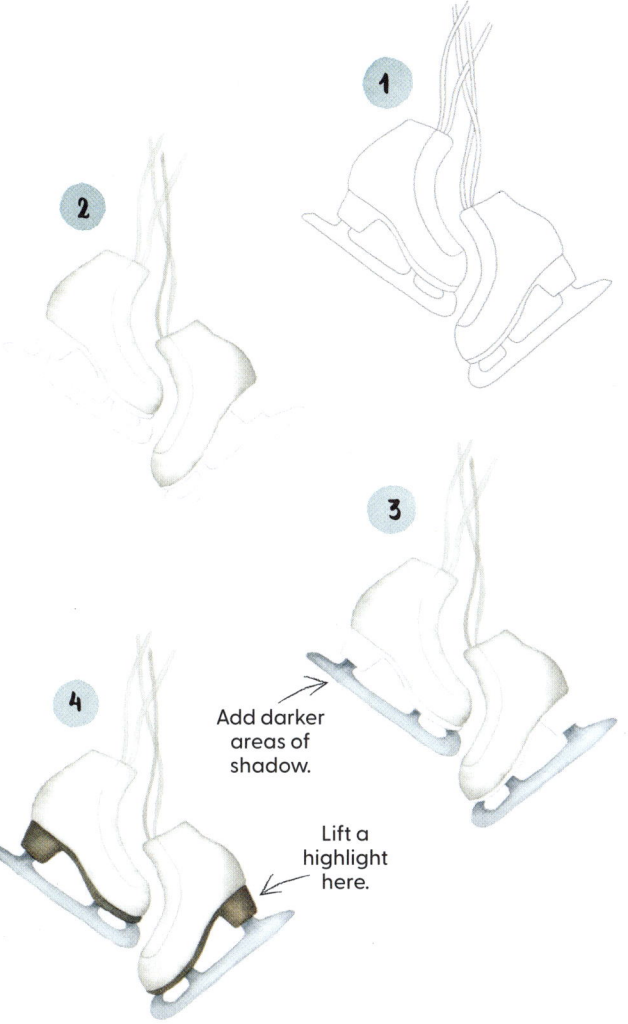

Add darker areas of shadow.

Lift a highlight here.

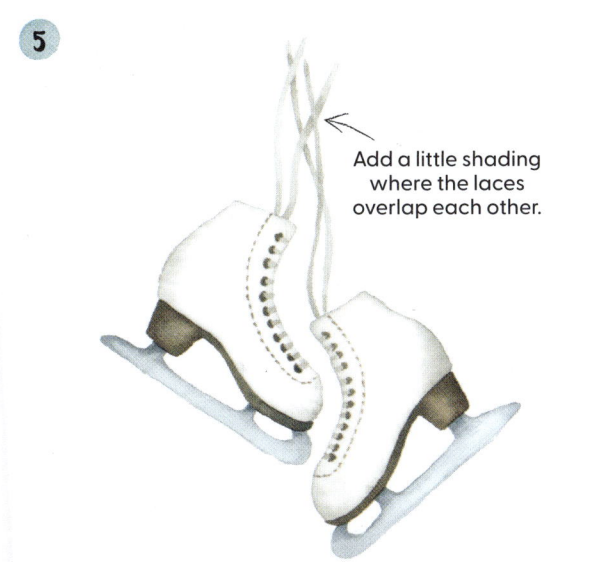

Add a little shading where the laces overlap each other.

With a paler subject like these boots, keep your pencil lines very light.

Celebrations

There is always something to celebrate or look forward to throughout the year; I love painting simple gift tags, greeting cards or place cards for these events. This can be a wonderful way to incorporate watercolor into your life and share your creativity with your friends and family.

From holidays like Easter, Halloween and Christmas to more intimate celebrations such as graduations, weddings, birthdays and new homes or babies, there are so many fun things that we can paint. For the more generic projects such as the bunting, balloons and candles, you can easily change the colors and patterns to suit your event or recipient. I hope these projects will inspire you to paint during these special occasions throughout the year and enable you to share more of your work with your loved ones!

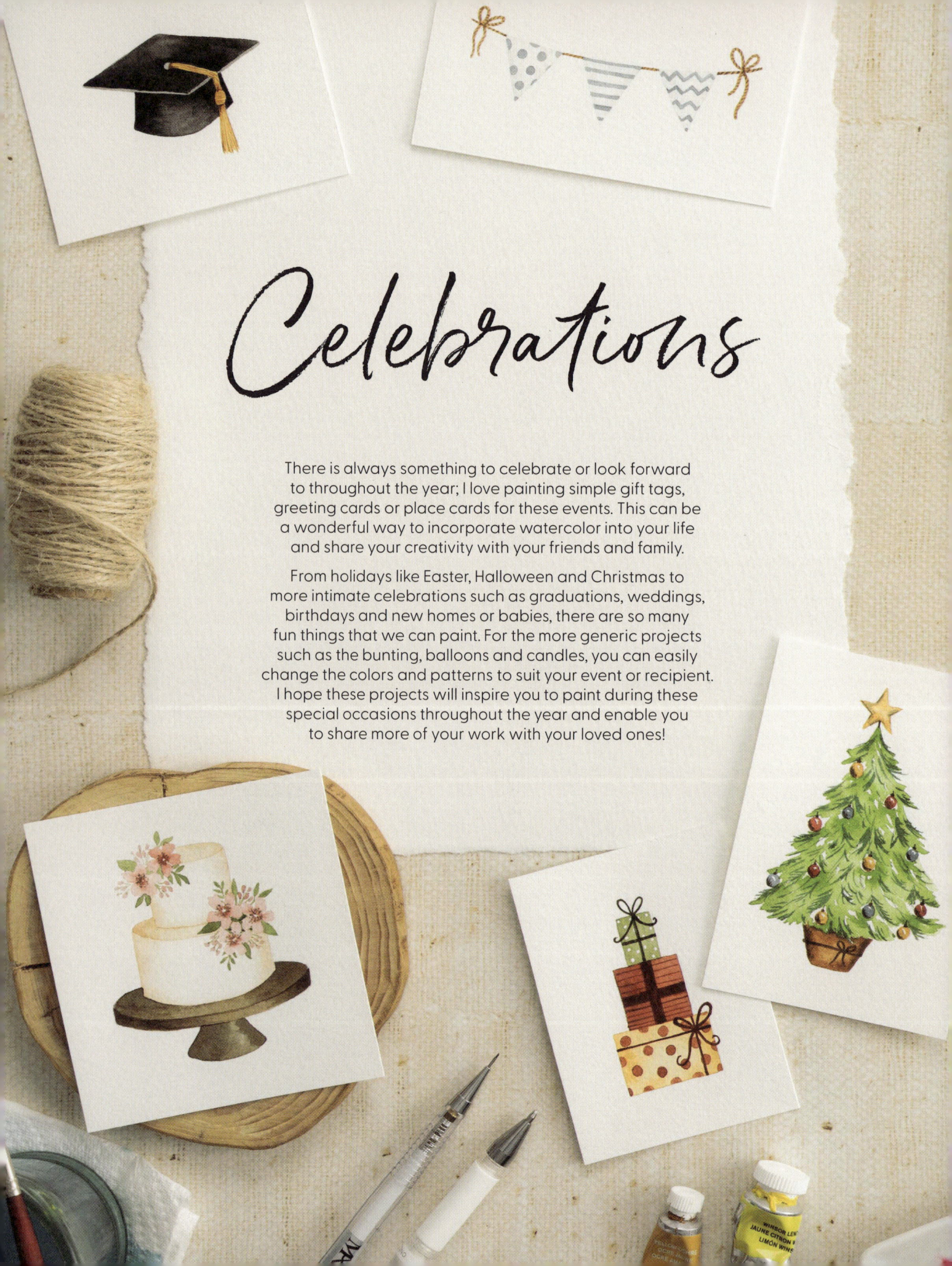

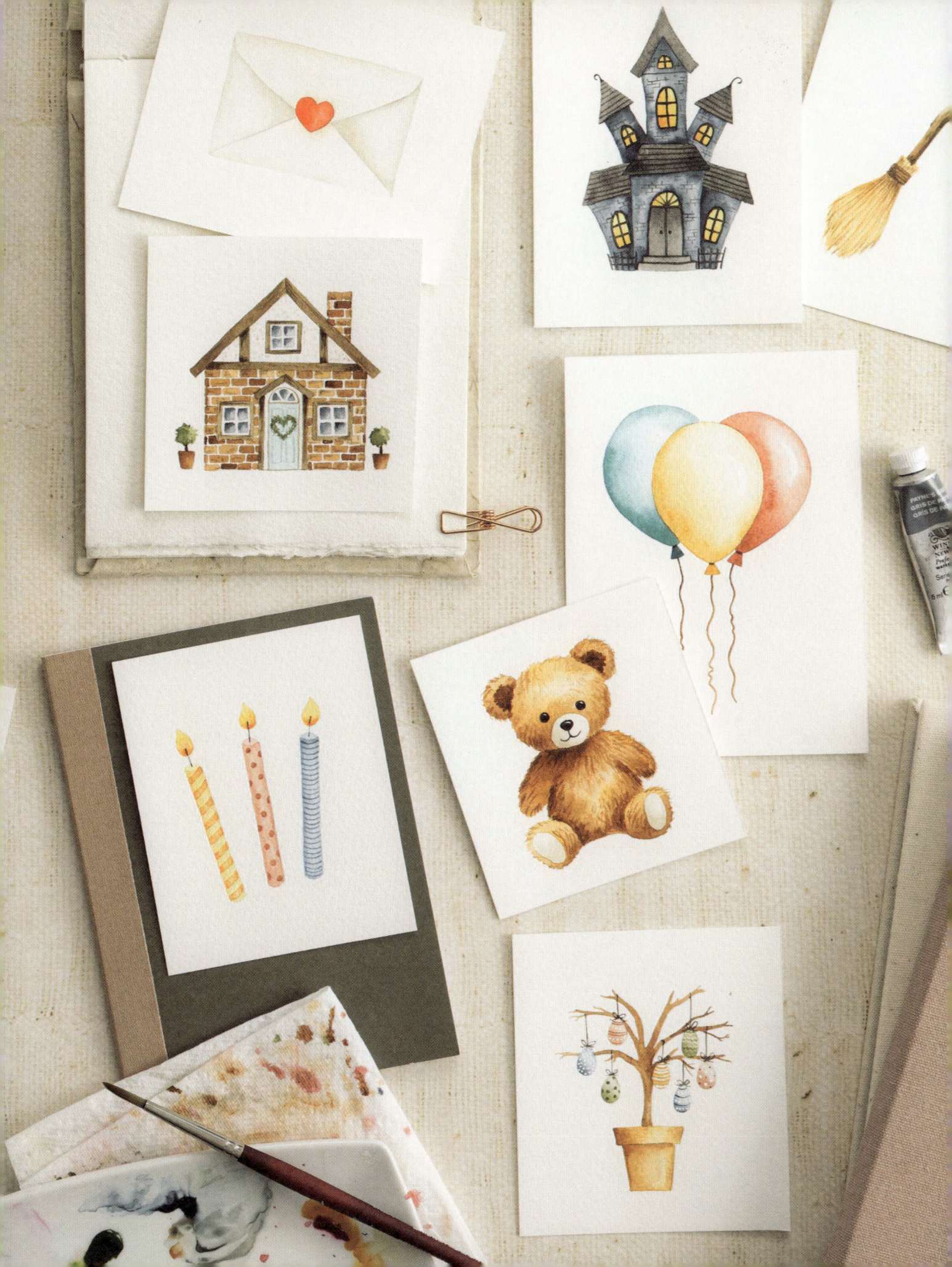

Indigo

Ivory Black

Mix 1: Winsor Lemon and a little Permanent Rose

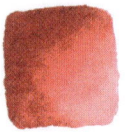
Mix 2: Permanent Rose and Burnt Umber

Mix 3: Winsor Lemon and Permanent Rose

Mix 4: Permanent Rose and Winsor Lemon

Candles

STEPS

1. Paint three candles, curving the top and bottom edges. If preferred, used the traceable pdf to sketch the shapes first.

2. With a slightly darker version of each mix, paint a downward curve at the top of each candle and blend out. Add shading to the edges.

3. Add patterns to each candle. For the first candle, lift a highlight on each stripe to add dimension. For the third candle, curve the lines so they are parallel with the top and bottom edge.

4. For the flames, paint a teardrop shape with mix 1 (yellow orange) and then, while still wet, add mix 4 (red orange) at the base. Once dry, paint a wick on each candle with Ivory Black.

Mix 1 (yellow orange)

Indigo

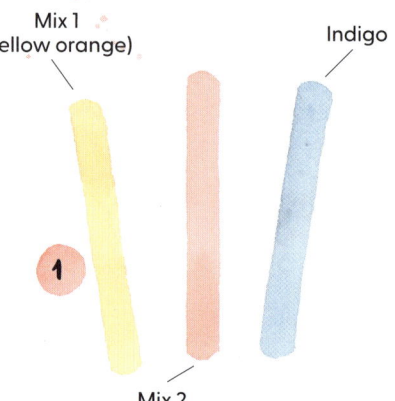

1

Mix 2 (brown red)

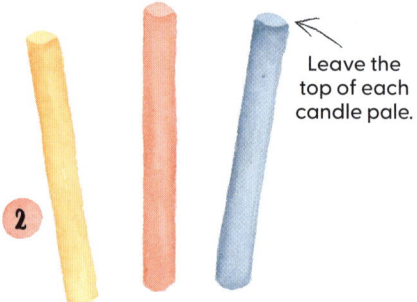

Leave the top of each candle pale.

2

Mix 2 (brown red)

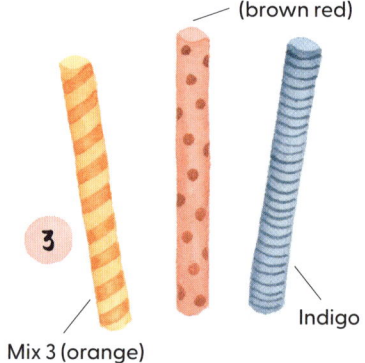
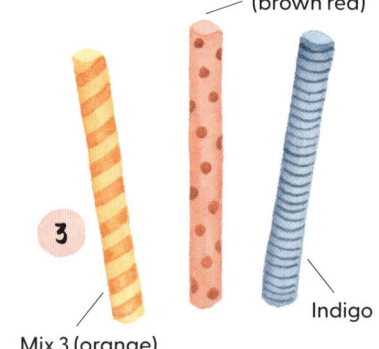

3

Mix 3 (orange)

Indigo

4

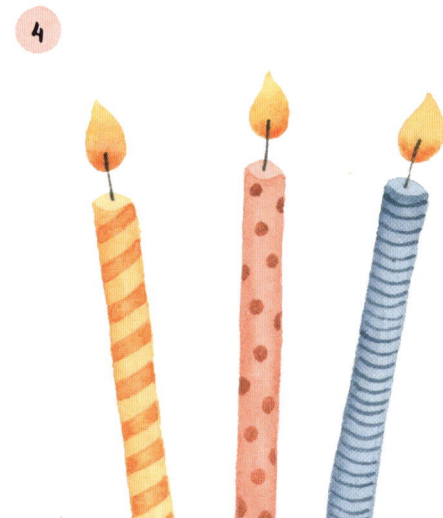

Practice flat washes, shading and delicate brushwork with this simple project!

Graduation Cap

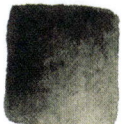
Ivory Black

Yellow Ochre

Burnt Umber

STEPS

1. Draw the outline lightly in pencil.

2. With a mid-value Ivory Black, paint the rim of the cap and the inner hole.

3. Once dry, paint the tassel with Yellow Ochre. Paint a jagged edge at the end of the tassel to represent each string.

4. Paint the remainder of the hat with darker Ivory Black.

5. With Burnt Umber, add lines and shadows to the tassel. Darken any areas of the hat as needed with Ivory Black.

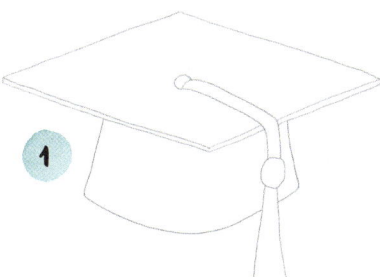

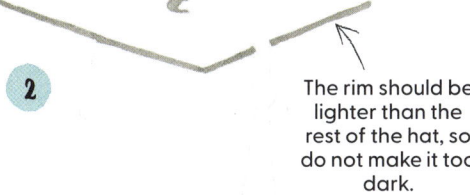

The rim should be lighter than the rest of the hat, so do not make it too dark.

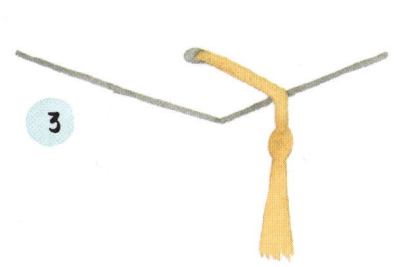

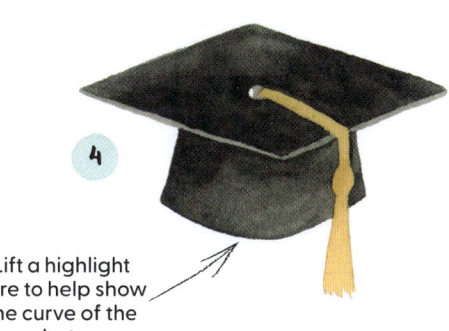

Lift a highlight here to help show the curve of the hat.

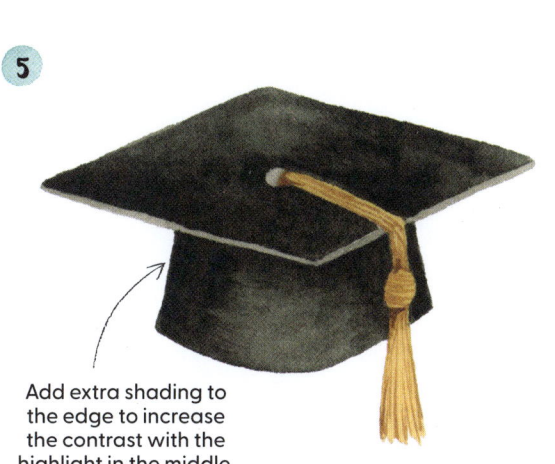

Add extra shading to the edge to increase the contrast with the highlight in the middle.

Add some black or Yellow Ochre splatters around the cap and use it on a greeting card!

Burnt Umber

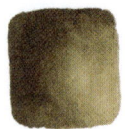

Mix 1: Burnt Umber and a little Indigo

Mix 2: Permanent Rose and a little Winsor Lemon

Love Letter

STEPS

1. Draw the outline lightly in pencil.

2. For the top and bottom sections, wet the inside and then add pale Burnt Umber to the top and bottom edges and around the heart.

3. Once dry, wet the inside of the side sections and add a pale mix 1 (dark brown) to the edges.

4. Once dry, paint the heart with mix 2 (red).

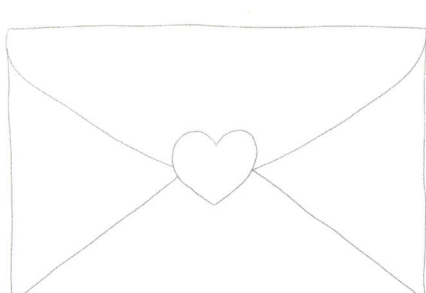

Keep your mixes pale for these shadows and leave plenty of whiter areas.

This project is great for practicing values and subtle shading. You could turn it into a cute Valentine's card with some lettering underneath!

Wedding Cake

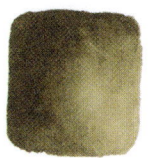

Burnt Umber

Mix 1: Burnt Umber and a little Indigo

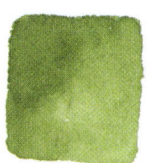

Mix 2: Permanent Rose and a little Burnt Umber

Mix 3: Permanent Sap Green and a little Permanent Rose

STEPS

1. Draw the outline lightly in pencil, with circle guides for where the flowers will be.

2. With a pale Burnt Umber, paint the shadow on the edges of the cake, avoiding the circles. With mix 1 (dark brown), paint the rim of the cake stand.

3. Once dry, paint the top of each cake with pale Burnt Umber, then paint the top and stem of the cake stand with mix 1.

4. With mix 2 (pink), paint some flowers and clusters of small buds.

5. With mix 3 (neutral green), add some leaves and stems to the buds. With mix 1, paint some delicate lines and dots inside each flower.

1

2

Leave white space in the middle.

Darken the edges to help show the curve of the stand.

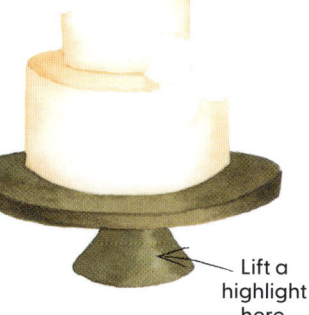

3

Lift a highlight here.

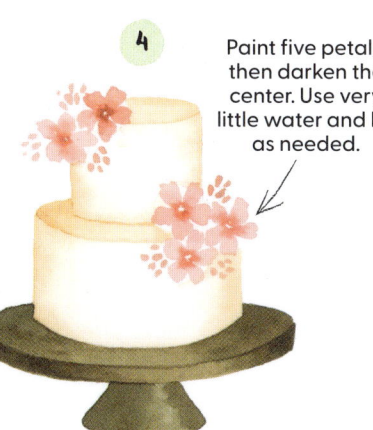

4

Paint five petals, then darken the center. Use very little water and lift as needed.

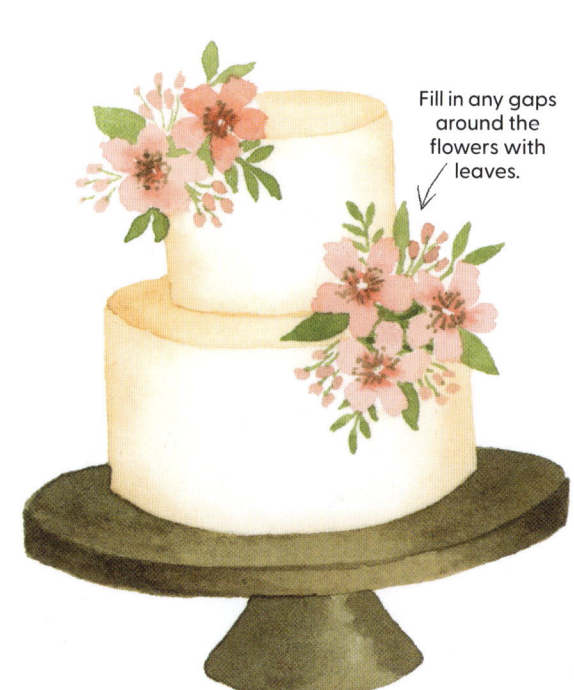

5

Fill in any gaps around the flowers with leaves.

Payne's Gray

Yellow Ochre

Burnt Umber

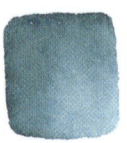

Mix 1: Winsor Blue
(Red Shade) and
a little Winsor
Lemon

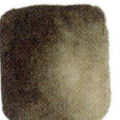

Mix 2: Burnt
Umber and a
little Indigo

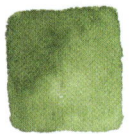

Mix 3: Permanent
Sap Green and a
little Permanent
Rose

New Home

STEPS

1. Draw the outline lightly in pencil.

2. Paint the door with a pale mix 1 (blue) and the windows with Payne's Gray. With mix 2 (dark brown), paint the beams and window frames. Paint fine lines around the door.

3. Paint rows of rectangles for the brickwork with Yellow Ochre and Burnt Umber, varying the values for a range of browns. Paint the plant pots with Burnt Umber. Add four rectangle outlines to the door with mix 1.

4. Add final details by painting the bay trees, using mix 2 for the trunks and mix 3 for the leaves, and the heart wreath with mix 3. Add speckling to the upper wall with a pale mix 3, and shading to the beams and brickwork with mix 2.

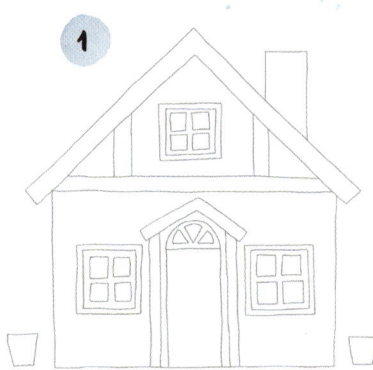

1

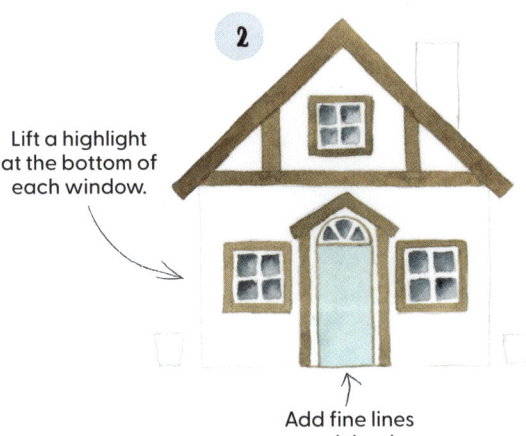

2

Lift a highlight at the bottom of each window.

Add fine lines around the door.

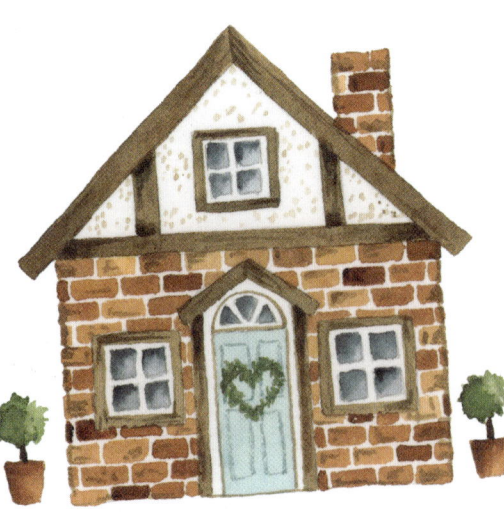

4

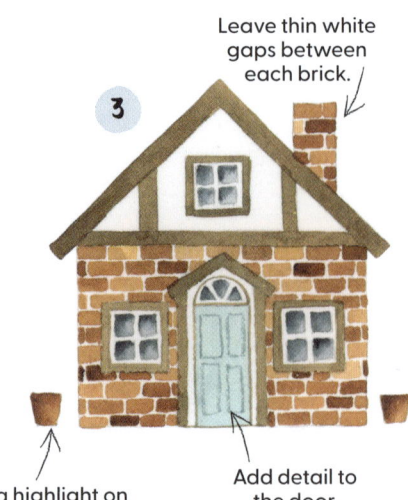

3

Leave thin white gaps between each brick.

Lift a highlight on the right-hand side of each pot.

Add detail to the door.

Bunting

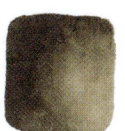
STEPS

1. Draw the outline lightly in pencil.

2. Paint the edge of each triangle with pale Payne's Gray and blend out, leaving plenty of white area.

3. Once dry, paint patterns on each triangle with Payne's Gray.

4. With Burnt Umber, paint the string and bows.

5. Once dry, paint dashes and shadows on the string with mix 1 (dark brown).

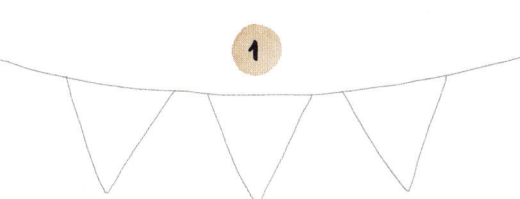

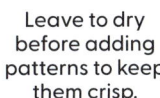

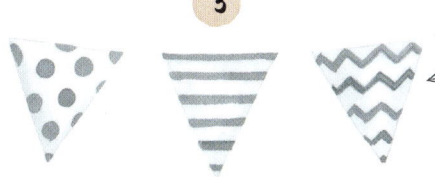

Leave to dry before adding patterns to keep them crisp.

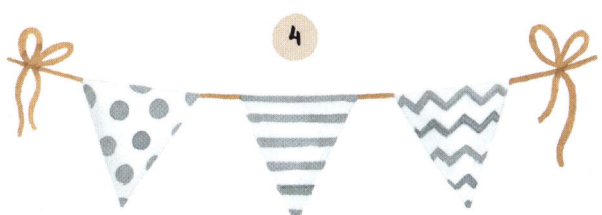

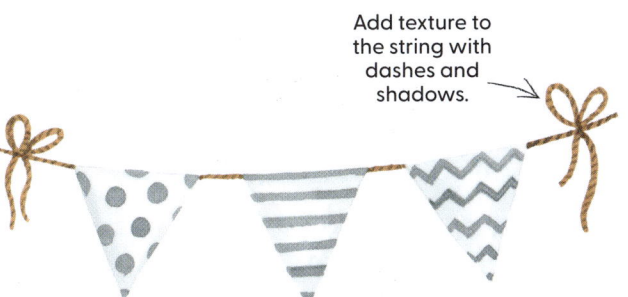

Add texture to the string with dashes and shadows.

Have fun trying this bunting with different colors and patterns!

Yellow Ochre

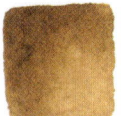

Burnt Umber

Ivory Black

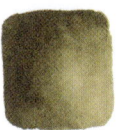

Mix 1: Burnt Umber and a little Indigo

Teddy Bear

STEPS

1. Draw the outline lightly in pencil.

2. Paint the snout and paws with a pale mix 1 (dark brown), leaving some white areas. Once dry, paint the head and the feet with Yellow Ochre, adding Burnt Umber to darken some areas. Make the edges ragged.

3. Once dry, paint the ears and body in the same way.

4. With a darker Burnt Umber, paint the inner ears and then add dashes all over for the fur.

5. With Ivory Black, paint the eyes, nose and mouth, leaving small highlights.

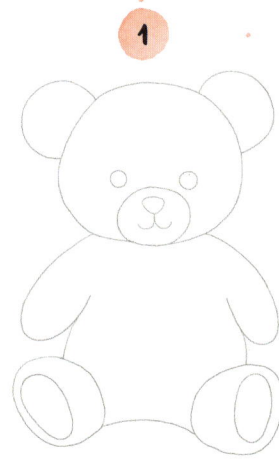

1

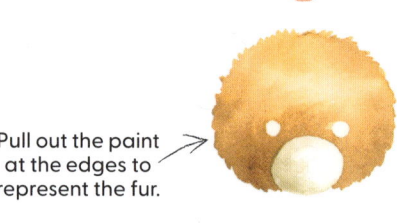

2

Pull out the paint at the edges to represent the fur.

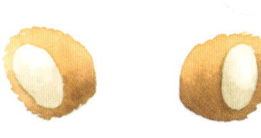

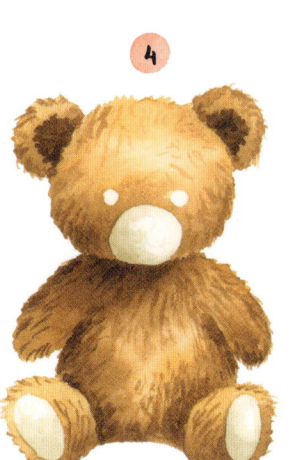

3

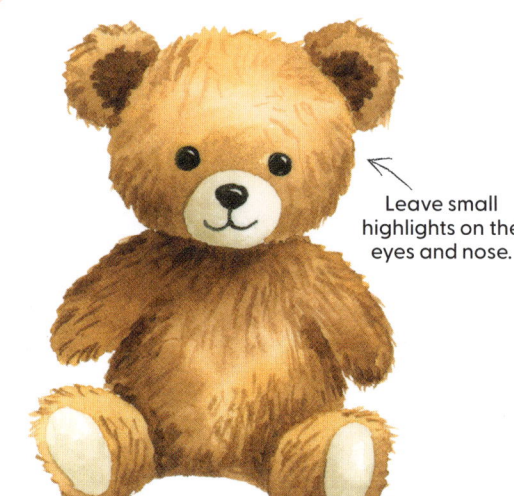

4

5

Leave small highlights on the eyes and nose.

Balloons

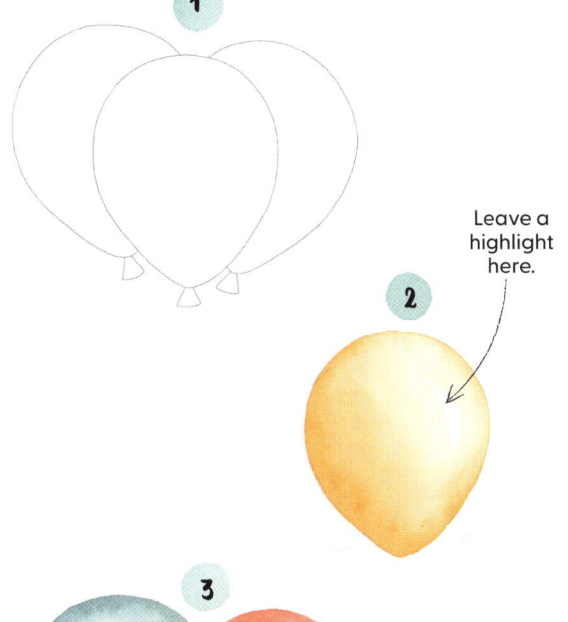

1

STEPS

1. Draw the outline lightly in pencil.

2. Wet the inside of the center balloon, leaving an area dry for a highlight, then add pale Yellow Ochre. Darken the left-hand and lower edges.

3. Once dry, paint one side balloon in mix 1 (green blue) and the other in mix 2 (brown red), leaving a highlight and darkening the left-hand edges on each as before.

4. Paint the triangle at the bottom of each balloon in the matching color.

5. Add strings with Burnt Umber.

Yellow Ochre

Burnt Umber

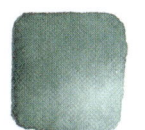

Mix 1: Winsor Blue (Red Shade) and a little Winsor Lemon

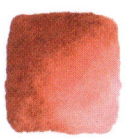

Mix 2: Permanent Rose and Burnt Umber

2

Leave a highlight here.

3

Leave a highlight here.

Darken the edges for dimension.

4

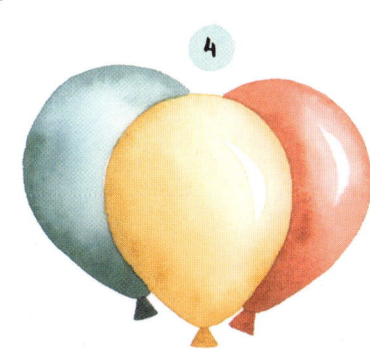

Leave most of the balloon quite pale and darken the edges to help create the shape!

5

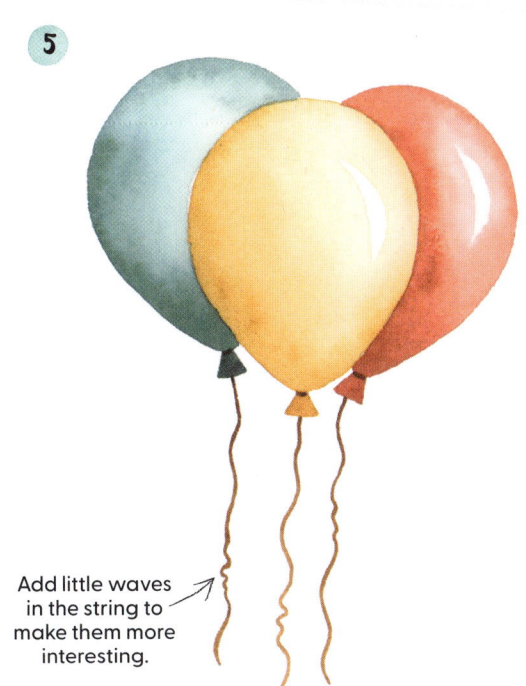

Add little waves in the string to make them more interesting.

Indigo

Yellow Ochre

Burnt Umber

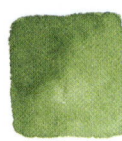
Mix 1: Permanent Sap Green and a little Permanent Rose

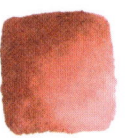
Mix 2: Permanent Rose and Burnt Umber

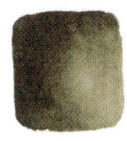
Mix 3: Burnt Umber and a little Indigo

Plus opaque white

Easter Tree

STEPS

1. Draw the outline lightly in pencil.

2. Paint the eggs, lifting a highlight at the top right of each one. Wet the pot and paint with Yellow Ochre, leaving a lighter area off-center on the right and darkening the edges.

3. Once dry, paint the tree with Burnt Umber, adding more, finer twigs on the branches. Add shadow to the pot with Burnt Umber.

4. Paint patterns on each egg with darker versions of each mix and opaque white. Add a string and bow to each egg with mix 3 (dark brown).

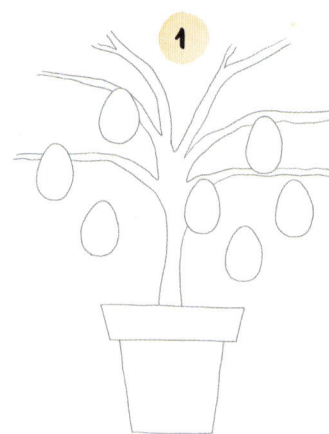

1

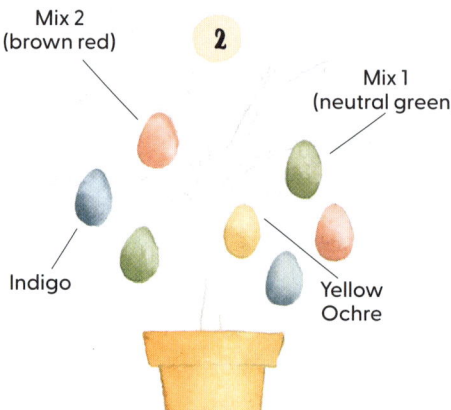

2

Mix 2 (brown red)

Mix 1 (neutral green)

Indigo

Yellow Ochre

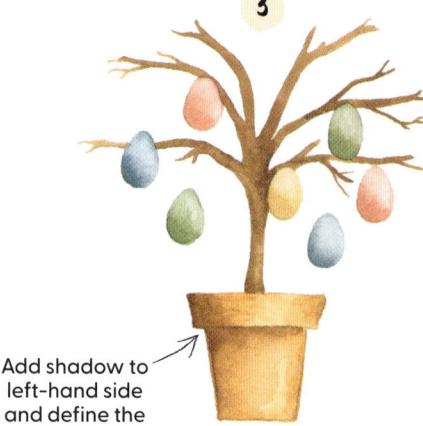

3

Add shadow to left-hand side and define the upper ridge.

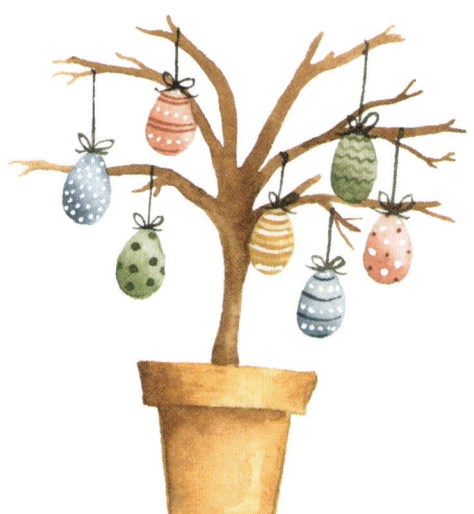

4

This would make a lovely addition to place cards for an Easter dinner!

Easter Bunny

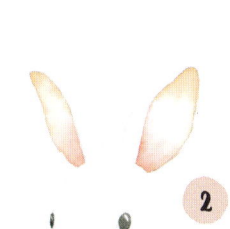

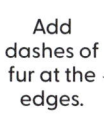

STEPS

1. Draw the outline lightly in pencil.

2. Wet the inside of the ears and then add a pale mix 1 (pink) to the bottom. Add pale Burnt Umber to the top and around the edges so the center remains pale. Paint the eyes with mid-value Ivory Black, leaving a small highlight.

3. Paint the head with Yellow Ochre, then add in some Burnt Umber, especially around the edges. Leave a white space around the eyes.

4. Once dry, paint the outer ears with Burnt Umber and mix 2 (dark brown). Paint the chest with Yellow Ochre and then add Burnt Umber around it, with a little mix 2 under the head for shadow.

5. Paint fur all over with Burnt Umber and mix 2. With mix 2, paint the mouth, whiskers and feet. With dark Ivory Black, paint the outer eyes.

Add dashes of fur at the edges.

Leave some white patches around the nose and mouth.

Add dashes of fur at the edges.

Burnt Umber

Ivory Black

Yellow Ochre

Mix 1:
Permanent
Rose and a little
Burnt Umber

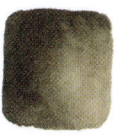

Mix 2: Burnt
Umber and a
little Indigo

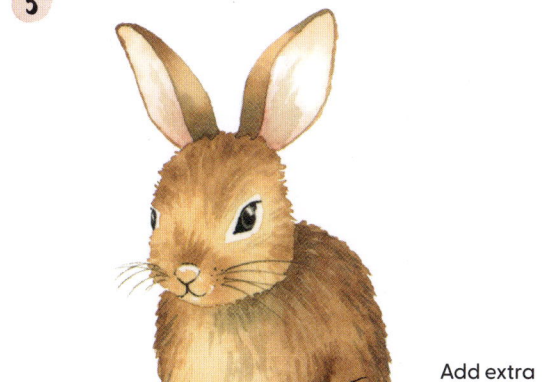

Add extra dashes of fur here to define the legs.

When adding the fur, use darker patches to help define the body and neck.

Payne's Gray

Ivory Black

Mix 1: Winsor Lemon and a little Permanent Rose

Mix 2: Winsor Lemon and Permanent Rose

Haunted House

STEPS

1. Draw the outline lightly in pencil.

2. Paint each window with mix 1 (yellow orange). While still wet, add a little mix 2 (orange) to the bottom.

3. One section at a time, paint the walls with pale Payne's Gray and then add darker Payne's Gray to the edges.

4. With Ivory Black, paint the door, steps and each roof.

5. With a dark Ivory Black, paint the final details: the window frames, door, steps, lines along each roof and curled spires and the brickwork and fences.

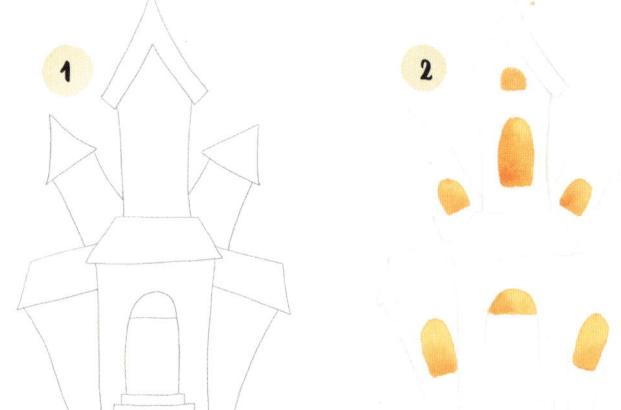

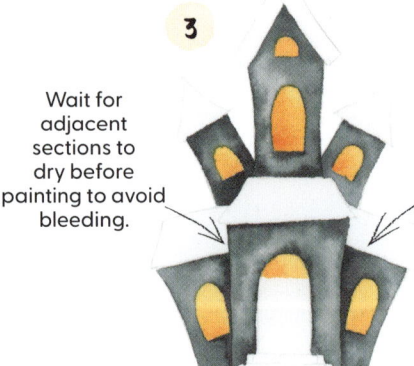

Wait for adjacent sections to dry before painting to avoid bleeding.

Darken these back walls to distinguish them from the front wall.

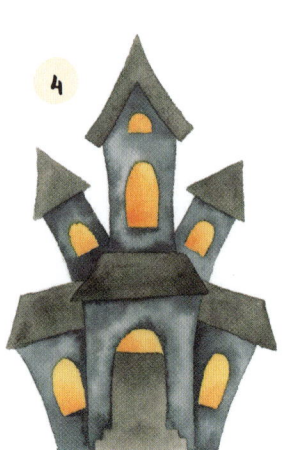

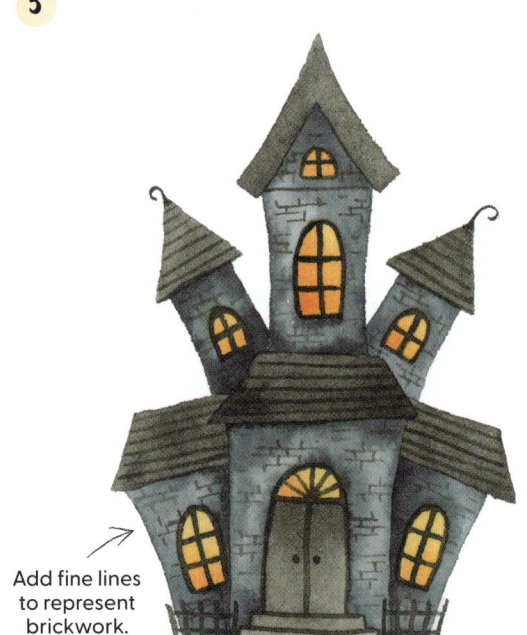

Add fine lines to represent brickwork.

Broomstick

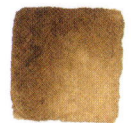
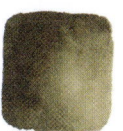
STEPS

1. Paint the base of the broom using Yellow Ochre.

2. Once dry, paint the rope and a crooked stick with Burnt Umber.

3. Add lines to the broom with more Burnt Umber.

4. With mix 1 (dark brown), add texture and shadow to the stick, lines on the rope and shadow and extra lines to the broom.

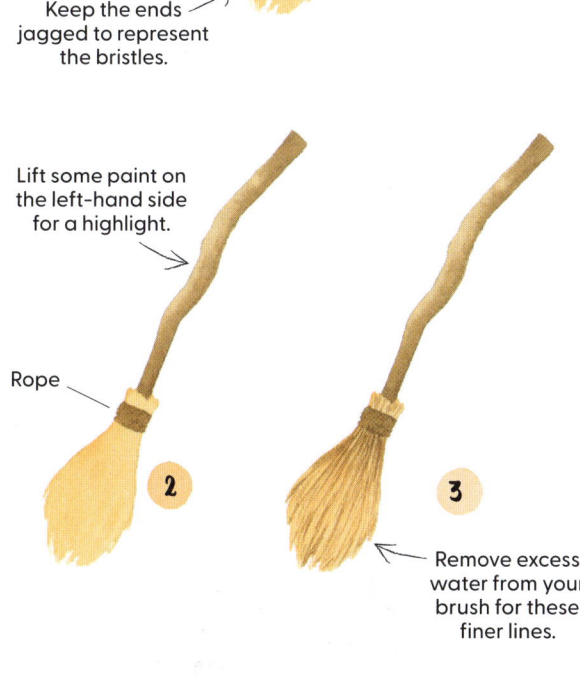

Keep the ends jagged to represent the bristles.

Lift some paint on the left-hand side for a highlight.

Rope

Remove excess water from your brush for these finer lines.

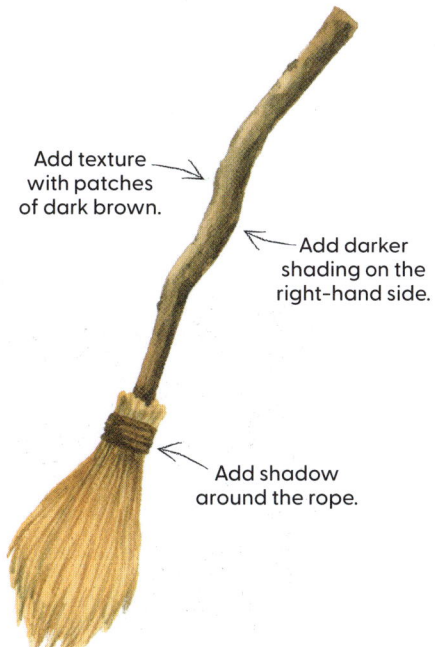

Add texture with patches of dark brown.

Add darker shading on the right-hand side.

Add shadow around the rope.

I have painted freehand here, but sketch the outline using the traceable download if you prefer!

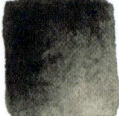

Ivory Black

Permanent
Sap Green

Mix 1: Permanent
Sap Green and
Winsor Lemon

Cauldron

STEPS

1. Draw the outline lightly in pencil.

2. With Ivory Black, paint the rim, handles and feet of the cauldron.

3. Once dry, paint the bowl, darkening the edges. As it is drying, pull the paint across the bowl horizontally to create lines and give it texture.

4. With a pale mix 1 (yellow green), paint the steam, adding Permanent Sap Green at the bottom.

5. Once dry, paint bubbles rising through the steam with Permanent Sap Green, leaving a small highlight in the top right of each. Darken the liquid in the bowl.

Leave the top lines off to fill with steam and bubbles later.

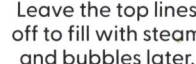

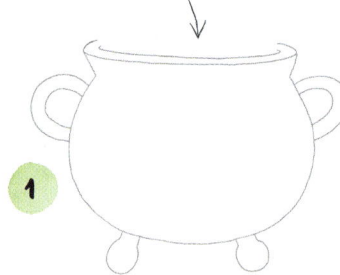

1

Paint the rim with quite a pale mix.

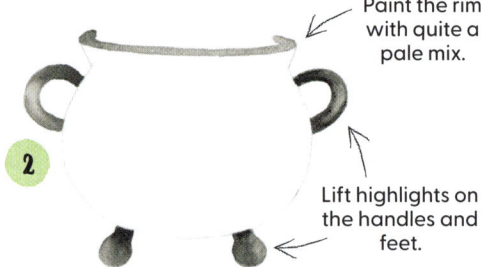

2

Lift highlights on the handles and feet.

3

Add texture across the bowl with lines.

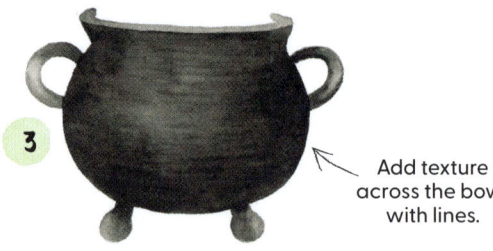

4

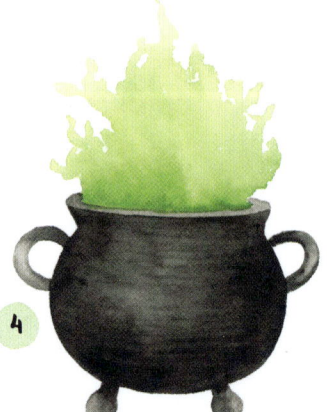

5

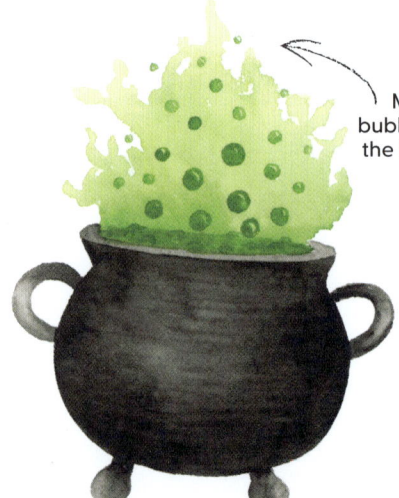

Make the bubbles smaller the higher they get.

Vary the values of your mixes to distinguish between sections. Here, note that the rim is paler than the bowl.

Witch's Hat

Yellow Ochre

Payne's Gray

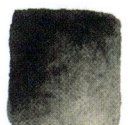

Ivory Black

STEPS

1. Draw the outline lightly in pencil.

2. Paint the buckle with Yellow Ochre.

3. Once dry, paint the strap with Payne's Gray, darkening the edges.

4. Once dry, wet the inside of the hat and add Ivory Black to the edges. Paint the rim under the buckle with dark Ivory Black and then blend out so it is lighter towards the outer rim.

5. Once dry, paint the underside of the hat with dark Ivory Black. Add folds and shading to the top of the hat.

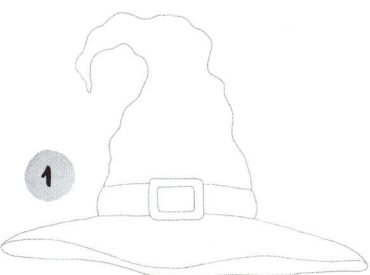

1

2

3

Lift lighter areas on the strap.

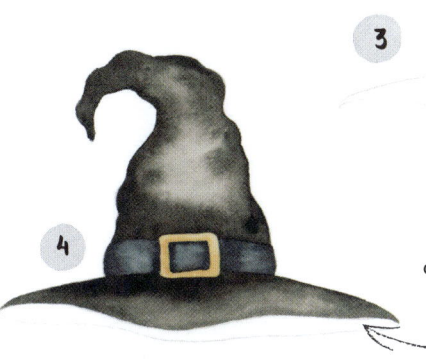

4

Keep the rim lighter on the lower edge to contrast with the dark underside added in the next step.

5

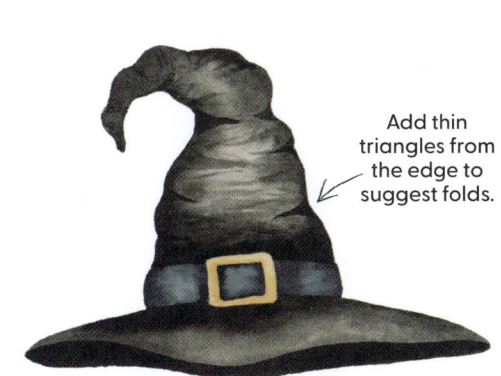

Add thin triangles from the edge to suggest folds.

This is a great project for practicing values and shading to achieve depth and dimension.

Yellow Ochre

Payne's Gray

Permanent Sap Green

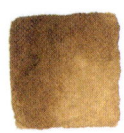
Burnt Umber

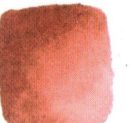
Mix 1: Permanent Rose and Burnt Umber

Mix 2: Permanent Sap Green and Indigo

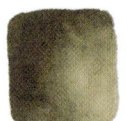
Mix 3: Burnt Umber and a little Indigo

Christmas Tree

STEPS

1. Sketch a triangle with a curved base lightly in pencil for a guide, or use the pdf download to trace the outline. Paint the baubles, leaving a small highlight in the top right of each circle.

2. Once dry, paint the tree branches around the baubles in Permanent Sap Green, using downward-curving strokes. Leave some white gaps.

3. Once dry, use mix 2 (blue green) to paint some darker branches.

4. Paint the star with Yellow Ochre and add the basket with Burnt Umber, lifting a highlight in the center.

5. With mix 3 (dark brown), paint a shadow on the bottom left of each bauble and a small square and string at the top. Add shading and a stem to the star, then add shading at the sides of the basket and a ribbon with a bow.

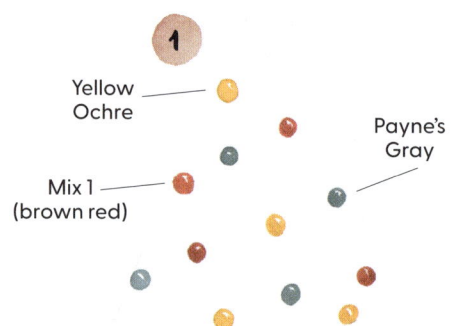

1

Yellow Ochre

Payne's Gray

Mix 1 (brown red)

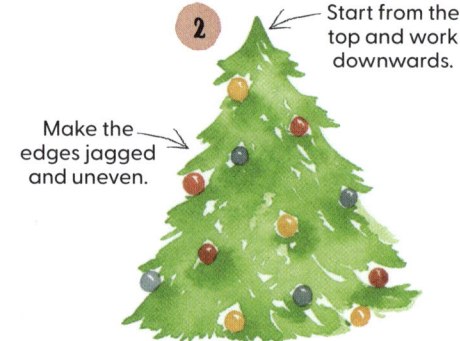

2

Start from the top and work downwards.

Make the edges jagged and uneven.

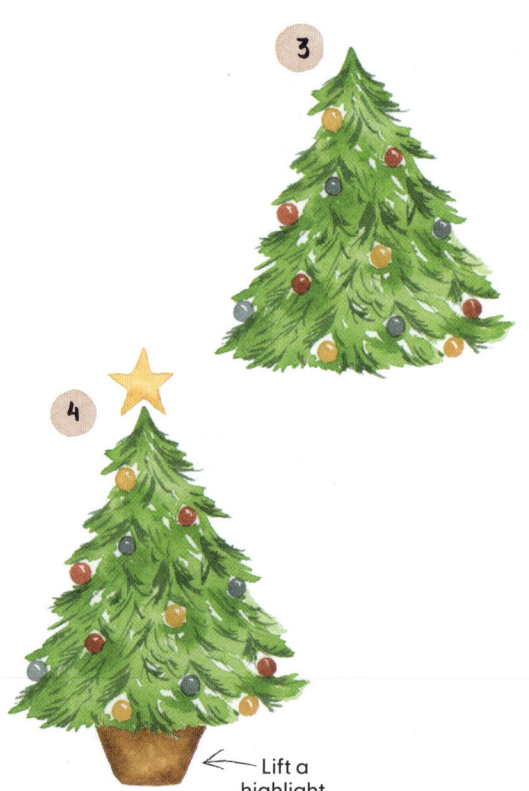

3

4

Lift a highlight.

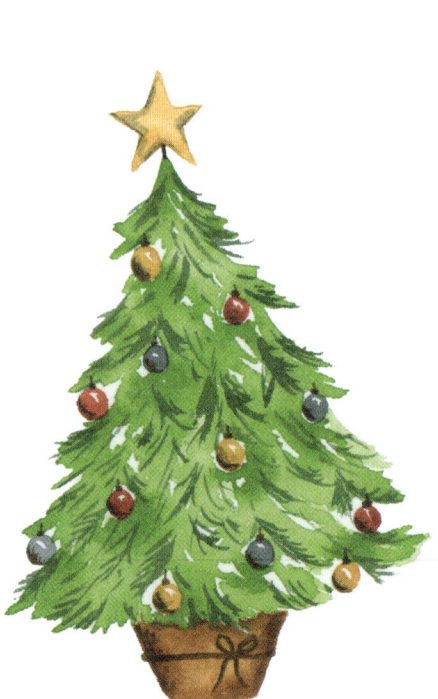

5

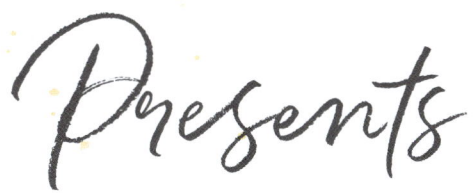

Presents

Yellow Ochre

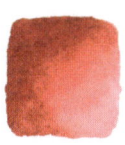

Mix 1: Permanent Sap
Green and a little
Permanent Rose

Mix 2: Permanent
Rose and Burnt
Umber

Plus opaque white

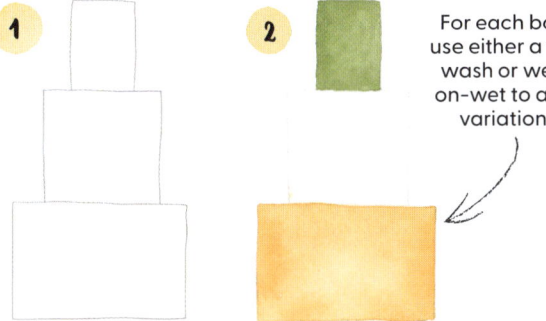

For each box,
use either a flat
wash or wet-
on-wet to add
variation.

STEPS

1. Draw the outline lightly in pencil.

2. Paint the top box in mix 1 (neutral green) and the bottom box in Yellow Ochre.

3. Once dry, paint the middle box in mix 2 (brown red).

4. Once dry, paint patterns onto the boxes with an opaque white and mix 2.

5. When the patterns are dry, paint a ribbon on each box using mix 1 and mix 2.

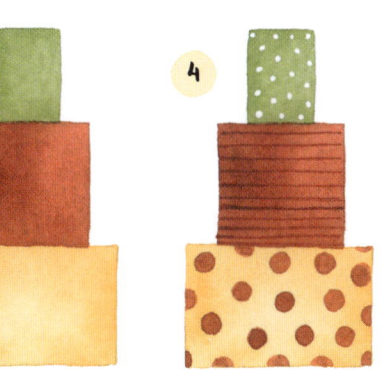

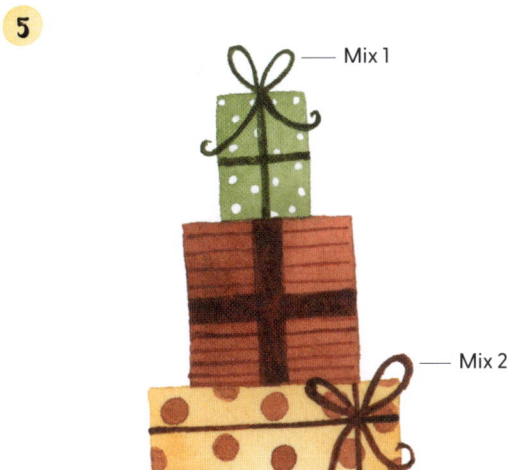

Mix 1

Mix 2

I love turning these
presents into mini
Christmas cards or gift
tags, each with different
colors and patterns!

Mix 1: Permanent Rose and a little Winsor Lemon

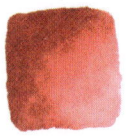

Mix 2: Permanent Rose and Burnt Umber

Candy Cane

STEPS

1. Draw the outline lightly in pencil.

2. With a pale mix 1 (red), paint a little shadow on the edge of the white areas, blending out. Leave plenty of white space in the middle of each stripe.

3. Once dry, paint the red stripes with mix 1, lifting a highlight in each.

4. Once dry, darken the edges of the red stripes with mix 2 (brown red) and blend out. If needed, add a little more shadow with mix 2 to the white areas.

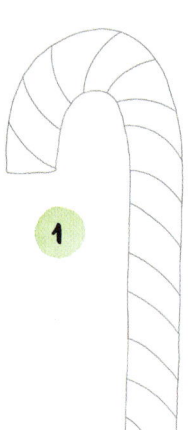

Add a pale shadow at the edges of the white stripes.

Lift a highlight in each red stripe.

Add some red splatters and cut out to turn your candy cane into a cute little gift tag at Christmas!

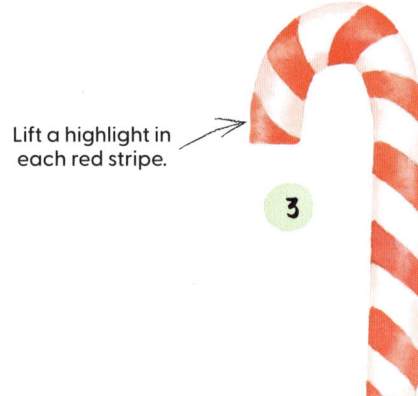

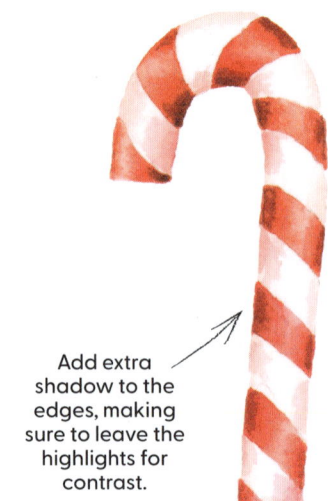

Add extra shadow to the edges, making sure to leave the highlights for contrast.

Christmas Pudding

STEPS

1. Draw the outline lightly in pencil.

2. With a pale mix 1 (dark brown), add shading to the icing. Leave plenty of white areas. When the icing is dry, wet the sections of the pudding one at a time, adding Burnt Umber around the edges. While the paint is still wet, dab in mix 1.

3. Paint the berries with mix 2 (red), leaving a small highlight in each. Once dry, paint the leaves with mix 3 (yellow green), adding mix 4 (neutral green) around the edges.

4. With Burnt Umber and mix 1, add shading to the bottom left of each berry and a little more shading on the icing, including under the berries. Add more patches and shading to the pudding. With mix 4, add veins to each leaf.

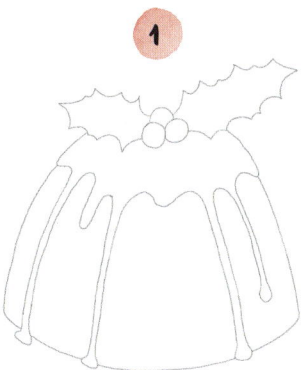

Burnt Umber

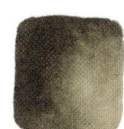
Mix 1: Burnt Umber and a little Indigo

Mix 2: Permanent Rose and a little Winsor Lemon

Mix 3: Permanent Sap Green and Winsor Lemon

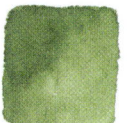
Mix 4: Permanent Sap Green and a little Permanent Rose

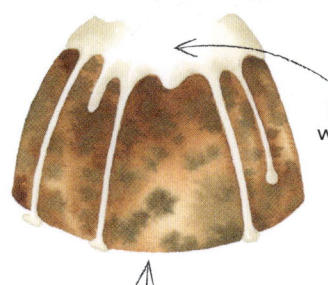

Leave lots of white areas on the icing.

Make sure the pudding is not too wet, otherwise these dabs will spread too far.

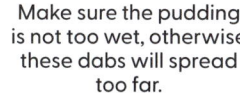

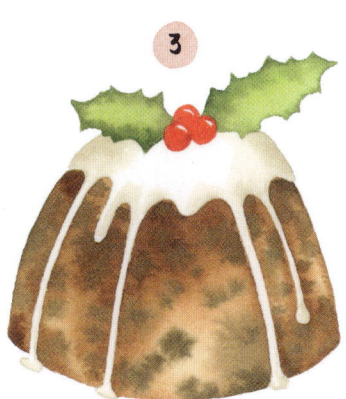

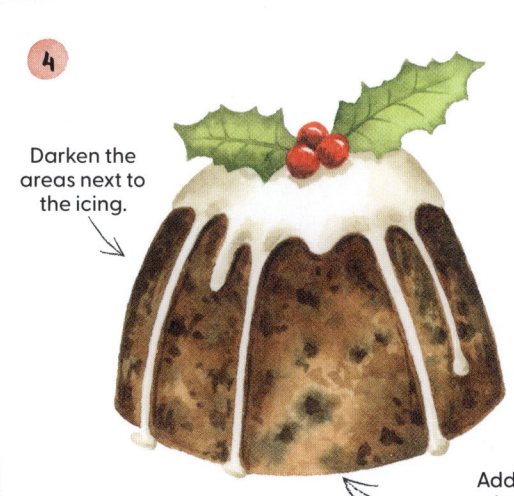

Darken the areas next to the icing.

Add darker marks on top of each dab from step 2.

Food & Drink

There are so many interesting shapes, patterns and colors in food and drink that there is no end to the inspiration to be found within this category. Fridge and cupboard staples can also be wonderful subjects for kitchen wall art or some cute little recipe cards!

So many foods have unique markings and details – these subjects give you a great opportunity to practice painting textures and building up contrast and definition through multiple layers. From the gorgeous red of the pomegranate to the variety of greens within a peapod, there are also many wonderful colors for you to practice mixing.

Have a go at these projects and then take a look around your kitchen for other interesting subjects that you could try painting.

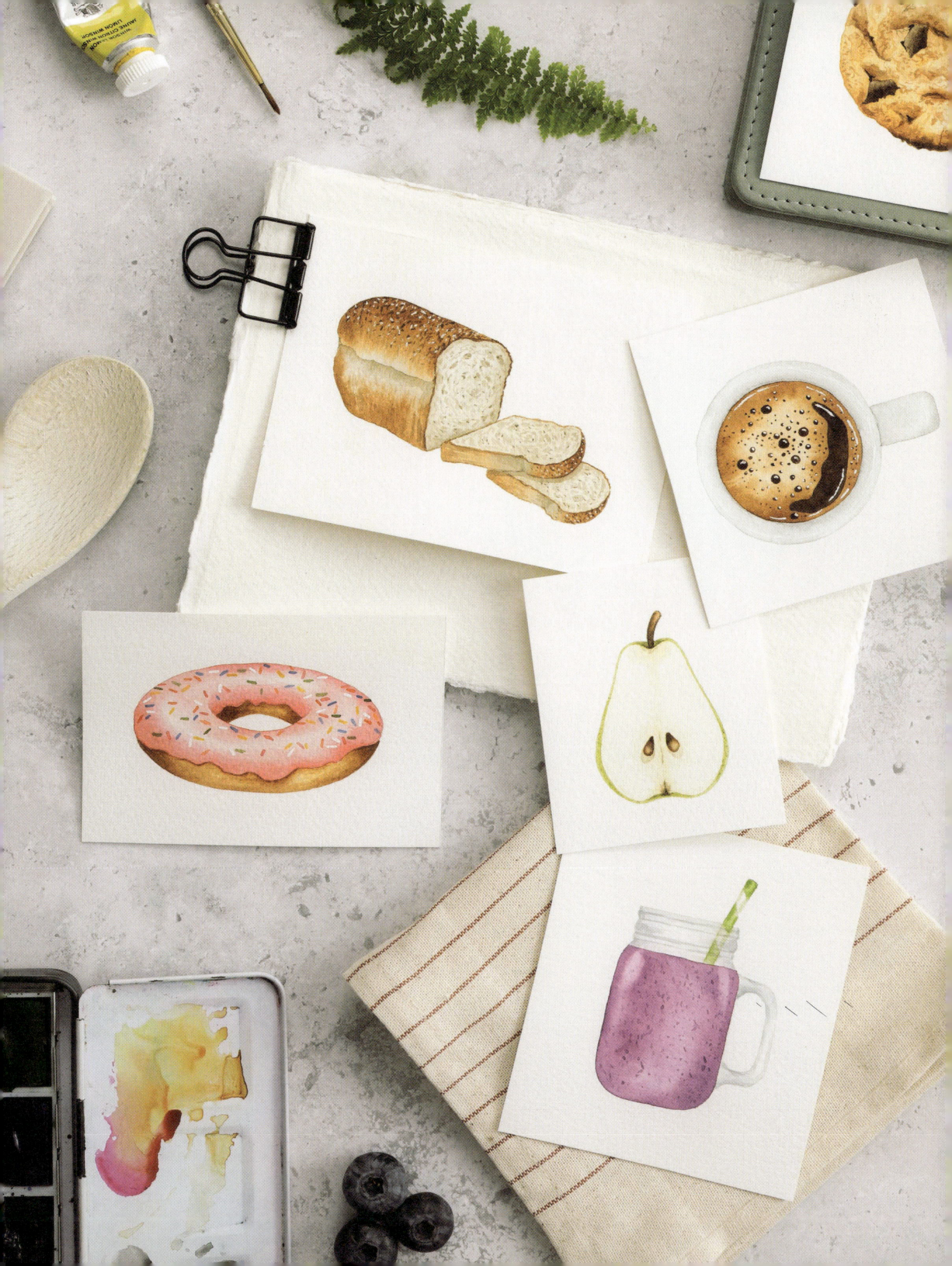

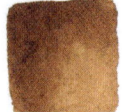

Burnt Umber

Mix 1: Payne's Gray and a little Burnt Umber

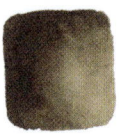

Mix 2: Burnt Umber and a little Indigo

Plus opaque white

Coffee

STEPS

1. Draw the outline lightly in pencil.

2. Wet the inside of the outer ring of the mug, then add mix 1 (gray) to the edges. Once dry, paint the handle in the same way.

3. Wet the inner circle, leaving a large area dry so it will remain white. Add dark Burnt Umber around the edges of the circle and the white area so it bleeds into the wet paper naturally.

4. With mix 2 (dark brown), fill in the white area and add circles and dots to the foam.

5. Once dry, use an opaque white to add highlights.

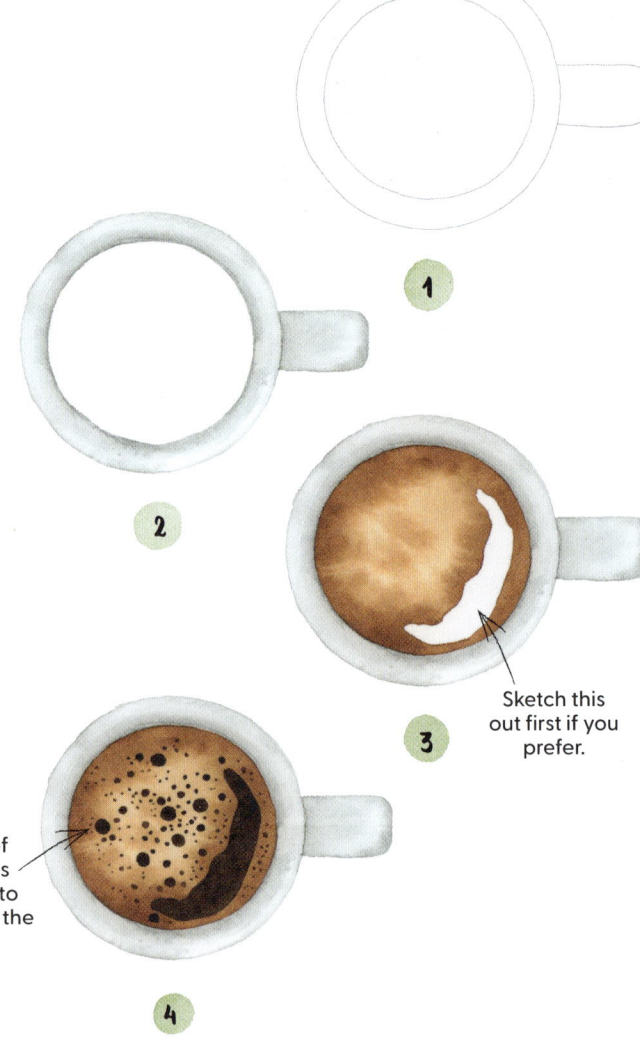

1

2

Sketch this out first if you prefer.

3

Add circles of different sizes and tiny dots to represent all of the bubbles.

4

5

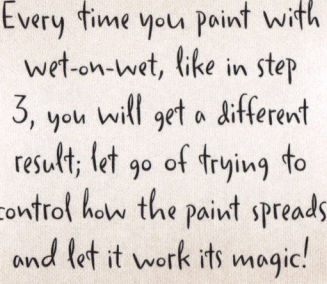

Every time you paint with wet-on-wet, like in step 3, you will get a different result; let go of trying to control how the paint spreads and let it work its magic!

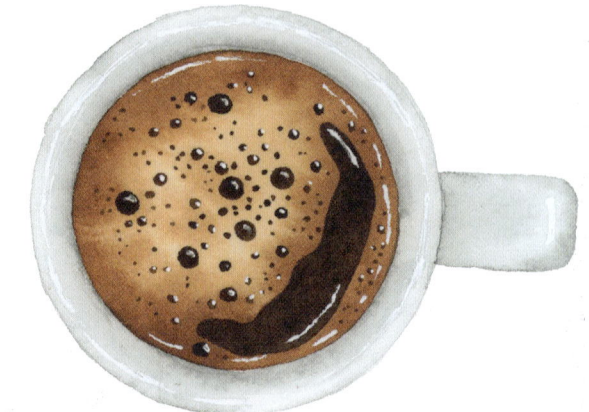

Smoothie

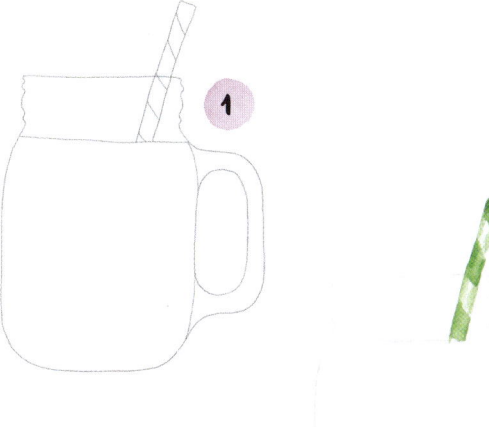

Permanent Sap Green

Mix 1: Payne's Gray and a little Burnt Umber

Mix 2: Permanent Rose and Winsor Blue (Red Shade)

STEPS

1. Draw the outline lightly in pencil.

2. With Permanent Sap Green, paint the stripes on the straw, lifting a highlight and darkening the edges. Pull a little of the green down the edges to act as shading on the white sections of the straw.

3. Once dry, with a pale mix 1 (gray), add shading to the top of the glass, working over the straw, and around the handle. Leave some white areas.

4. Paint the drink with mix 2 (pink purple), lifting a slightly curved highlight at the top left and top right-hand corners.

5. Add more shading to the glass with mix 1, including lines across the top. Paint small dots all over the drink with mix 2.

Leave white areas.

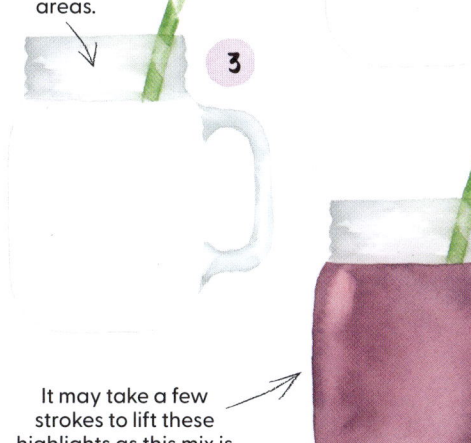

It may take a few strokes to lift these highlights as this mix is quite staining.

Add lines here.

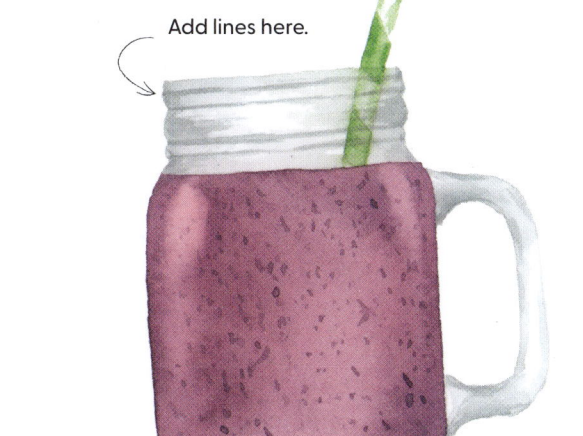

Try this project with other colors for different flavors of smoothie!

Burnt Umber

Mix 1: Payne's Gray and a little Burnt Umber

Mix 2: Winsor Lemon and a little Winsor Blue (Red Shade)

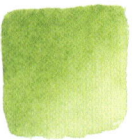

Mix 3: Winsor Lemon and Winsor Blue (Red Shade)

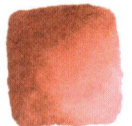

Mix 4: Permanent Rose and Burnt Umber

Cocktail

STEPS

1. Draw the outline lightly in pencil.

2. With a pale mix 1 (gray), paint the shadows on the glass.

3. Paint the umbrella with mix 2 (yellow green), adding mix 3 (green) to the sides. Lift a highlight.

4. With mix 4 (brown red), paint the drink with a slight upwards curve at the top. Darken the sides and lift a highlight in the middle.

5. Paint the sticks on the umbrella with Burnt Umber, then add shading and patterns to the umbrella with mix 3. With mix 4, darken the top of the drink. If needed, darken the edges as well.

Avoid painting the area that will be covered by the umbrella.

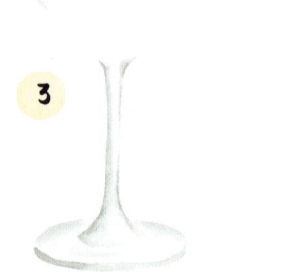

1

2

3

4

5

With your green, add fine lines to the umbrella for crinkles, before adding darker marks on top.

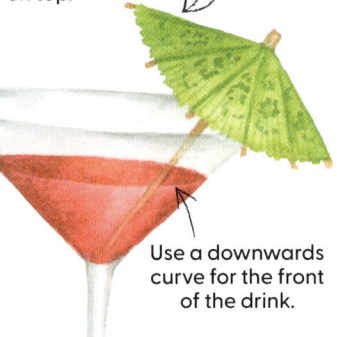

Use a downwards curve for the front of the drink.

Play around with different colors of drinks and umbrellas!

Jar of Honey

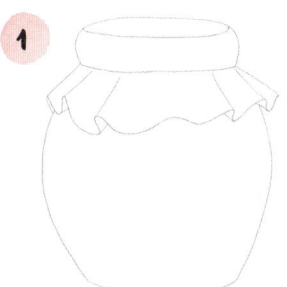

Burnt Umber

Mix 1: Payne's Gray and a little Burnt Umber

Mix 2: Winsor Lemon and a little Permanent Rose

Mix 3: Winsor Lemon and Permanent Rose

Mix 4: Burnt Umber and a little Indigo

STEPS

1. Draw the outline lightly in pencil.

2. Paint the shadows on the fabric cover with a pale mix 1 (gray).

3. Once dry, paint the honey. Start with mix 2 (yellow orange) on the right-hand side, blending to mix 3 (orange) and Burnt Umber towards the edges.

4. Add a little extra shadow to the dips in the fabric with a pale mix 4 (dark brown). Paint the underside of the fabric with a dark mix 4.

5. Once dry, paint the string with Burnt Umber. If needed, darken the left-hand side and edges of the honey with Burnt Umber.

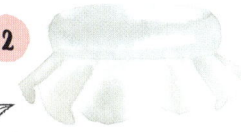

Leave white areas where the fabric rises up.

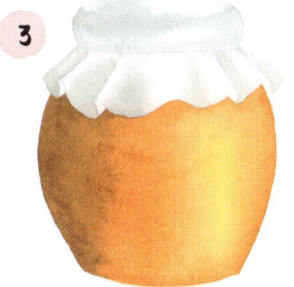

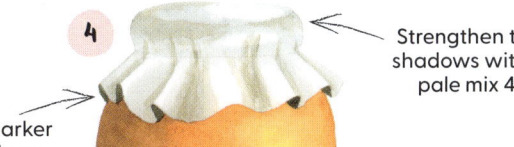

Add darker shadows underneath.

Strengthen the shadows with a pale mix 4.

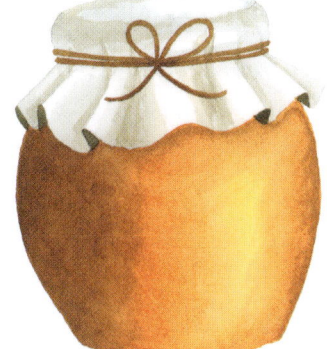

For areas where you are blending multiple colors together, like in step 3, remember to prepare your mixes beforehand.

Permanent Rose

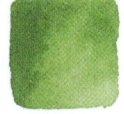
Permanent Sap Green

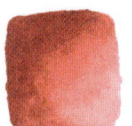
Mix 1: Permanent Rose and Burnt Umber

Mix 2: Permanent Rose and Winsor Blue (Red Shade)

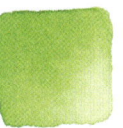
Mix 3: Permanent Sap Green and Winsor Lemon

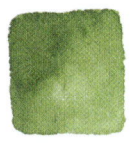
Mix 4: Permanent Sap Green and a little Permanent Rose

Beetroot

STEPS

1. Work freehand, or sketch the shape first using the traceable download, as preferred. Paint the beetroot with a pale mix 1 (brown red). Dab in a darker mix 1 and Permanent Rose for a variety of pinks and browns, leaving a highlight. Add a dark mix 2 (deep purple) to the edges.

2. One at a time, paint each leaf with mix 3 (yellow green) and then, with the paint still wet, add Permanent Sap Green and mix 4 (neutral green) to the edges.

3. With mix 1, paint the stalks and the veins of the leaves.

4. With mix 1 and mix 2, add some shadow to the beetroot and stalks. Paint curved lines across the beetroot for extra texture with both mixes.

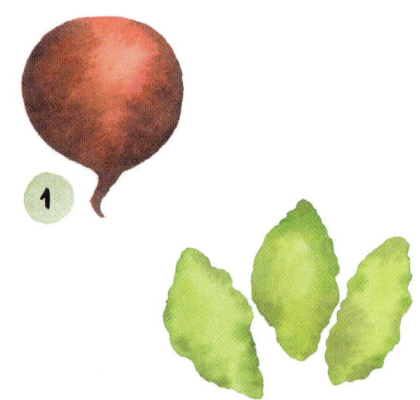
1

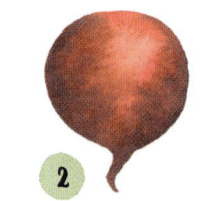

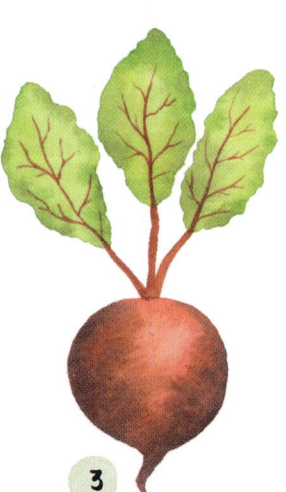
2

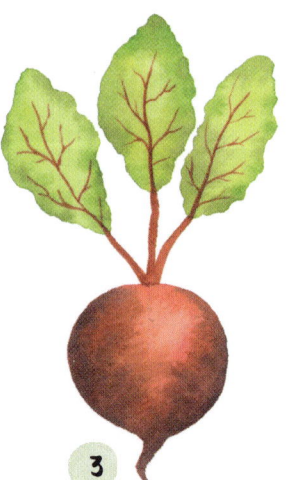
3

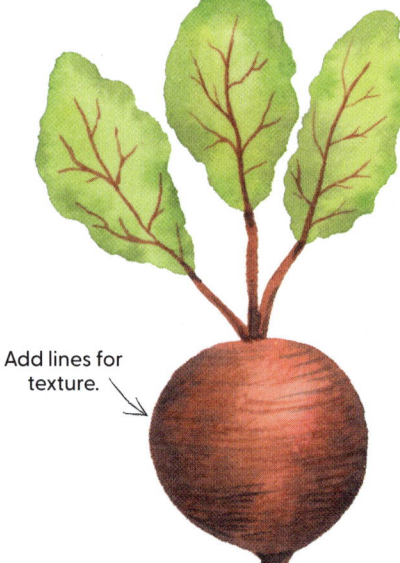
4

Add lines for texture.

Remember to prepare your mixes before you start painting with the wet-on-wet technique in steps 1 and 2.

Peapod

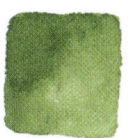

Permanent Sap Green

Mix 1: Permanent Sap Green and Winsor Lemon

Mix 2: Permanent Sap Green and a little Permanent Rose

STEPS

1. Draw the outline lightly in pencil.

2. Paint the top right of alternating peas in mix 1 (yellow green), leaving a highlight. While still wet, add in Permanent Sap Green to the bottom left of the peas.

3. Once dry, paint the remaining peas in the same way.

4. With a pale Permanent Sap Green, paint the outer pod. While still wet, darken the outer edges.

5. Once dry, paint the inside with a dark mix 2 (neutral green).

6. With mix 2, darken the bottom left of each pea and the edges of the outer pod to add more dimension.

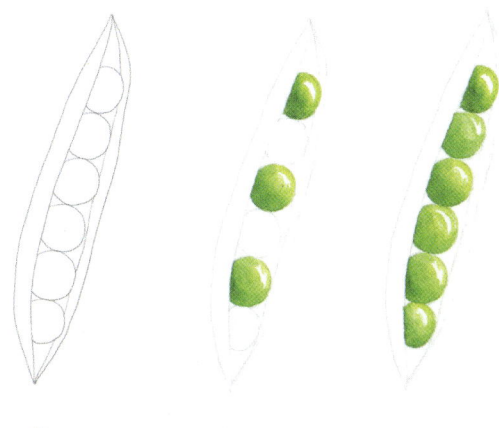

1　　2　　3

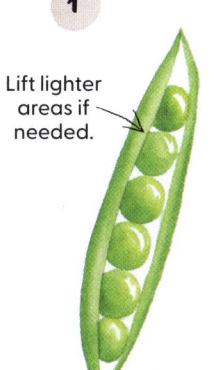

Lift lighter areas if needed.

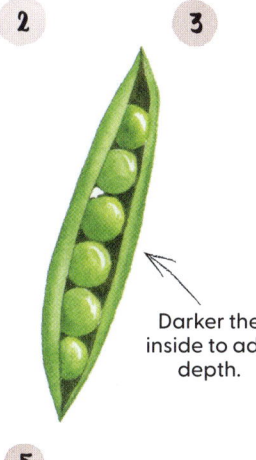

Darker the inside to add depth.

4　　5

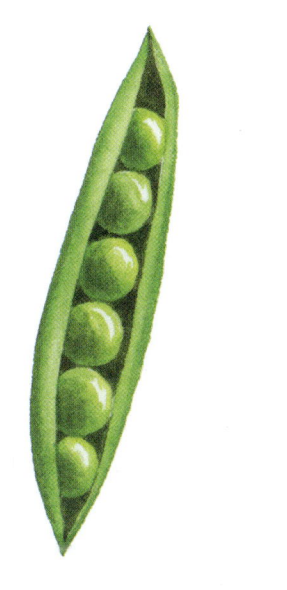

6

Practice mixing a range of values to contrast between the lighter areas and the very dark shading, which has a lot of paint and only a little water.

Ivory Black

Burnt Umber

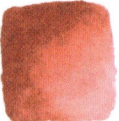
Mix 1: Winsor
Lemon and
Permanent Rose

Mix 2: Permanent
Rose and a little
Winsor Lemon

Mix 3: Permanent
Rose and Burnt
Umber

Pomegranate

STEPS

1. Using mix 1 (orange) and leaving patches of white paper, paint a circle with a bump at the stem end and an opening at the top. Paint around the edge with mix 2 (red).

2. Paint three groups of seeds with mix 2, leaving a highlight in each seed.

3. Add a darker mix 2 to each seed for a shadow. Paint a line around the pomegranate and add little dots inside the edge.

4. With mix 3 (brown red) and Ivory Black, fill in the background of each section of seeds, adding smaller marks around the edge of each section.

5. Add more mix 3 as shadow where needed and Burnt Umber to the top.

1
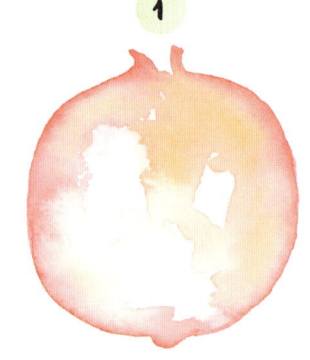

2
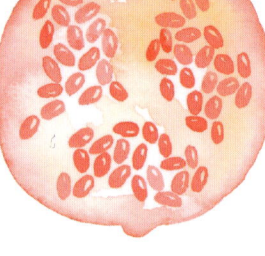

3
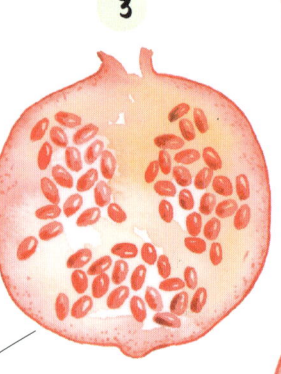
Outline

4
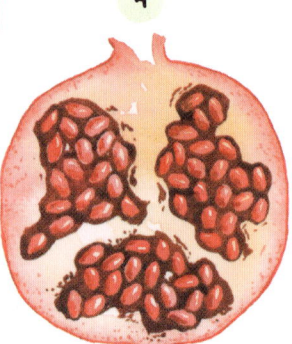

5
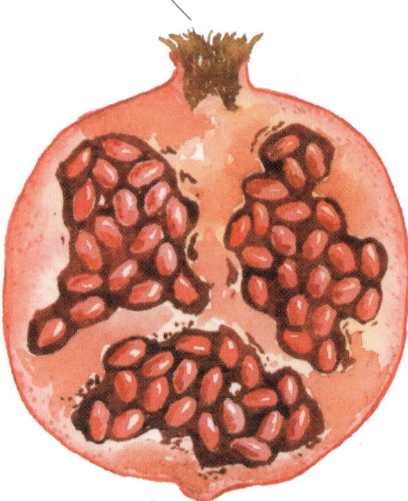
Dashes of Burnt Umber

Sketch this out first if you are more comfortable doing so — there's a traceable outline on the downloadable pdf.

Pear

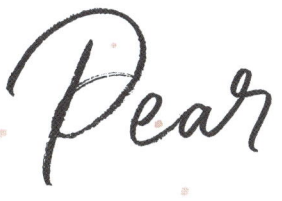

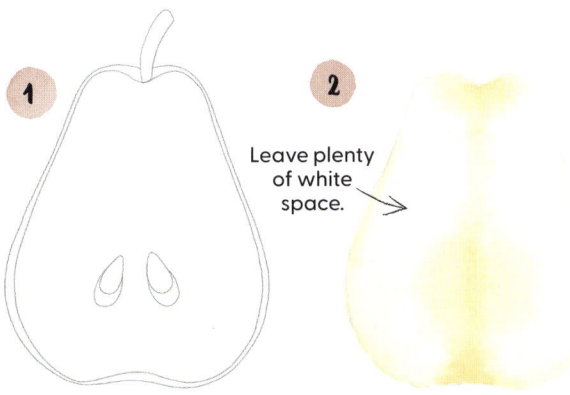

1

2

Leave plenty of white space.

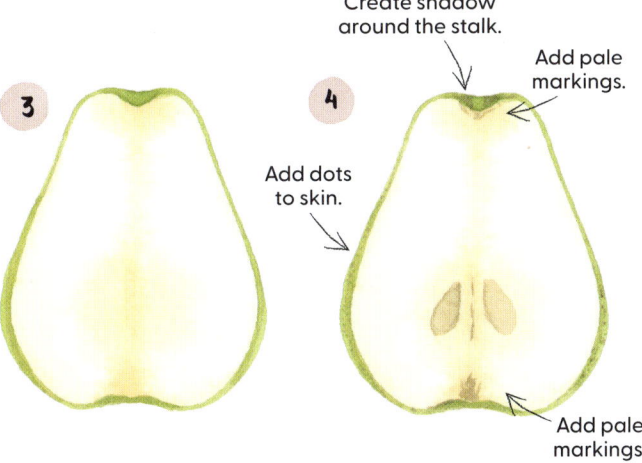

3

4

Create shadow around the stalk.

Add pale markings.

Add dots to skin.

Add pale markings.

STEPS

1. Draw the outline lightly in pencil.

2. Wet the body of the pear and then add a pale mix 1 (yellow brown) around the edges and down the center, concentrating at the top and bottom and where the pips will be.

3. Once dry, paint around the edge of the skin using mix 2 (neutral yellow green).

4. With a pale mix 3 (dark brown), paint the indents where the pips will sit. Add delicate dashes down the center in between the indents and some extra markings and shadows as shown.

5. Paint the pips and stalk with Burnt Umber, lifting a highlight and adding shading with mix 3.

Burnt Umber

Mix 1: Winsor Lemon and Burnt Umber

Mix 2: Permanent Sap Green, Winsor Lemon and a little Permanent Rose

Mix 3: Burnt Umber and a little Indigo

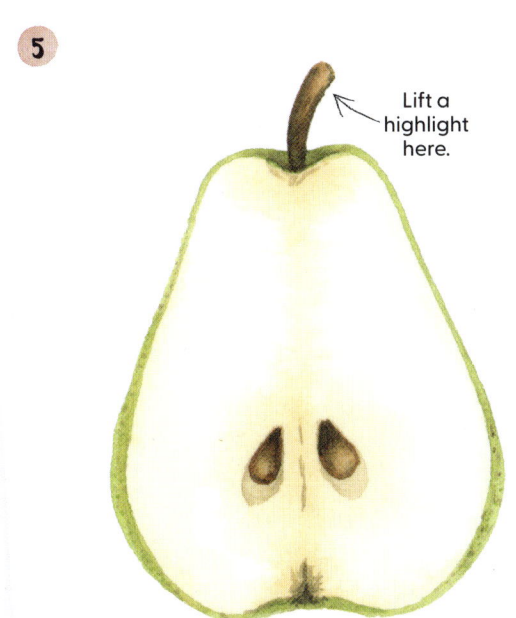

5

Lift a highlight here.

Fruits have so many interesting textures and markings; keep an eye out for more that inspire you!

Winsor Lemon

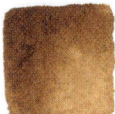

Burnt Umber

Mix 1: Winsor Lemon and Permanent Rose

Mix 2: Burnt Umber and a little Indigo

Egg

STEPS

1. Paint the yolk, starting with Winsor Lemon and leaving a highlight. With the paint still wet, add mix 1 (orange) and a little Burnt Umber to the bottom left.

2. Using very pale Burnt Umber, paint the edge of the egg white and blend inwards.

3. With a pale mix 2 (dark brown), add some shadow under the yolk and to some areas around the edge.

4. With mix 2, add more shading to the lower part of the yolk and very pale dots and marks around the egg white. Add Burnt Umber to some of the edges.

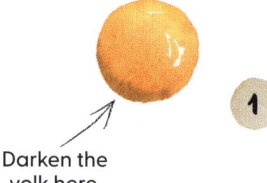

Darken the yolk here.

1

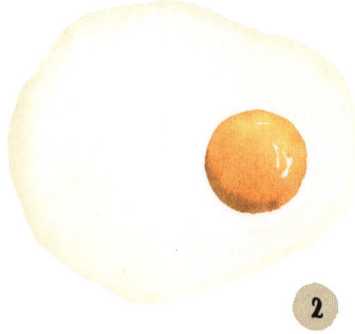

2

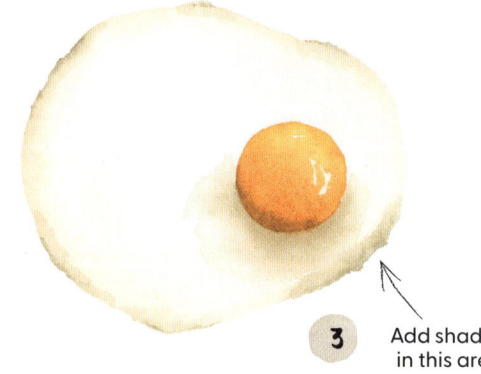

3

Add shadow in this area.

4

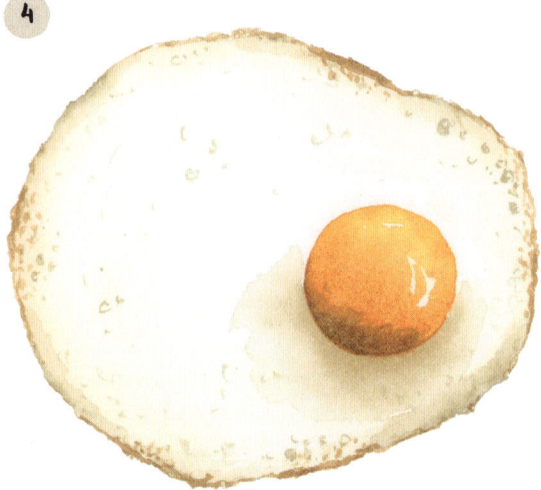

Subjects with simple shapes like this can be painted with no need for drawing. If you are more comfortable doing so, you can trace or sketch it out first.

Bread

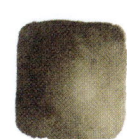

Burnt Umber

Mix 1: Burnt Umber and a little Indigo

Plus opaque white

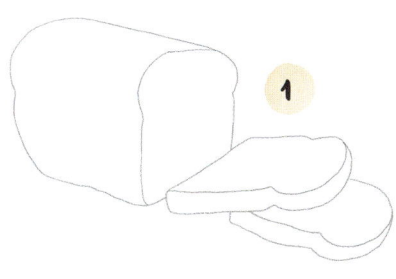

STEPS

1. Draw the outline lightly in pencil.

2. With a pale mix 1 (dark brown), paint the inside of the bread.

3. Once dry, paint the outside of the bread. Begin with a pale mix 1 across the dip in the middle, then add Burnt Umber above and below. Darken the top with more Burnt Umber. Repeat this for the edges of each slice.

4. Once dry, paint an uneven line across the side of the loaf in mix 1, then blend out underneath. With pale Burnt Umber and a pale mix 1, add markings to the side of the loaf and slices. With a pale mix 1, add markings inside the bread.

5. Paint the seeds on the top of the loaf and slices with Burnt Umber, mix 1 and an opaque white. Add seeds to the inside of the bread with mix 1.

Leave the first area to dry before painting the adjacent section.

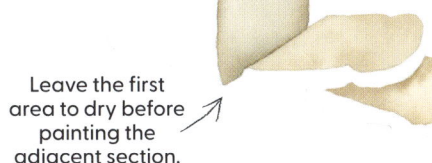

Start here with a strip of pale mix 1.

Paint an uneven line.

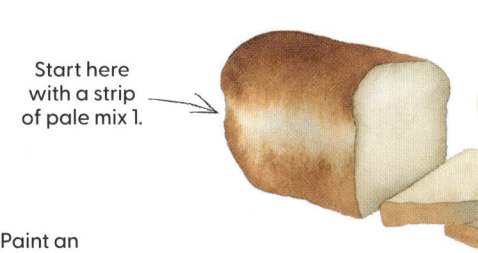

Add an edge around the bread with Burnt Umber.

Add shadow here with mix 1.

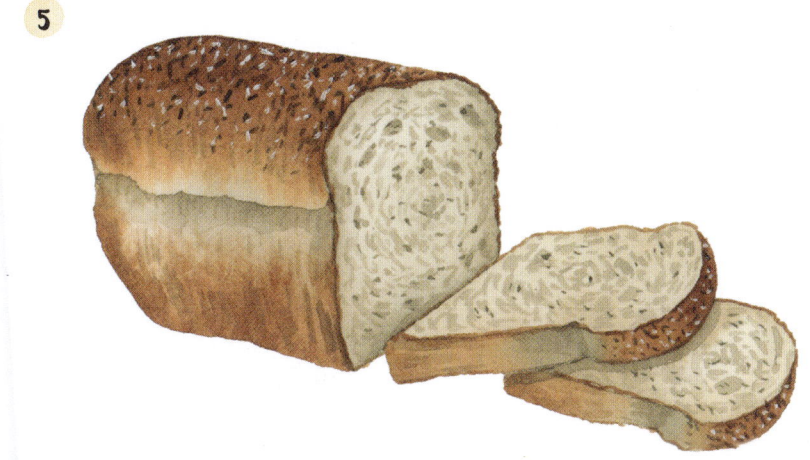

Yellow Ochre

Burnt Umber

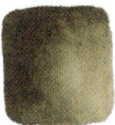

Mix 1: Burnt Umber and a little Indigo

Cookie

STEPS

1. Draw the outline lightly in pencil.

2. With Yellow Ochre, paint the base layer, avoiding the chocolate chips. Add in Burnt Umber around the edges and along some of the crack lines.

3. Once dry, paint the chocolate chips with mix 1 (dark brown), lifting a highlight on each.

4. Build up shadows with Burnt Umber.

5. Darken some of the cracks with mix 1. Add small dots and finer cracks with Burnt Umber all over.

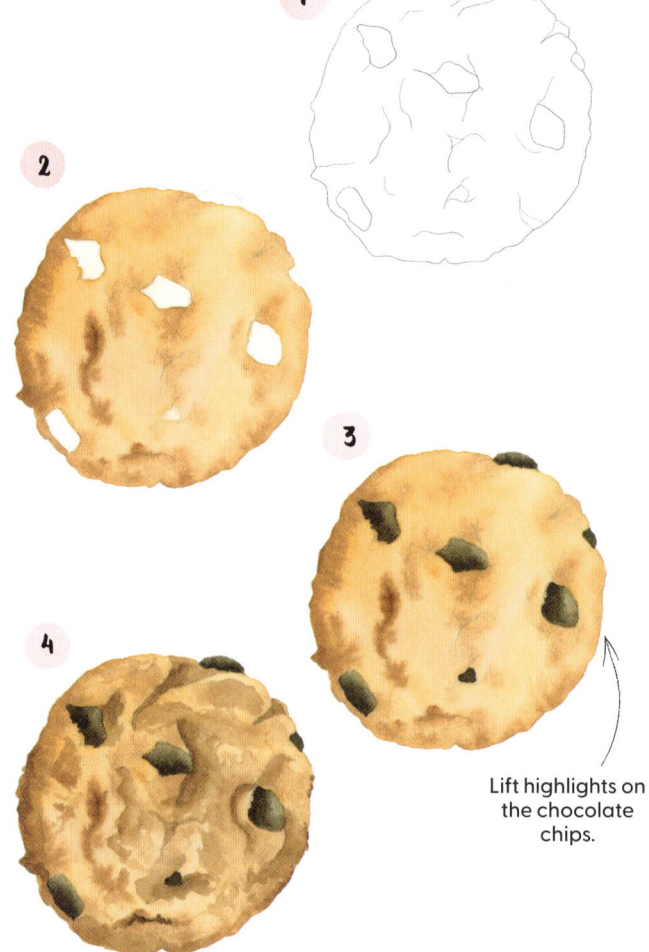

Lift highlights on the chocolate chips.

Use a larger brush to cover the area in the early stages, then switch to a smaller brush for the delicate details at the end.

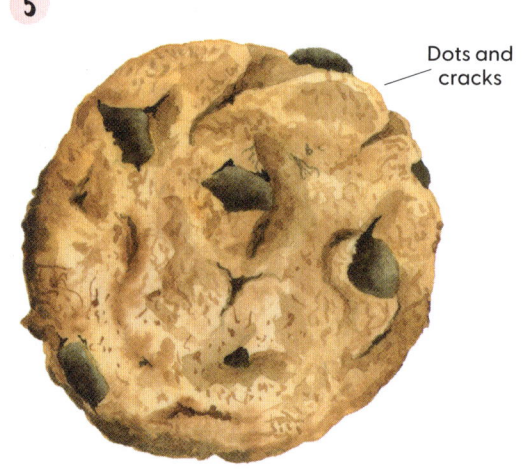

Dots and cracks

Donut

STEPS

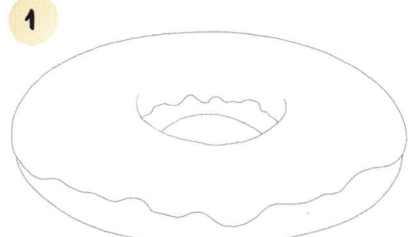
1

1. Draw the outline lightly in pencil.

2. With mix 1 (pink), paint the icing, darkening the edges and lifting curved highlights in the middle.

3. Once dry, paint the donut with Yellow Ochre, adding Burnt Umber for darker areas.

4. Build up the shadow on the icing with mix 1, especially around the highlights for contrast. Add shadow to the donut with Burnt Umber.

5. Paint the sprinkles with mix 1, mix 2 (orange), Permanent Sap Green, Winsor Lemon, Winsor Blue (Red Shade) and an opaque white.

 Yellow Ochre

 Burnt Umber

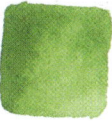 Permanent Sap Green

 Winsor Lemon

 Winsor Blue (Red Shade)

 Mix 1: Permanent Rose and a little Winsor Lemon

 Mix 2: Winsor Lemon and Permanent Rose

Plus opaque white

2
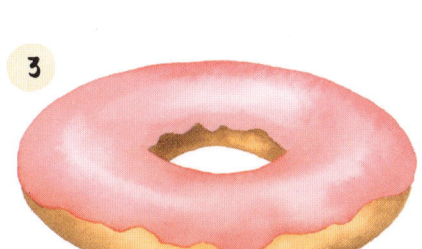

3

4
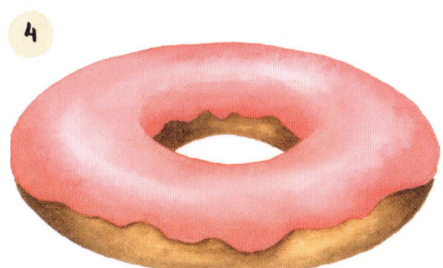

5
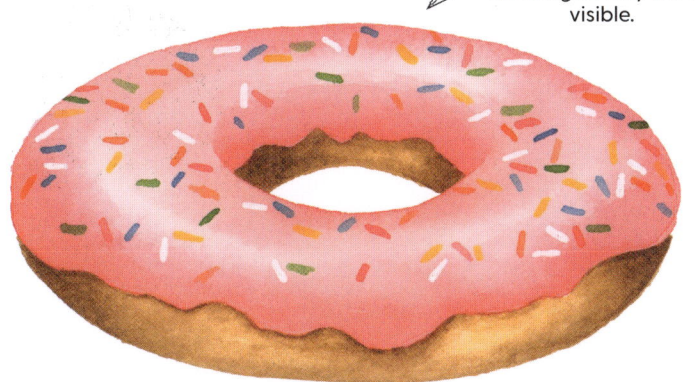

Paint the yellow sprinkles in the lighter areas of the icing so they will be visible.

Botanical

In this section, I have chosen a variety of botanical subjects, from houseplants and flowers to trees, cacti and tropical leaves. I have also included some fun compositions with a berry wreath and a floral letter to show you how I would approach them.

There were so many options to choose from when picking these projects! I could not resist the delicate markings on the lily or the contrast on the snake plant. If botanical subjects are something particularly appealing to you, it can be wonderful to visit garden centers or take walks in the countryside to find more inspiration.

One of my favorite colors to paint with is green, because there are so many endless varieties, from the cooler, bluer greens that are great for painting winter foliage and leaves like the eucalyptus, to the brighter, warmer greens that are well suited to vibrant cacti and tropical leaves. Have fun mixing and exploring different colors!

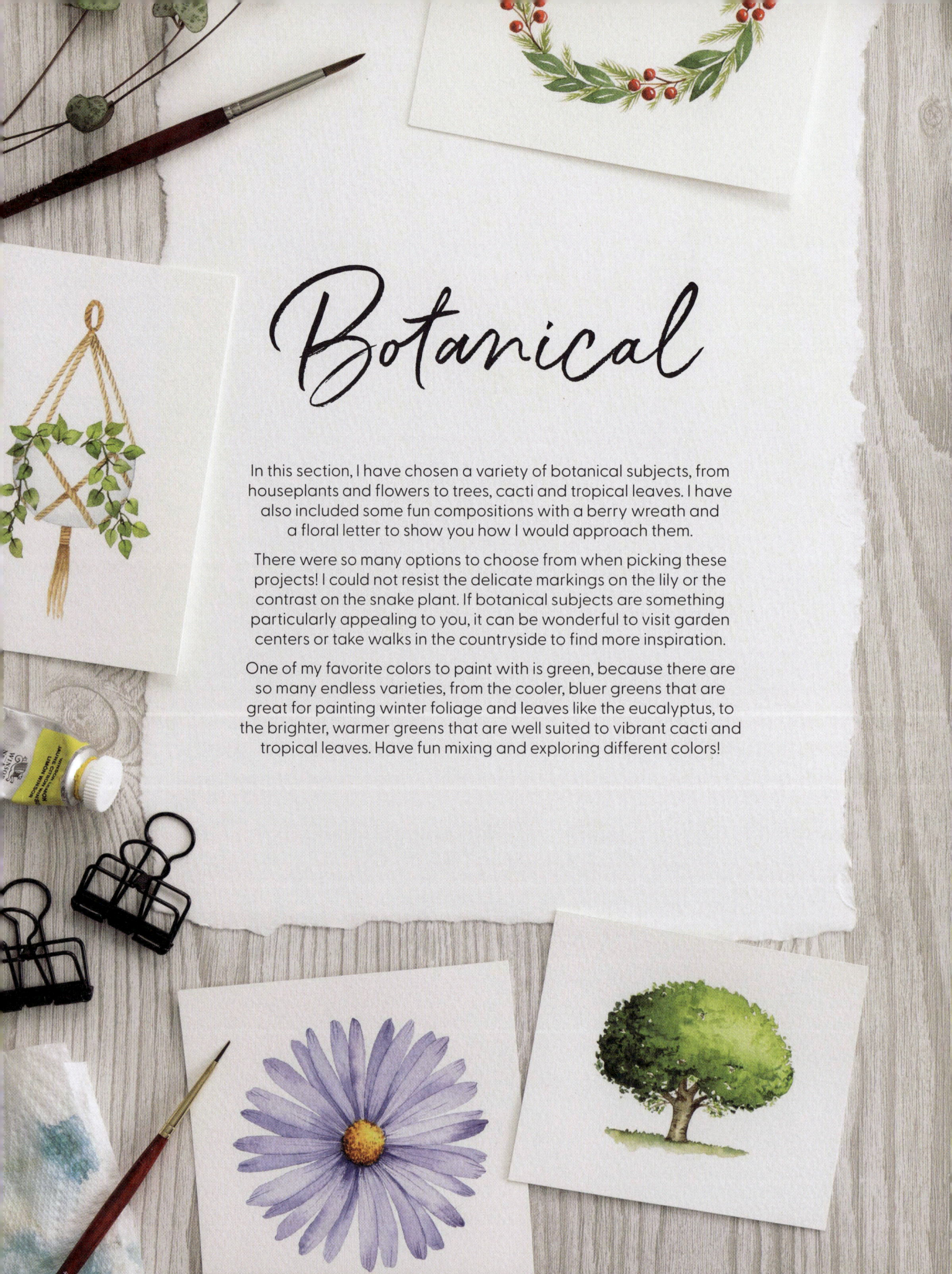

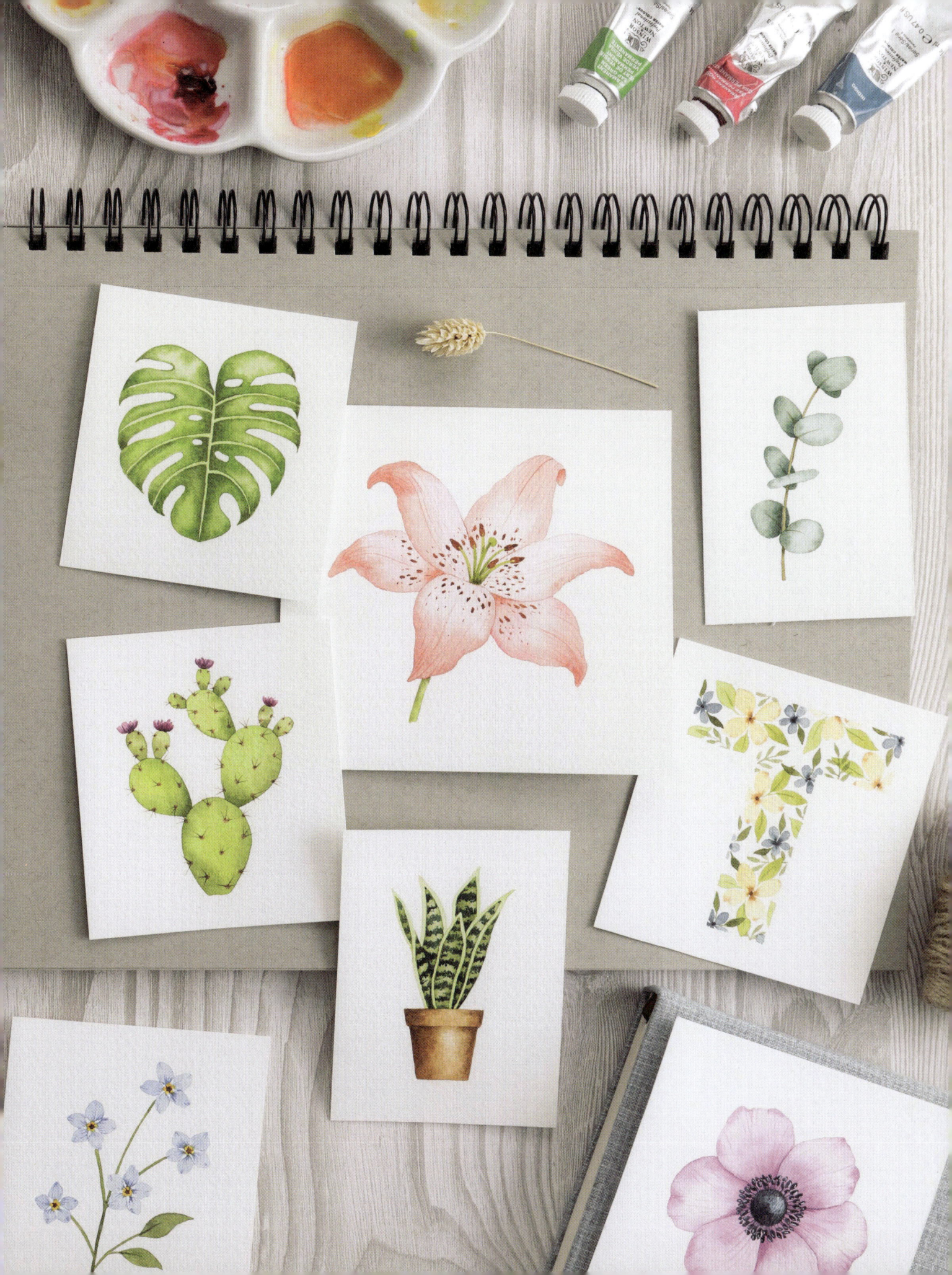

**Permanent
Sap Green**

**Mix 1: Permanent
Sap Green and
Winsor Lemon**

**Mix 2: Permanent
Sap Green and a
little Permanent Rose**

Gingko

STEPS

1. Draw the outline lightly in pencil.

2. Paint the leaf with mix 1 (yellow green), adding in Permanent Sap Green at the edges. With the paint still wet, add the stalk in a dark mix 2 (neutral green), ending at the base of the leaf so it bleeds in.

3. With mix 2, add shading at the base and where the top edges dip in.

4. Using more mix 2, add fine lines fanning out from the base to the top.

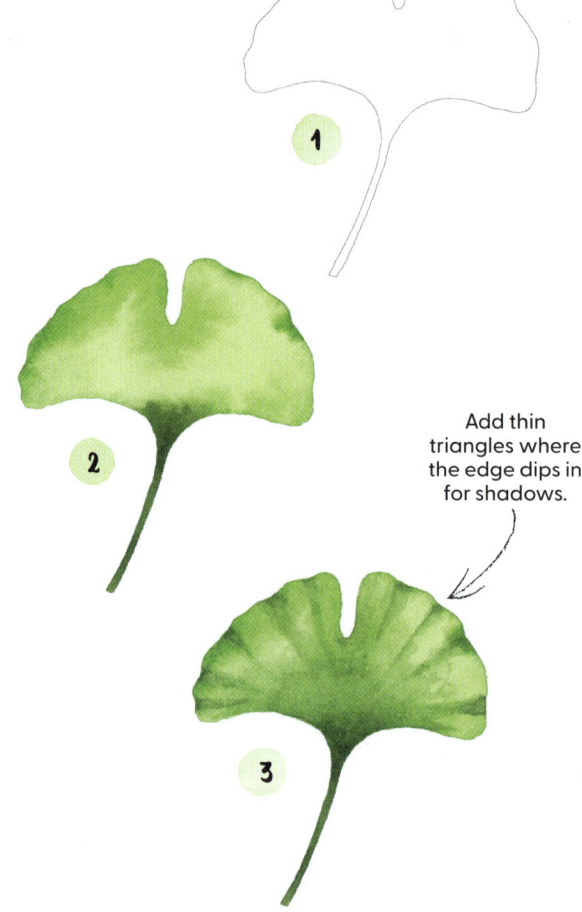

Add thin triangles where the edge dips in for shadows.

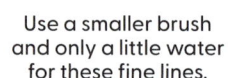

Create a fun page of gingko leaves for a repeating pattern. This can be very therapeutic!

Use a smaller brush and only a little water for these fine lines.

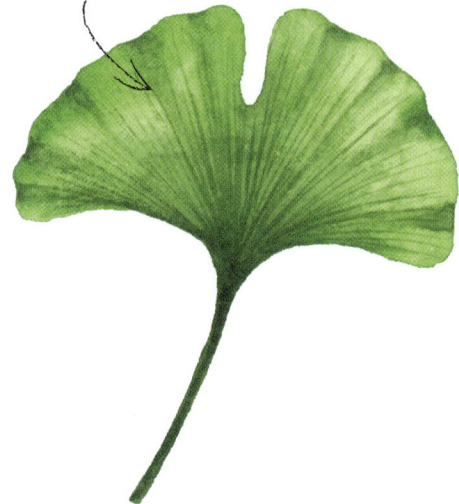

Monstera

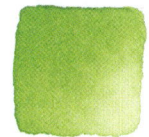

Permanent
Sap Green

Mix 1: Permanent
Sap Green and
Winsor Lemon

Mix 2: Permanent Sap
Green and a little
Permanent Rose

STEPS

1. Draw the outline lightly in pencil.

2. With mix 1 (yellow green), paint the veins.

3. Paint the middle of each section one at a time, using a pale mix 1, then adding Permanent Sap Green to the edges.

4. Once dry, use mix 2 (neutral green) to add shading, especially next to the main vein and at the outer edges.

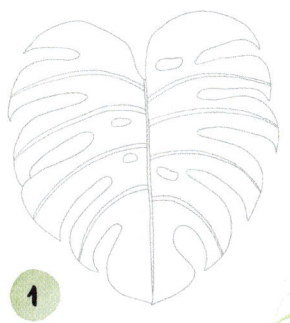

1

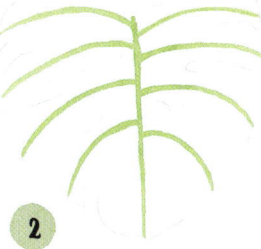

2

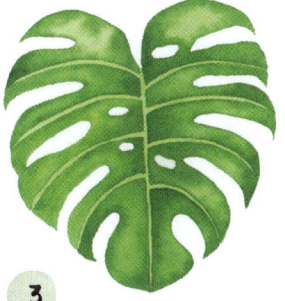

3

Paint each section
one by one with
wet-on-wet.

4

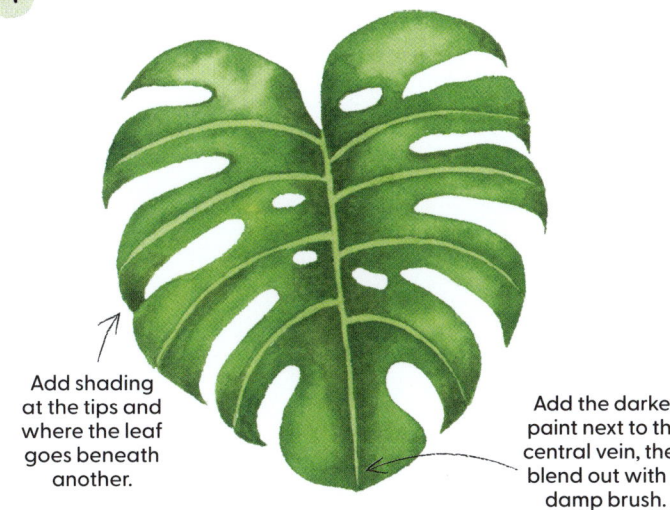

Add shading
at the tips and
where the leaf
goes beneath
another.

Add the darker
paint next to the
central vein, then
blend out with a
damp brush.

Experiment with
mixing a variety of
different greens to use
for your foliage.

Payne's Gray

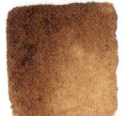
Burnt Umber

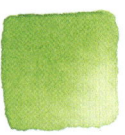
Mix 1: Permanent
Sap Green and
Winsor Lemon

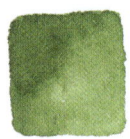
Mix 2: Permanent
Sap Green and a
little Permanent Rose

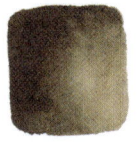
Mix 3: Burnt Umber
and a little Indigo

Hanging Plant

STEPS

1. If preferred, sketch or trace your outline. With pale Payne's Gray, paint the pot. While still wet, add a little darker paint to the edges.

2. With mix 1 (yellow green), paint the leaves, adding a little mix 2 (neutral green) to darken the tips and edges.

3. Paint the stems and veins with more mix 2.

4. With pale Burnt Umber, paint the ropes, adding a hanging loop at the top.

5. With mix 3 (dark brown), add dashes and shadow to the ropes.

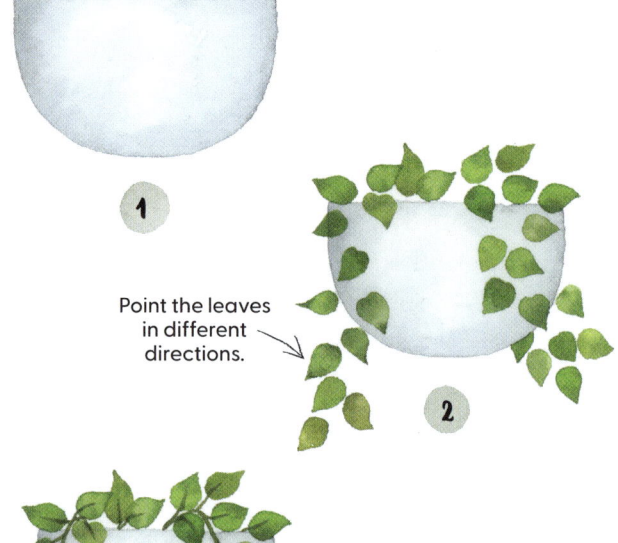

Point the leaves in different directions.

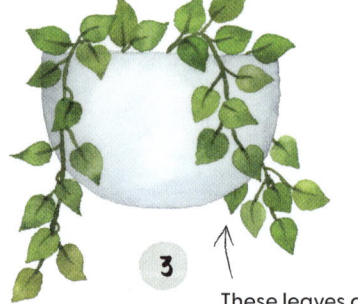

These leaves come from behind the pot.

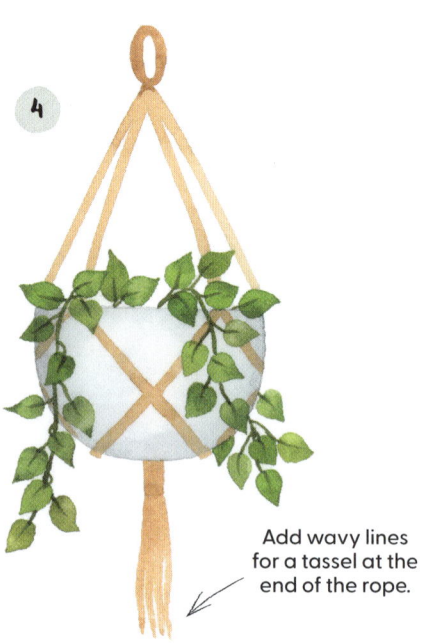

Add wavy lines for a tassel at the end of the rope.

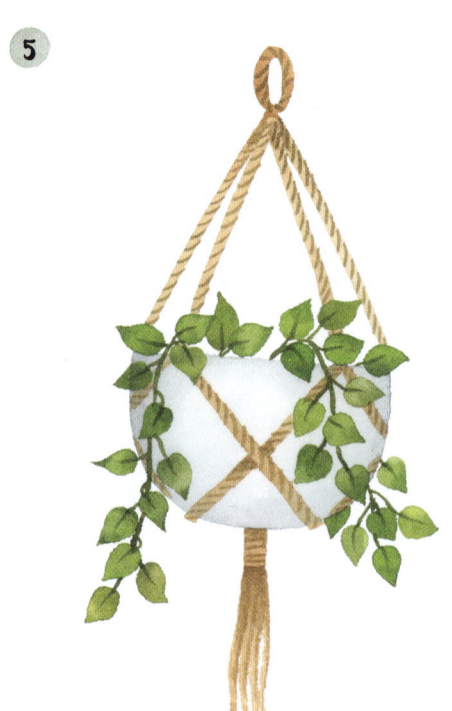

Snake Plant

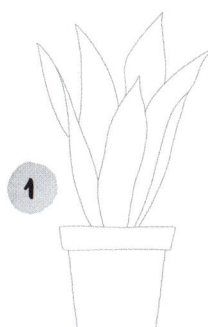

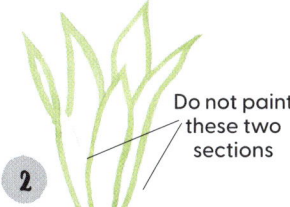

Do not paint these two sections

STEPS

1. Draw the outline lightly in pencil.

2. Paint the outer edge of each leaf with mix 1 (neutral yellow green). Leave a section of each folded leaf unpainted as shown.

3. Use a pale mix 2 (neutral green) to paint the inside of each leaf and then add darker paint to the edges.

4. Paint the pot with Burnt Umber, lifting a highlight in the center right and darkening the sides.

5. With mix 3 (blue green), paint the patterns on the leaf, using dabs and dashes. Add shading to the pot with Burnt Umber.

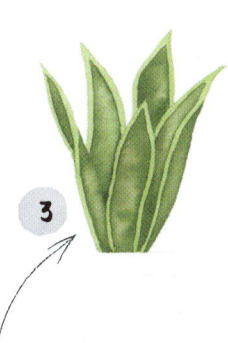

Using wet-on-wet to achieve different values makes your painting less flat.

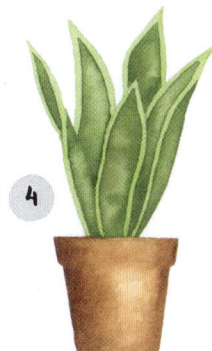

Burnt Umber

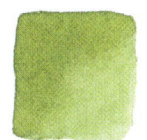

Mix 1: Permanent Sap Green, Winsor Lemon and a little Permanent Rose

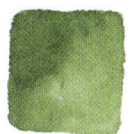

Mix 2: Permanent Sap Green and a little Permanent Rose

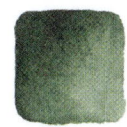

Mix 3: Indigo and Winsor Lemon

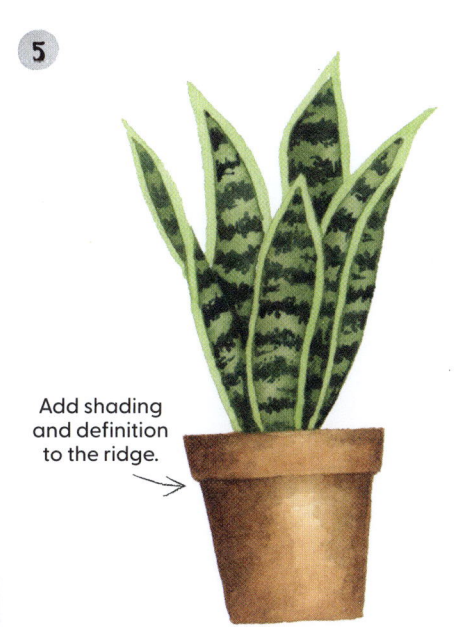

Add shading and definition to the ridge.

Turn these botanical paintings into thoughtful greeting cards for a new home or as a sweet thank you note to a loved one.

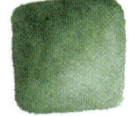

Mix 1: Permanent
Sap Green and
Indigo

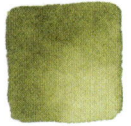

Mix 2: Permanent
Sap Green and
Burnt Umber

Eucalyptus

STEPS

1. Draw the outline lightly in pencil, starting with the stem followed by the front leaves and then the back leaves.

2. With a pale mix 1 (blue green), paint the front leaves. While still wet, add some darker paint to the outer edges.

3. Once dry, use mix 2 (green brown) to paint the stalk, going over the outlines of the back leaves.

4. Once dry, paint the back leaves with mix 1. Make each back leaf darker where it sits beneath the top leaf or stalk to distinguish between the parts.

5. Once dry, add a vein to the leaves using mix 2.

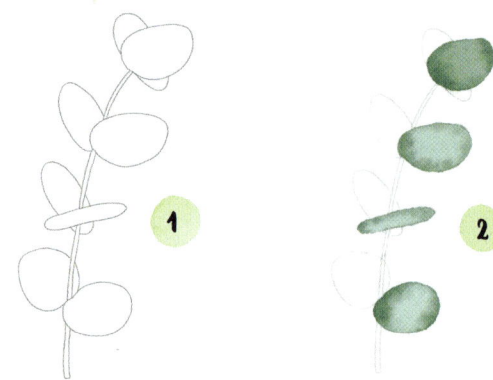

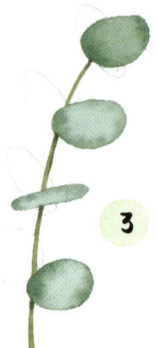

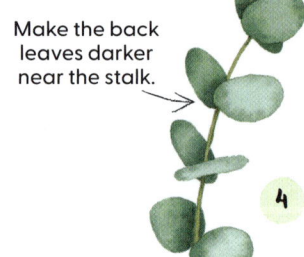

Make the back leaves darker near the stalk.

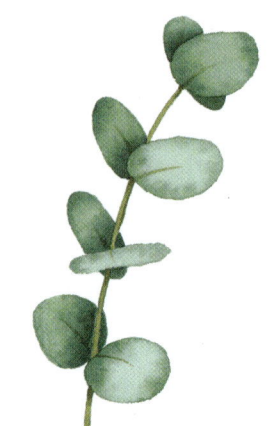

The height of this project would work perfectly for turning it into a bookmark for yourself or a loved one!

Tree

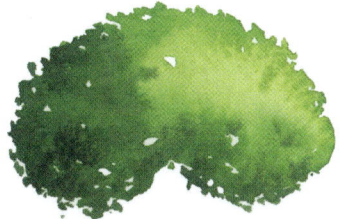

Use quick dabbing strokes with the brush to get this effect.

1

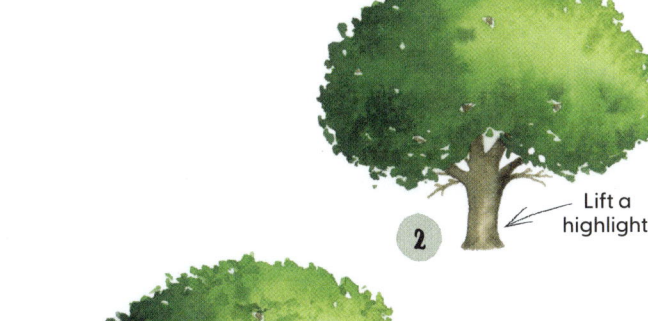

2

Lift a highlight.

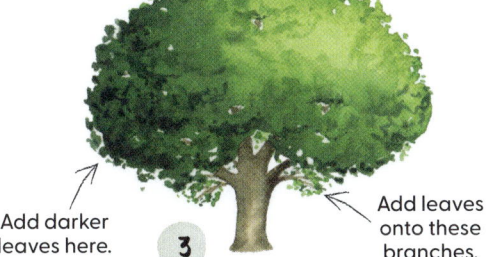

Add darker leaves here.

3

Add leaves onto these branches.

STEPS

1. If preferred, sketch or trace your outline. Paint the top right of the tree with mix 1 (neutral yellow green), blending to mix 2 (neutral green) as you get to the middle and mix 3 (blue green) as you get to the bottom left. As the paint starts to dry, dab the paint around the edges and inside the shape to create the leafy effect.

2. Once dry, paint the trunk and branches with mix 4 (dark brown), lifting a highlight on the right.

3. Add more defined leaves by dabbing different greens onto the tree, especially around the lower branches.

4. With mix 4, add details to the trunk. With mix 2, add a line of dashes for the grass and then blend out underneath.

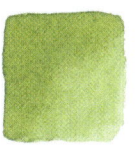

Mix 1: Permanent Sap Green, Winsor Lemon and a little Permanent Rose

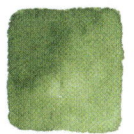

Mix 2: Permanent Sap Green and a little Permanent Rose

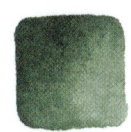

Mix 3: Indigo and Winsor Lemon

Mix 4: Burnt Umber and a little Indigo

4

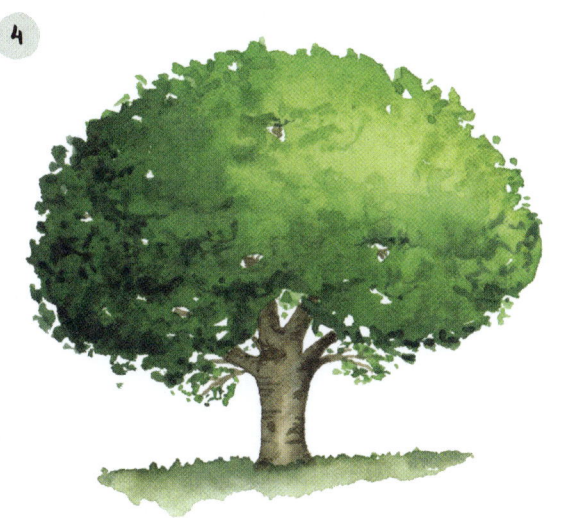

In step 1, continue to add dabs of color as the paint starts to dry so they spread less.

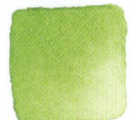

Mix 1: Permanent Sap Green and Winsor Lemon

Mix 2: Permanent Sap Green and a little Permanent Rose

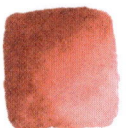

Mix 3: Permanent Rose and Burnt Umber

Mix 4: Permanent Rose and Winsor Blue (Red Shade)

Mix 5: Permanent Rose and Winsor Blue (Red Shade)

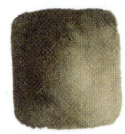

Mix 6: Burnt Umber and a little Indigo

Mixes 4 and 5 are a good example of how the same paints can make a variety of shades.

Cactus

STEPS

1. Draw the outline lightly in pencil.

2. Paint alternating sections with mix 1 (yellow green) and then add mix 2 (neutral green) at some of the edges to darken.

3. Once dry, paint the remaining sections in the same way.

4. Once dry, paint small circles on the cactus with a pale mix 3 (brown red). With mix 4 (pink purple), paint flowers at the top of some of the smaller sections, adding a little mix 5 (purple) at the base of each flower.

5. With mix 6 (dark brown), paint two or three spines coming out of each circle. With a darker mix 5, add a little more detail to the flowers to separate the petals.

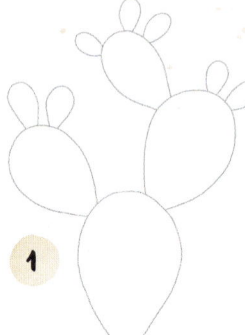

1

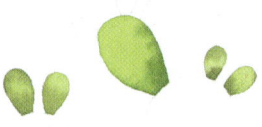

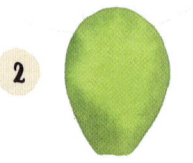

2

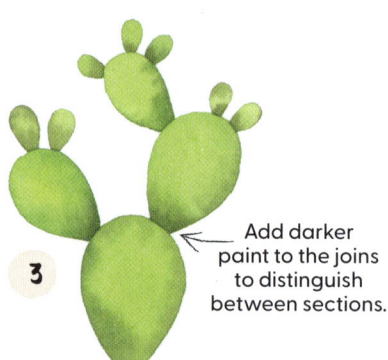

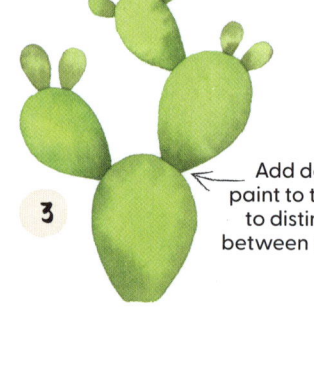

3

Add darker paint to the joins to distinguish between sections.

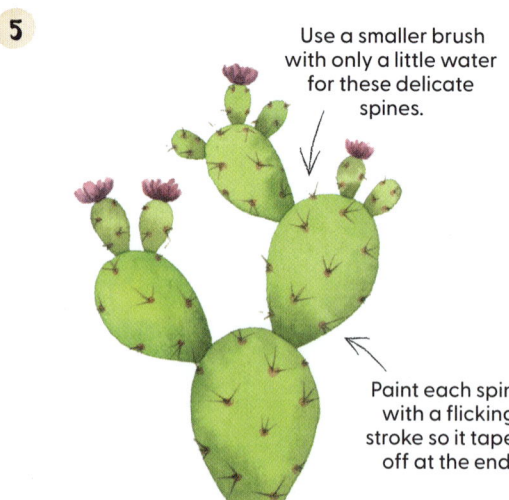

5

Use a smaller brush with only a little water for these delicate spines.

Paint each spine with a flicking stroke so it tapers off at the end.

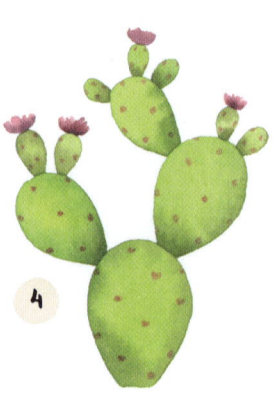

4

Palm Tree

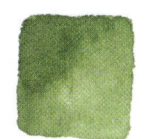

Burnt Umber

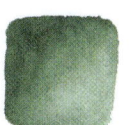

Mix 1: Permanent Sap Green and a little Permanent Rose

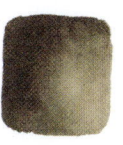

Mix 2: Permanent Sap Green and Indigo

Mix 3: Burnt Umber and a little Indigo

STEPS

1. Draw the outline lightly in pencil.

2. With mix 1 (neutral green), paint the branches. For each branch, start with a curved line and then paint shorter strokes either side.

3. With Burnt Umber, paint the trunk and coconuts, lifting a highlight on the right-hand side of the trunk.

4. With a darker mix 1 and mix 2 (blue green), add darker leaves to the branches.

5. Add shadow and markings to the coconuts and trunk with mix 3 (dark brown). With a pale mix 3, add a little area of ground.

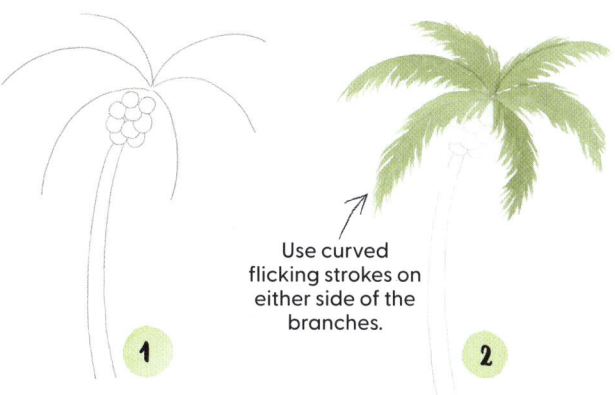

Use curved flicking strokes on either side of the branches.

1

2

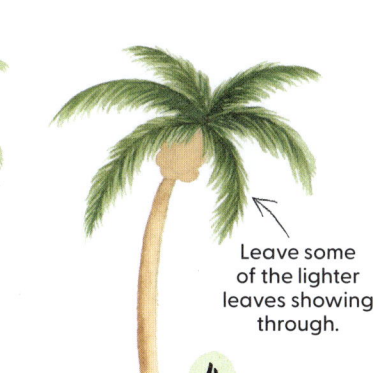

Leave some of the lighter leaves showing through.

3

4

5

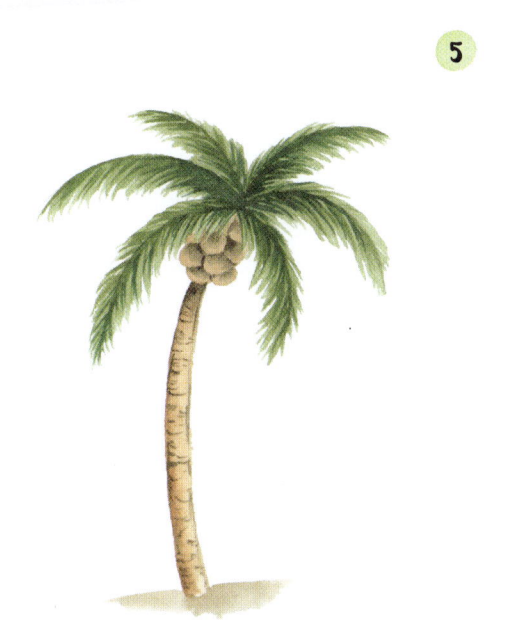

Sometimes the final steps can be quite subtle, but it is these small details that bring the subject to life!

PALM TREE · *Botanical*

73

Burnt Umber

Mix 1: Winsor Lemon and Burnt Umber

Mix 2: Winsor Blue (Red Shade) and a little Permanent Rose

Mix 3: Permanent Sap Green and a little Permanent Rose

Plus opaque white

Forget-Me-Nots

STEPS

1. Draw a guide for the branch very lightly in pencil.

2. With mix 1 (yellow brown), paint a ring of five small circles for each flower center.

3. Once dry, paint five petals on each flower with mix 2 (blue).

4. Once dry, with mix 3 (neutral green), paint the stem and leaves, avoiding the front flower.

5. With mix 2, paint delicate shading on each petal and add a triangle of opaque white between each petal. Add a dot of Burnt Umber to each flower center, then paint a vein onto each leaf with mix 3.

Leave a gap here for a flower that will overlap the branch.

1

2

Make sure each petal is touching to allow space for the white marks later on.

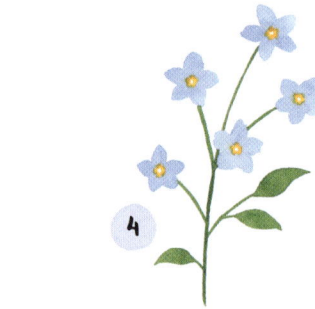

3

4

5

For more delicate subjects like this, use a finer brush and less water in your mixes.

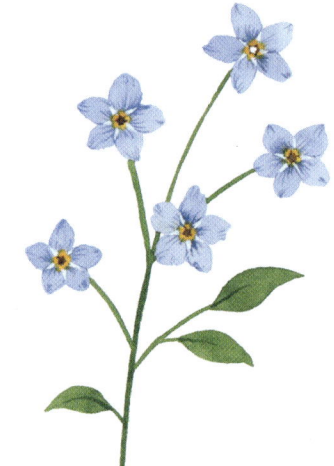

Aster

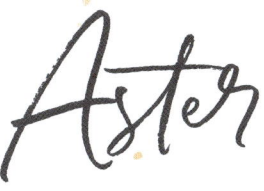

STEPS

1. Paint a circle in Winsor Lemon. While the paint is still wet, add dots of mix 1 (orange), leaving a yellow area at the top right. Add dots of Burnt Umber around the edge and on the bottom left.

2. Once dry, paint thin petals around the circle with mix 2 (blue purple).

3. Once dry, paint more petals in between the first layer, to look as though they are underneath.

4. With mix 2, add delicate shading and lines to the petals. Darken the lower left-hand side of the center with Burnt Umber.

Winsor Lemon

Burnt Umber

Mix 1: Winsor Lemon and Permanent Rose

Mix 2: Permanent Rose and Winsor Blue (Red Shade)

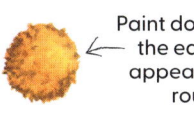

Paint dots around the edge so it appears a little rough.

1

2

Curve some of the petals slightly to show movement.

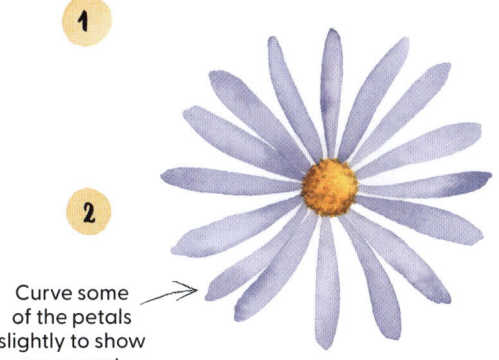

3

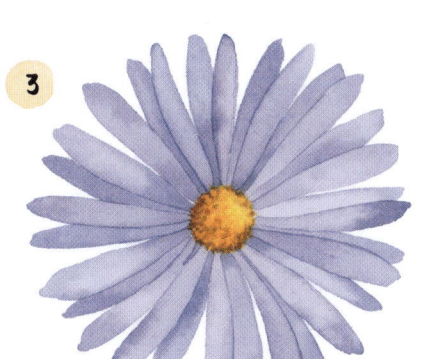

4

Add fine lines to the tips of each petal.

If helpful, sketch a large circle to give you a guide for the length of each petal, or trace the outline provided.

Payne's Gray

Mix 1: Permanent Rose and Winsor Blue (Red Shade)

Plus opaque white

Anemone

STEPS

1. Draw the outline lightly in pencil.

2. With a pale mix 1 (pink purple), paint alternating petals, adding darker paint to some of the edges.

3. Once dry, paint the remaining petals in the same way.

4. Once dry, add delicate shading and lines to the petals with mix 1. Paint the central mound with Payne's Gray, lifting a highlight in the top right-hand corner and darkening the lower left.

5. With Payne's Gray, paint tiny 'hairs' on the central mound. Paint tiny ovals around the center, giving each one a line to connect it to the mound. Once dry, add a highlight to each oval with an opaque white.

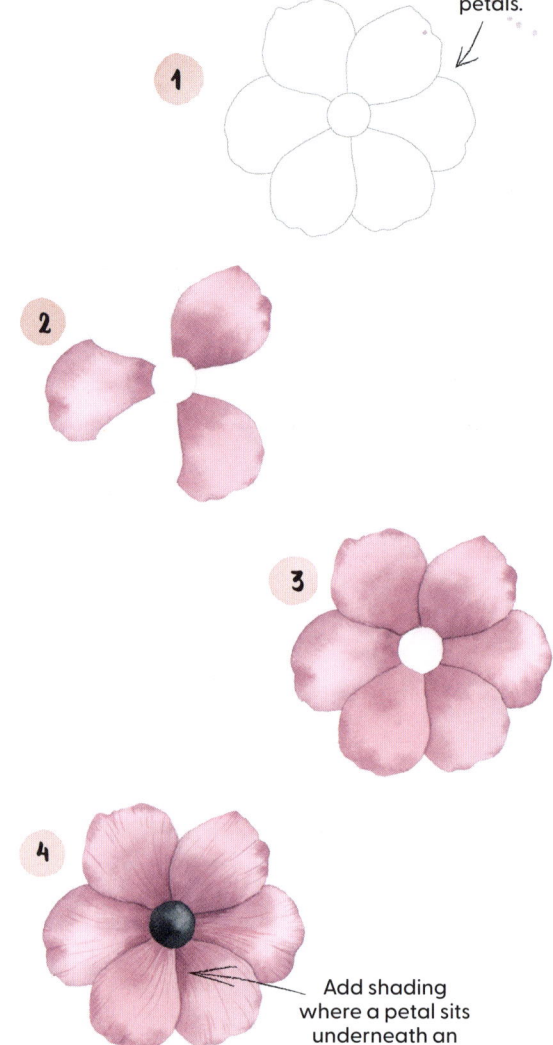

Overlap six petals.

Add shading where a petal sits underneath an adjacent petal.

When sketching out flowers like this, start with a large outer circle for a guide.

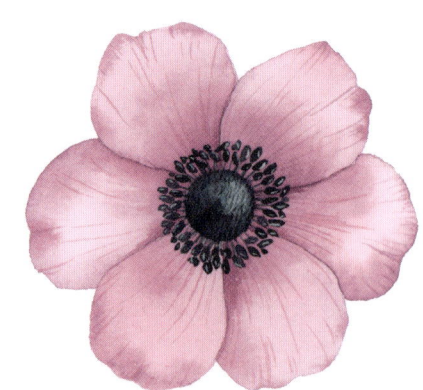

Lily

Mix 1: Permanent Rose and Burnt Umber

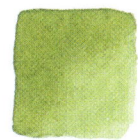

Mix 2: Permanent Sap Green, Winsor Lemon and a little Permanent Rose

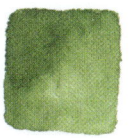

Mix 3: Permanent Sap Green and a little Permanent Rose

STEPS

1. Draw the outline lightly in pencil, with three petals on top overlapping the three underneath.

2. One by one, paint the top three petals with a pale mix 1 (brown red). With this paint still wet, add some darker paint to the ends and edges of the petals. Paint the underside of the far petal.

3. Once dry, paint the remaining petals in the same way.

4. Once dry, paint delicate curved lines onto the petals with mix 1. With mix 2 (neutral yellow green), paint seven lines from the center for the filaments, with an oval on top of the one in the middle for the stigma. With a dark mix 1, paint teardrop shapes on top of the remaining lines.

5. Paint the stem with mix 2, adding a little mix 3 (neutral green) at the edge to darken. Add a little shadow to the filaments in the center of the flower with mix 3. Finally, paint small dots and marks on the petals with a dark mix 1.

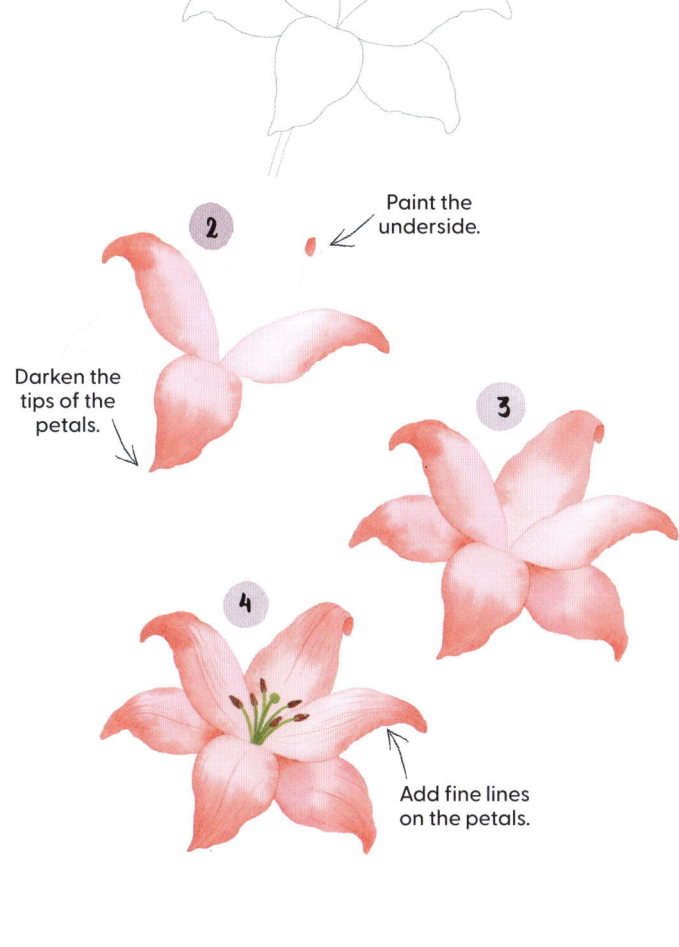

Paint the underside.

Darken the tips of the petals.

Add fine lines on the petals.

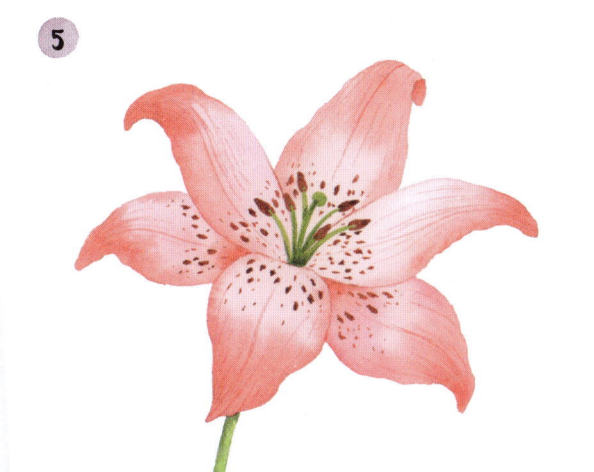

Keep the center of the flower very pale so the green structures can be painted on top.

Burnt Umber

Mix 1: Permanent Rose and a little Winsor Lemon

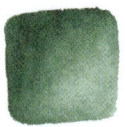

Mix 2: Permanent Sap Green and Indigo

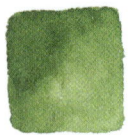

Mix 3: Permanent Sap Green and a little Permanent Rose

Berry Wreath

STEPS

1. Draw a circle lightly in pencil – or trace your outline using the downloadable guide, if preferred. Paint clusters of berries in mix 1 (red), leaving a small highlight at the top right of each berry.

2. With Burnt Umber, paint the stems of the berries and add a little shading to the bottom left of each berry.

3. Paint in the large leaves with mix 2 (blue green). For each leaf, start with the stem and then, as you drag the brush along, gradually press down and then release to come to a fine tip. Paint a second stroke in the same way, starting at the top of the stem and meeting the tip, leaving a thin gap in the middle.

4. Fill the gaps with pine branches using mix 3 (neutral green).

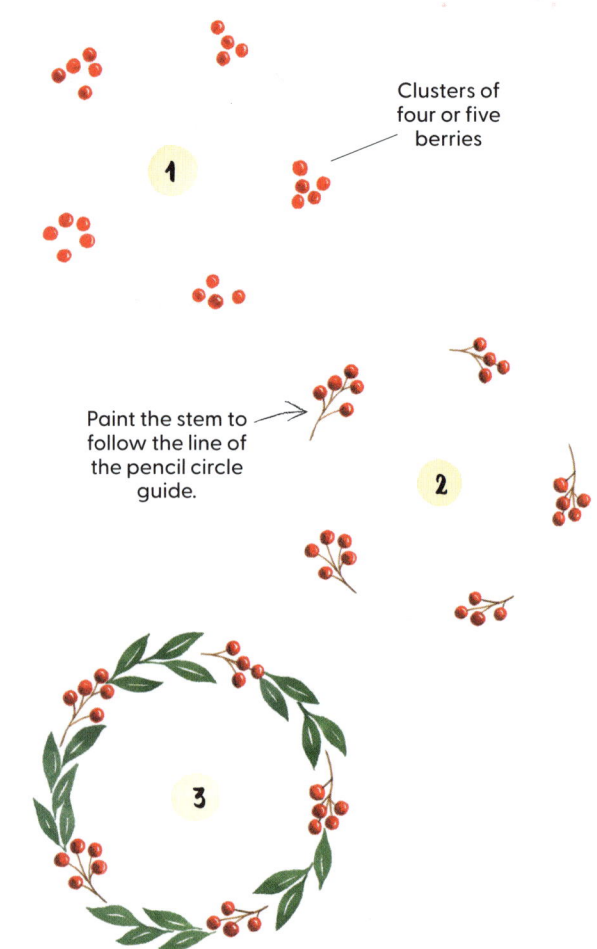

Clusters of four or five berries

Paint the stem to follow the line of the pencil circle guide.

Experiment with different styles of leaf and different greens to make a variety of wreaths!

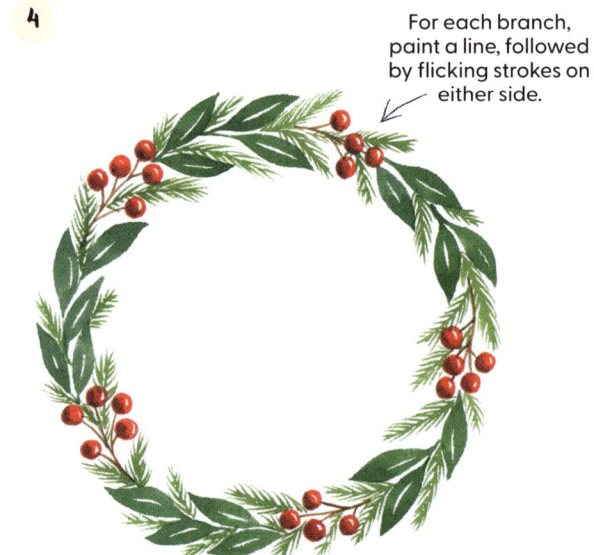

For each branch, paint a line, followed by flicking strokes on either side.

Floral Letter

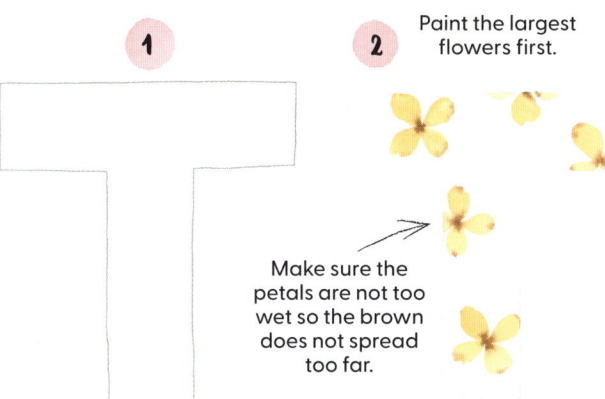

1

2 Paint the largest flowers first.

Make sure the petals are not too wet so the brown does not spread too far.

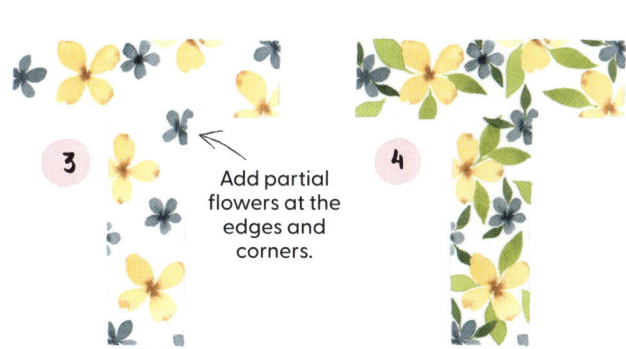

3 Add partial flowers at the edges and corners.

4

STEPS

1. Draw the outline of your letter lightly in pencil.

2. Paint simple four-petalled flowers with mix 1 (yellow brown), dropping a little Burnt Umber into the centers. Add a little Burnt Umber to the edges of the petals, too.

3. With Payne's Gray, paint some smaller five-petalled flowers, adding a darker dot of paint into their centers.

4. With mix 2 (neutral yellow green), paint leaves coming out from the yellow flowers. Once dry, paint some smaller leaves for the blue flowers, using mix 3 (neutral green).

5. With more mix 3, add small sprigs of leaves to fill in any gaps, especially around the edges of the letter. Add veins to the leaves. Using a darker Burnt Umber, add a small dot to the center of each yellow flower. Finally, erase your pencil outline of the letter.

Burnt Umber

Payne's Gray

Mix 1: Winsor Lemon and Burnt Umber

Mix 2: Permanent Sap Green, Winsor Lemon and a little Permanent Rose

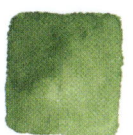
Mix 3: Permanent Sap Green and a little Permanent Rose

5

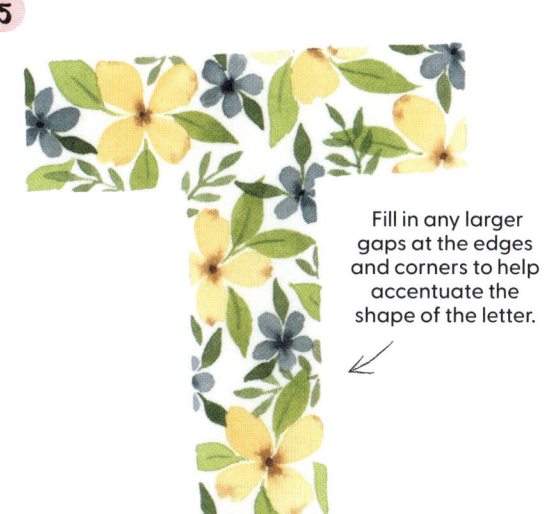

Fill in any larger gaps at the edges and corners to help accentuate the shape of the letter.

This would make a lovely gift or greeting card, choosing the appropriate letter or number for your recipient!

Animals

This section covers animals: mammals, sea life, insects and birds. It can be so much fun recreating the different patterns and textures that you see in these creatures using watercolor, and it is great exploring the different colors and techniques. You do not need to capture every detail to make your painting look recognizable or wonderful. Using techniques such as wet-on-wet can help to give the illusion of fur or feathers, and building layers on top of that with simple strokes can achieve impressive results.

From the shell of a snail to the patterns on a seahorse, each step allows you to build up color and contrast for striking results. I hope you will enjoy painting these projects as much as I did!

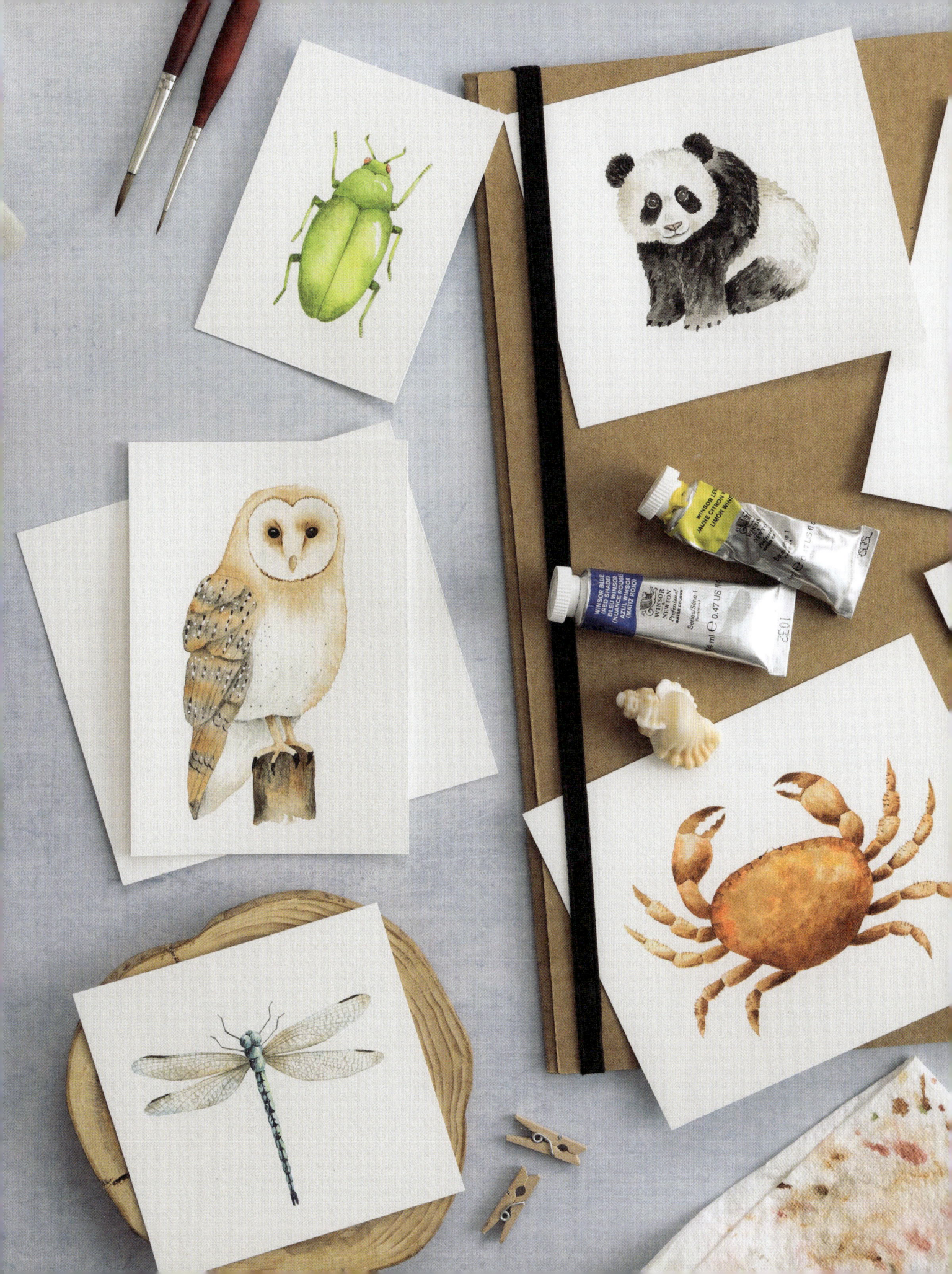

Ivory Black

Mix 1: Payne's Gray and a little Burnt Umber

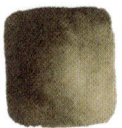

Mix 2: Burnt Umber and a little Indigo

Mix 3: Permanent Rose and a little Burnt Umber

Panda

STEPS

1. Draw the outline lightly in pencil.

2. For the areas of white fur, wet the inside and add a pale mix 1 (gray) and a pale mix 2 (dark brown) to the edges for shadows, leaving white patches.

3. With Ivory Black, paint the eyes, leaving a small highlight. Paint the black sections of fur on the body as shown. With mix 3 (pink), paint the nose.

4. With Ivory Black, paint the ears, the patches around the eyes, the edges of the nose, the mouth and the claws on the feet.

5. Paint dashes on the white fur with mix 1 and mix 2. Darken patches of black fur with Ivory Black, especially around the edges to distinguish the legs.

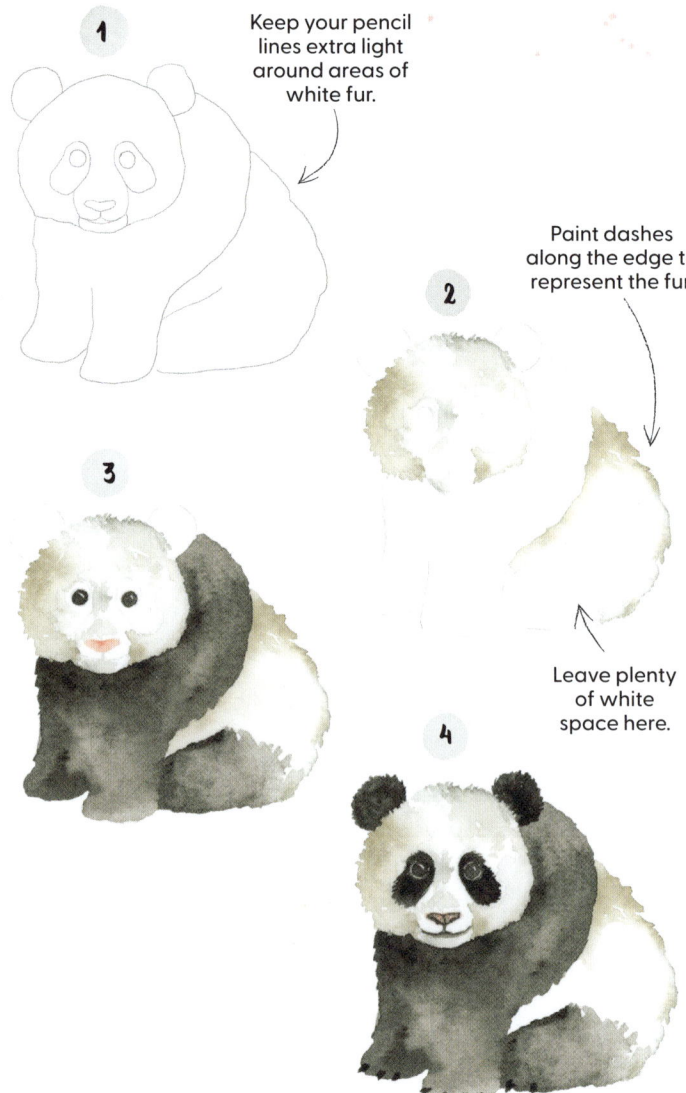

Keep your pencil lines extra light around areas of white fur.

Paint dashes along the edge to represent the fur.

Leave plenty of white space here.

Spend time practicing diluting your mixes so you feel confident adding pale shadows to these white areas.

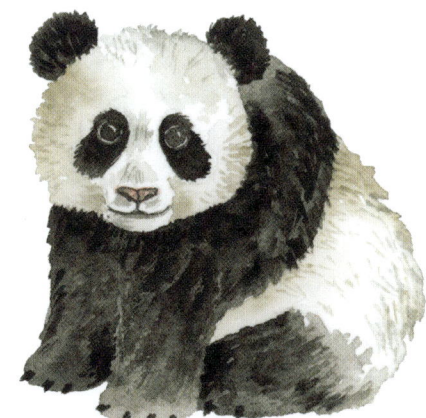

Elephant

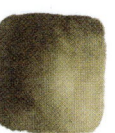

Ivory Black

Mix 1: Payne's Gray and a little Burnt Umber

Mix 2: Burnt Umber and a little Indigo

STEPS

1. Draw the outline lightly in pencil.

2. Wet the middle of the head and trunk and then add mix 1 (gray) and a little mix 2 (dark brown) to the edges and the tops of the ears. Darken around the eyes.

3. Once dry, paint the inner ears by wetting the inside and then adding a dark mix 1 to the top and a pale mix 2 to the outer edges.

4. Wet the middle of the legs and then add mix 1 and 2 to the edges, darkening beneath the head.

5. With mix 1, add a little shadow to the toes and tusks. Build up shadow to define other areas, including the back legs, the bottom of the head and around the eyes.

6. With Ivory Black, paint the eyes, leaving a small highlight in each. With mix 1, add short lines to the edge of the ears, curved lines down the trunk and legs, and small hairs on top of the head.

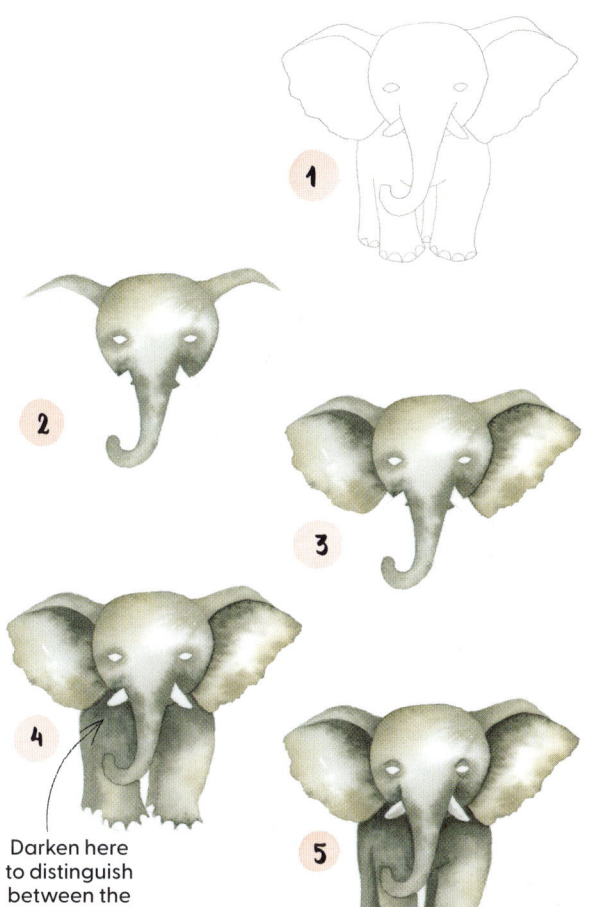

Darken here to distinguish between the head and body.

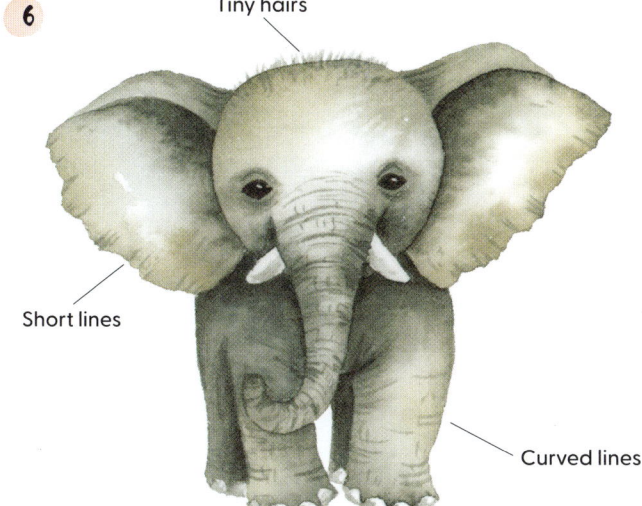

Tiny hairs

Short lines

Curved lines

Switch to a smaller brush for the finer details in step 6.

Yellow Ochre

Burnt Umber

Ivory Black

Mix 1: Permanent
Rose and a little
Burnt Umber

Mix 2: Payne's
Gray and a little
Burnt Umber

Plus opaque white

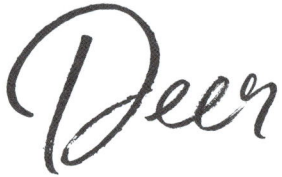

Deer

STEPS

1. Draw the outline lightly in pencil.

2. Wet the inside of the ears and add a pale mix 1 (pink) and mix 2 (gray). Wet the body and front legs and add in mix 2 under the head and at the edge of the belly. Add Yellow Ochre and Burnt Umber to the rest of the body and front legs leaving some white areas on the belly and chest.

3. Once dry, paint the head with Burnt Umber, avoiding the eyes and nose, followed by the outer edge of the ears and the back legs.

4. Once dry, paint dashes of fur across the head and body with Burnt Umber.

5. With Ivory Black, paint the eyes, nose, mouth and hooves. With opaque white, add some dashes to the body. Add any extra shadow and details as needed.

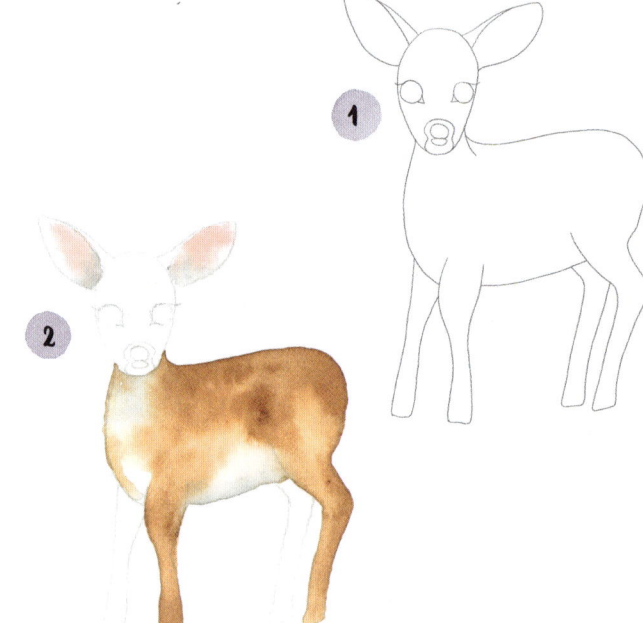

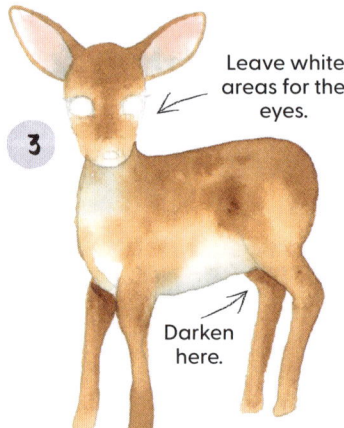

Leave white areas for the eyes.

Darken here.

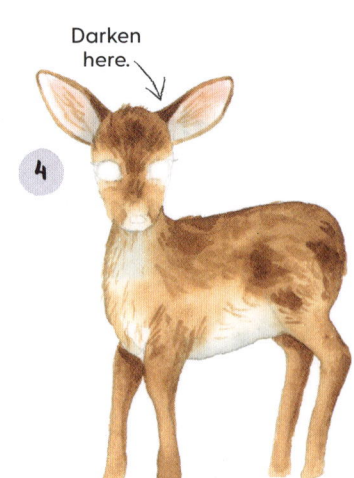

Darken here.

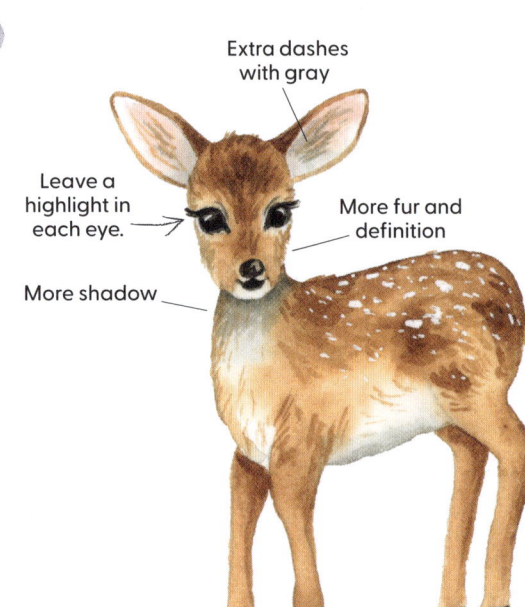

Extra dashes with gray

Leave a highlight in each eye.

More fur and definition

More shadow

Chicken

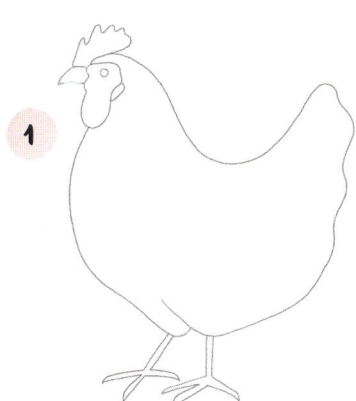

STEPS

1. Draw the outline lightly in pencil.

2. Wet the inside of the body. Add pale Payne's Gray to the bottom edge and mix 1 (yellow orange) to the top, followed by Burnt Umber.

3. With mix 2 (brown red), paint the head sections and the feet.

4. Using Payne's Gray, define the top of the legs. With Burnt Umber, paint dashes over the body to represent feathers.

5. Paint the beak with mix 1, the eye with Payne's Gray (leaving a small highlight), and add dashes on the feet with mix 2. Add any extra shading as needed.

Payne's Gray

Burnt Umber

Mix 1: Winsor Lemon and a little Permanent Rose

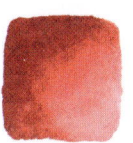
Mix 2: Permanent Rose and Burnt Umber

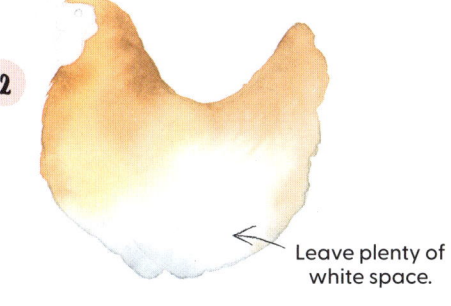
Leave plenty of white space.

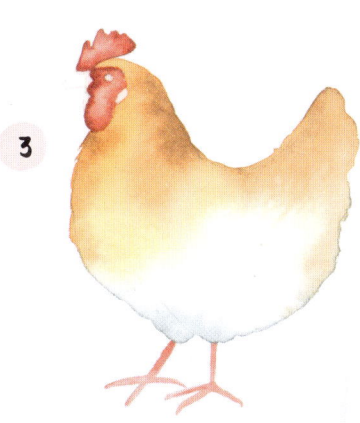

Paint dashes along the edge to represent the hair.

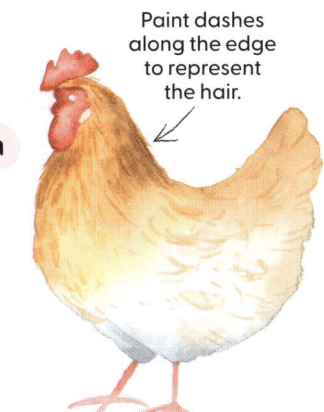

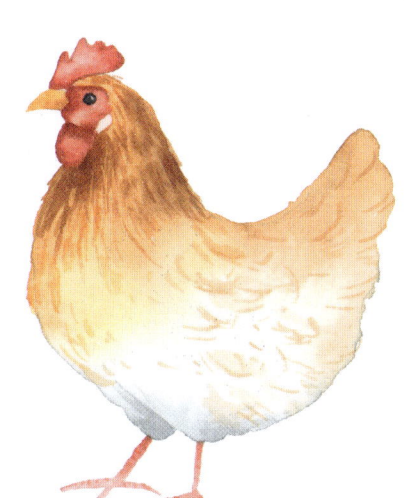

Winsor Lemon

Ivory Black

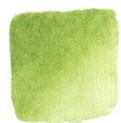

Mix 1: Winsor
Lemon and Winsor
Blue (Red Shade)

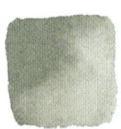

Mix 2: Payne's
Gray and a little
Burnt Umber

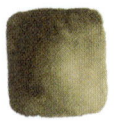

Mix 3: Burnt Umber
and a little Indigo

Budgerigar

STEPS

1. Draw the outline lightly in pencil.

2. Wet the head and upper belly, avoiding the eye and nose. Add Winsor Lemon to the head and blend to mix 1 (green) towards the belly. Add a little shadow with mix 2 (gray) under the eye and around the beak and the edge of the head.

3. Once dry, paint the wing with Winsor Lemon. With mix 2, paint the claws and nose, then darken the shadow under the eye.

4. Once dry, paint shadows under each feather on the wing with mix 2. Paint the beak and branch with mix 3 (dark brown). Add dashes to the belly with mix 1. Paint the eye with Ivory Black, leaving a small highlight and a white gap around the lower edge.

5. With Ivory Black, paint the patterns on the head and wing and add a nostril to the nose. Add lines to the tail (mix 1) and details to the claws (mix 2) and branch (mix 3).

1

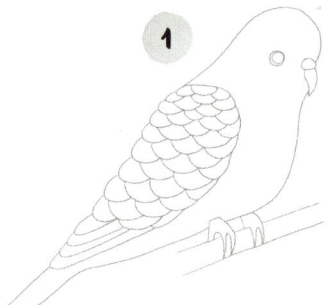

2

Add feathers at the edges.

3

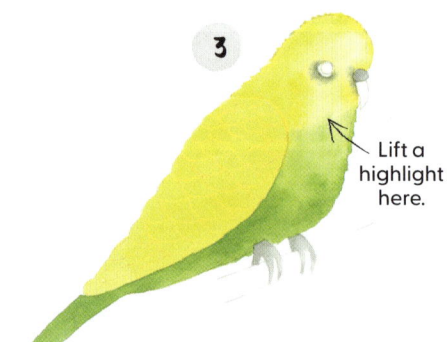

Lift a highlight here.

5

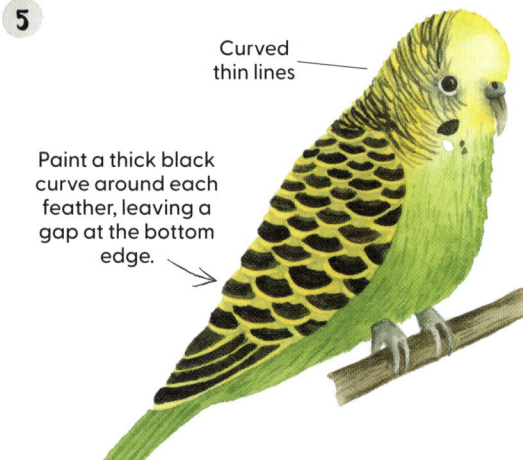

Curved thin lines

Paint a thick black curve around each feather, leaving a gap at the bottom edge.

4

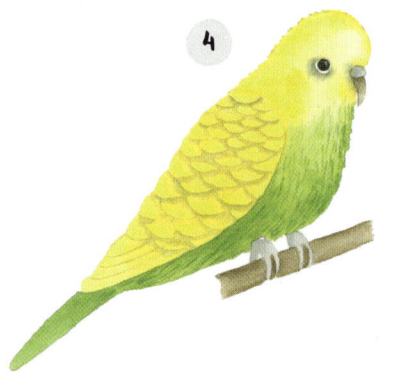

Owl

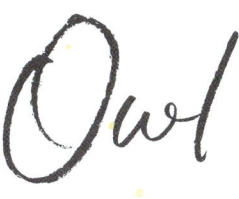

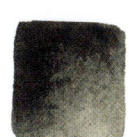
Burnt Umber

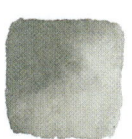
Ivory Black

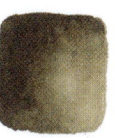
Mix 1: Payne's Gray and a little Burnt Umber

Mix 2: Burnt Umber and a little Indigo

Plus opaque white

STEPS

1. Draw the outline lightly in pencil.

2. Wet the face, excluding the eyes, then add Burnt Umber around the eyes. Add a little pale mix 1 (gray) to the face as well. Paint the legs with Burnt Umber.

3. Once dry, wet the head and body (avoiding the face) and add Burnt Umber and mix 1. Once those are dry, wet the wings and add Burnt Umber and Ivory Black in stripes. Paint the log with Burnt Umber and a dark mix 2 (dark brown).

4. Once dry, add shadow and feathers to the body with pale Burnt Umber and mix 1. Paint the nose with Burnt Umber and add definition to the wings with mix 1. Darken the log with mix 2.

5. With Burnt Umber, outline the face and add definition around the eyes and nose. Paint the eyes with Ivory Black, leaving a small highlight on each. Add the claws and some tiny dots on the belly. Add markings to the wings with Ivory Black and an opaque white.

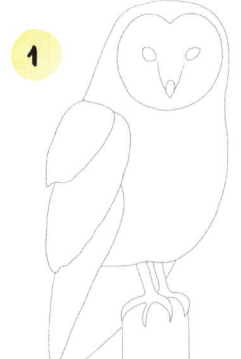

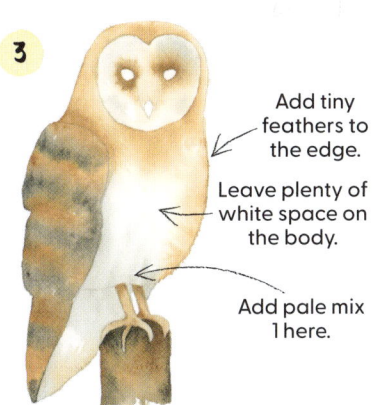

Add tiny feathers to the edge.

Leave plenty of white space on the body.

Add pale mix 1 here.

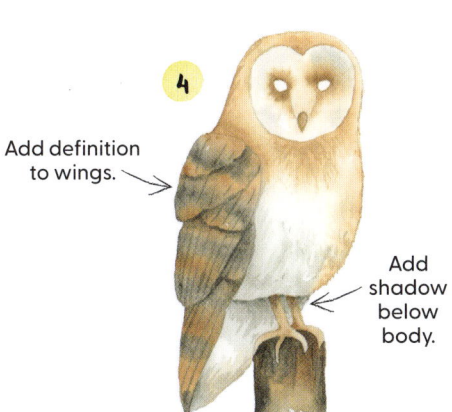

Add definition to wings.

Add shadow below body.

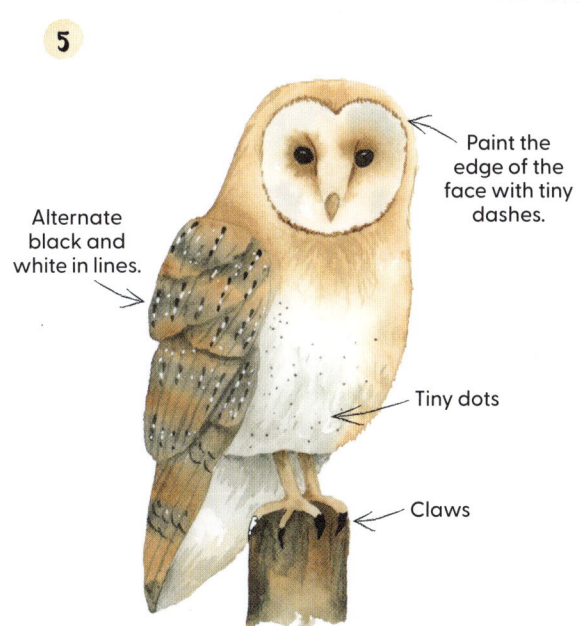

Paint the edge of the face with tiny dashes.

Alternate black and white in lines.

Tiny dots

Claws

Burnt Umber

Indigo

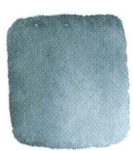
Mix 1: Winsor Blue
(Red Shade) and a
little Winsor Lemon

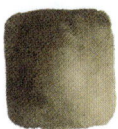
Mix 2: Burnt
Umber and a
little Indigo

Mix 3: Winsor
Lemon and a
little Winsor Blue
(Red Shade)

Dragonfly

STEPS

1. Draw the outline lightly in pencil.

2. Wet each wing and then add a little mix 1 (blue), Burnt Umber and mix 2 (dark brown) to the edges.

3. Paint the body with mix 3 (yellow green) and mix 1, leaving or lifting small highlights. With mix 2, paint the legs and fine lines on the wings. Add a mark at the top end of each wing.

4. With mix 2, fill in each section of the wings with dashes or rows of semi-circles.

5. With Indigo, paint the shadows and markings on the body.

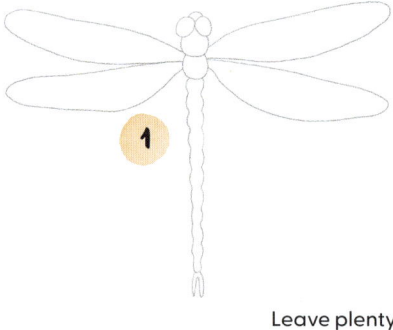

1

Leave plenty of white space to show the transparency of the wings.

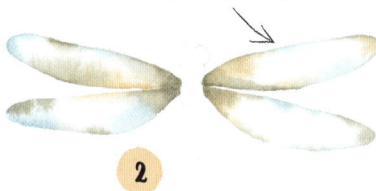

2

Add a bolder marking to each wing.

Legs

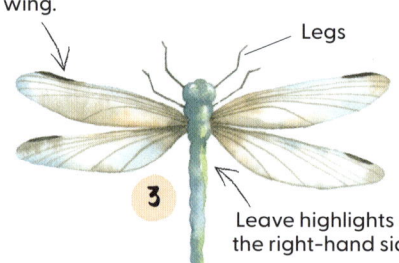

3

Leave highlights on the right-hand side.

5

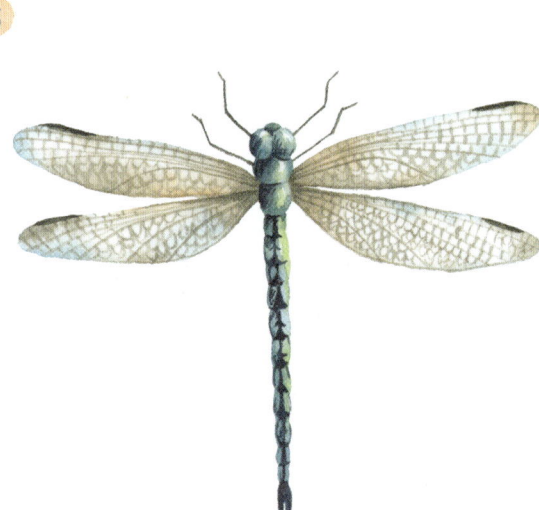

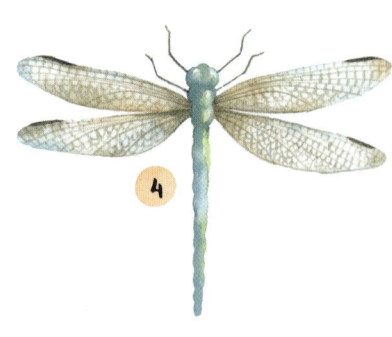

4

Moth

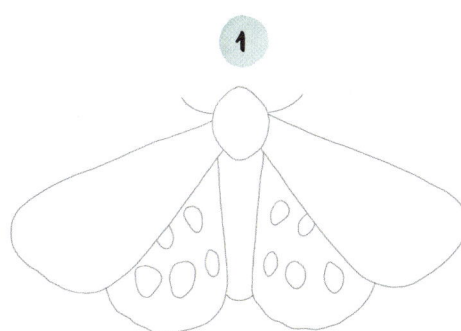

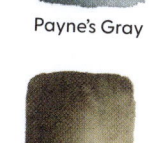

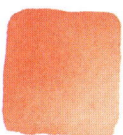

Burnt Umber

Payne's Gray

Ivory Black

Mix 1: Burnt Umber and a little Indigo

Mix 2: Winsor Lemon and a little Permanent Rose

Mix 3: Winsor Lemon and Permanent Rose

Mix 4: Permanent Rose and Winsor Lemon

STEPS

1. Draw the outline lightly in pencil.

2. With a pale mix 1 (dark brown), paint the antennae and shadows on the forewings. Paint the rim of the hindwings with mix 2 (yellow orange) and the body with mix 3 (orange).

3. Once dry, paint the hindwings, blending from mix 2 to mix 3 and mix 4 (red orange). Paint the head with mix 1, adding hairs to the edge.

4. Paint hairs on the body and hindwings with little dashes in mix 4 and Burnt Umber. Add more shadow to the forewings with mix 1 and more hairs to the head with a darker mix 1.

5. Paint the spots on the hindwings with Payne's Gray, lifting a highlight in the center of each and darkening the edges with Ivory Black. Paint stripes on the body with vertical dashes and more hairs on the head with Ivory Black. Paint the legs and the markings on the forewings with mix 1.

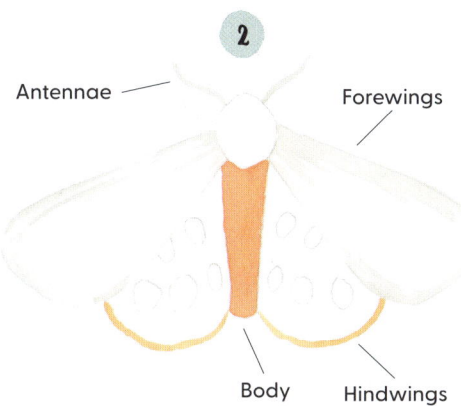

Antennae

Forewings

Body

Hindwings

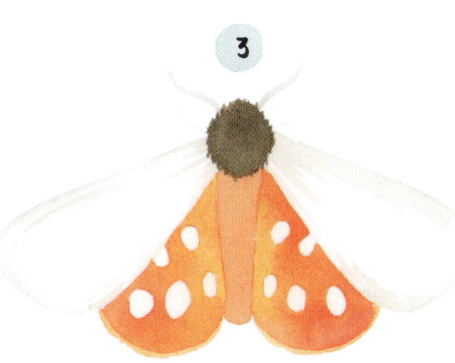

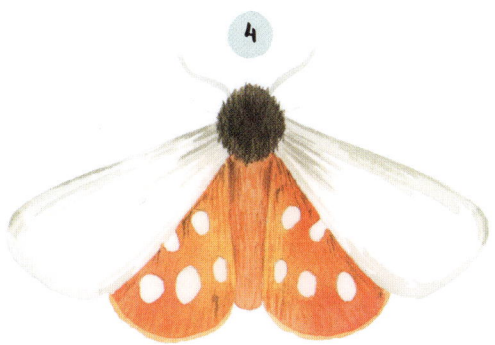

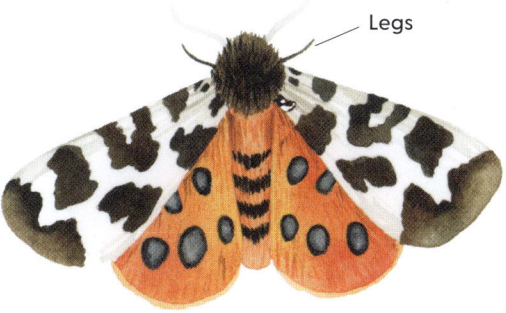

Legs

Permanent
Sap Green

Mix 1: Permanent
Sap Green and
Winsor Lemon

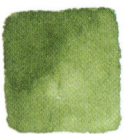

Mix 2: Permanent
Sap Green and a
little Permanent
Rose

Mix 3: Permanent
Rose and Winsor
Lemon

Beetle

STEPS

1. Draw the outline lightly in pencil.

2. Paint the main body with mix 1 (yellow green), leaving a highlight in the top right, and then add Permanent Sap Green to the edges. Add some green to the center line as the paint starts to dry so it does not spread as much.

3. Once dry, paint the middle section in the same way. Leave to dry and then paint the head.

4. Using mix 1 and Permanent Sap Green, paint the legs and antennae.

5. With mix 2 (neutral green), paint a line down the center of the body. Add shading at the edges and in between sections. With mix 3 (red orange), paint the eyes, leaving a small highlight on each.

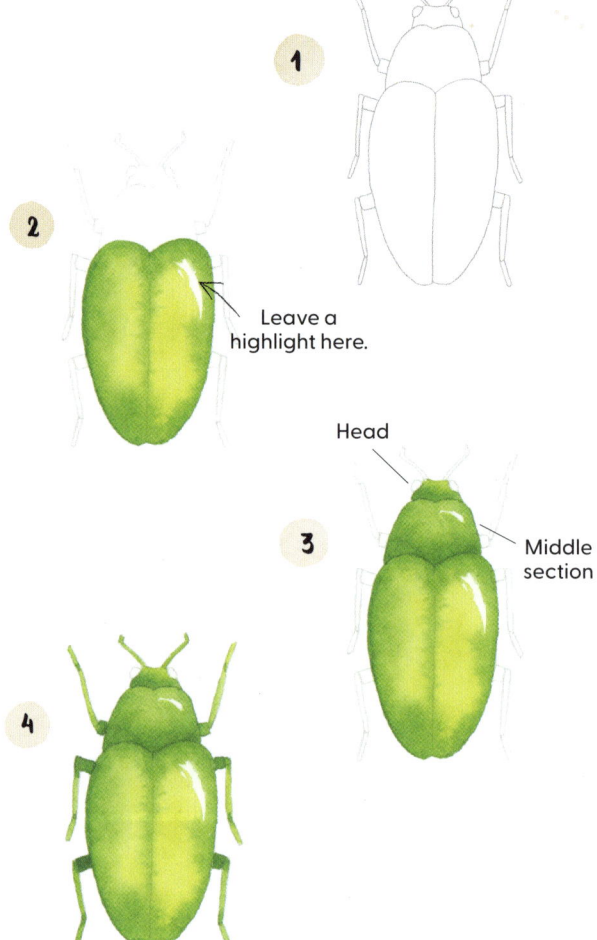

Leave a highlight here.

Head

Middle section

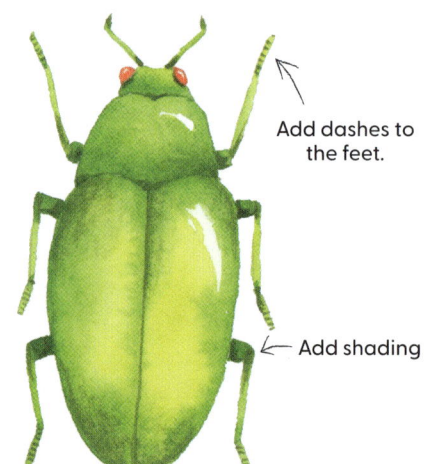

Add dashes to the feet.

Add shading

Leaving white space creates a bolder highlight compared to lifting the paint. This is useful for shinier surfaces.

Snail

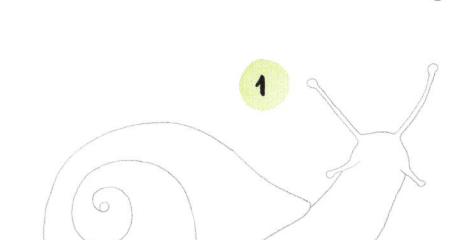

Yellow Ochre

Burnt Umber

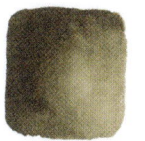
Mix 1: Burnt Umber and a little Indigo

STEPS

1. Draw the outline lightly in pencil.

2. Paint the shell with Yellow Ochre, leaving thin curved areas for highlights. While still wet, add Burnt Umber to darken the edges.

3. Once dry, use Burnt Umber to add shadows, focusing on the bottom right edges of each spiral.

4. Once dry, paint slightly curved stripes all over the shell using Burnt Umber.

5. Paint the snail body using mix 1 (dark brown) leaving small highlights.

6. Once dry, add shadow and details to the body using Burnt Umber and a darker mix 1.

Leave multiple curved highlights.

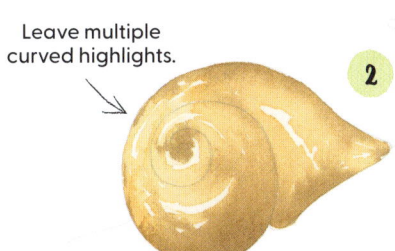

Darken lower right edges of each spiral.

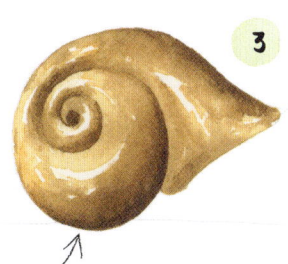

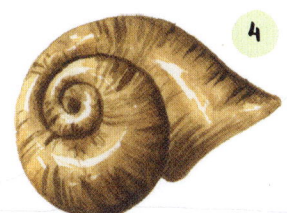

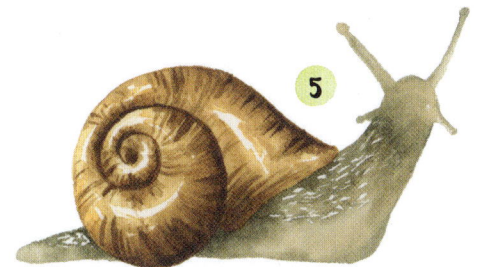

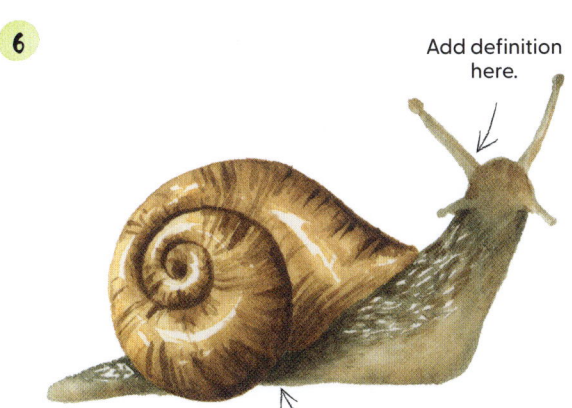

Add definition here.

Add shadow here.

Burnt Umber

Mix 1: Winsor Lemon and a little Permanent Rose

Mix 2: Winsor Lemon and Permanent Rose

Mix 3: Permanent Rose and Winsor Lemon

Crab

STEPS

1. Paint the shell with a pale mix 1 (yellow orange). While still wet, dab in a range of darker oranges (mix 1, mix 2 and mix 3) and Burnt Umber.

2. Paint the claws using a pale mix 1. While still wet, add mixes 2 and 3 and Burnt Umber at the edges. Using the same process, paint eight legs with three to four sections, ending in a point.

3. Once dry, use Burnt Umber to add shading to the legs and claws, especially around the edges and at the bottom of each section.

4. With Burnt Umber, darken the lower half of the shell and blend out roughly. Add some tiny eyes and antennae and some ridges around the top edge of the shell. Finally add some tiny hairs to the legs.

If you prefer, sketch this project out first before painting. A traceable outline is provided in the PDF download for you.

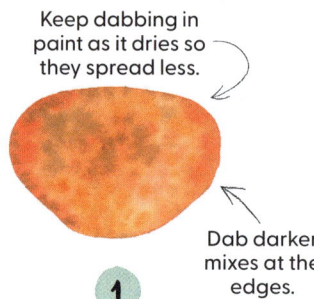

Keep dabbing in paint as it dries so they spread less.

Dab darker mixes at the edges.

1

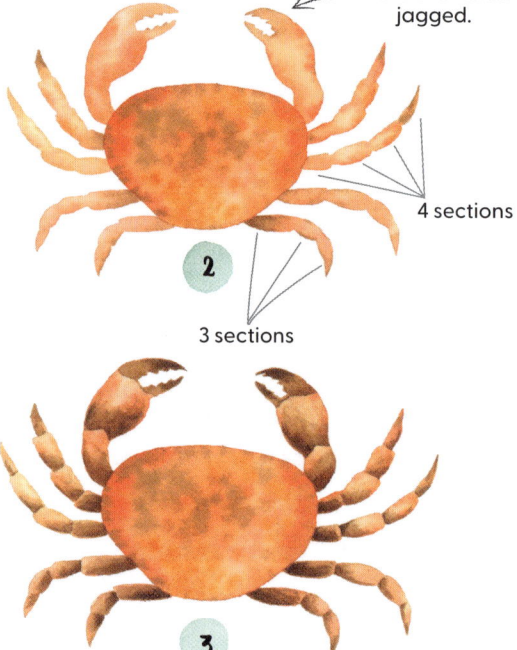

Make the inside jagged.

4 sections

3 sections

2

3

4

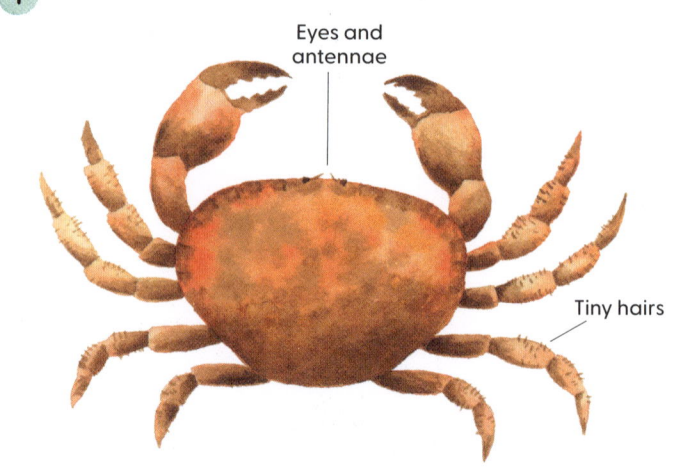

Eyes and antennae

Tiny hairs

Seahorse

STEPS

1. Draw the outline lightly in pencil.

2. Wet the inside and then add a pale mix 1 (yellow green) and a pale mix 2 (blue green), building up the colors at the edges.

3. Once dry, use mix 2 to paint rectangles all over the body. Paint the face, leaving a circle for the eye.

4. Using a darker mix 2, paint lines on the fin and a dot in the center of the eye.

5. With more mix 2, add shading and marks on the rectangles, fin and face.

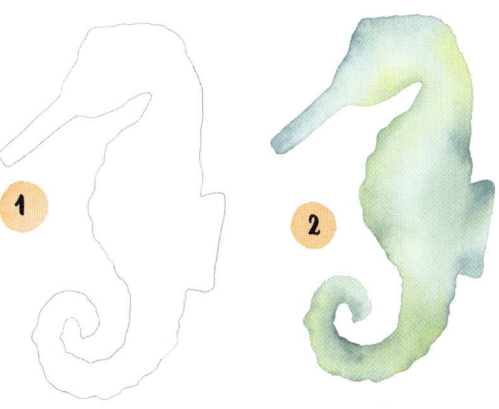

1

2

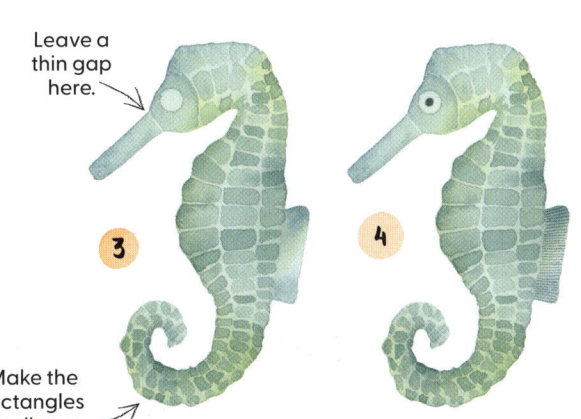

Leave a thin gap here.

3

4

Make the rectangles smaller on the tail.

5

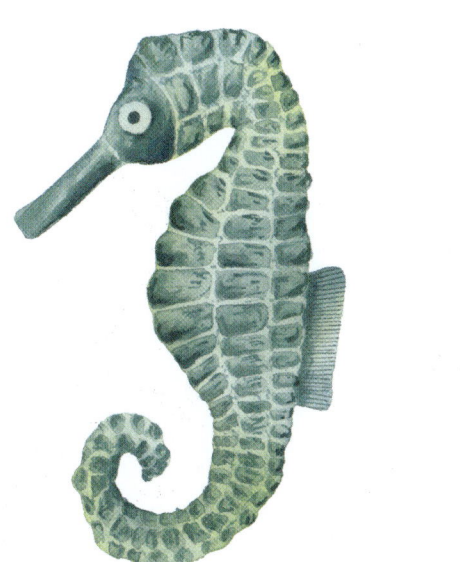

This project uses only two colors but achieves a lot of interest and contrast by varying the values of those colors.

Payne's Gray

Mix 1: Payne's
Gray and a little
Burnt Umber

Whale

STEPS

1. Draw the outline lightly in pencil.

2. Add a pale mix 1 (gray) to the edge of the underbelly and blend out. Add a little shading to the white patch as well.

3. Paint the top of the whale with a pale Payne's Gray and then add a very dark Payne's Gray to the edges.

4. Once dry, paint the tail fins and back fin in the same way. Add some light shading marks to the underbelly and then paint the eye and mouth in a dark Payne's Gray.

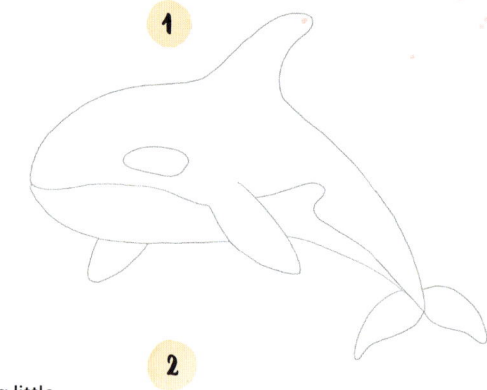

Add a little shading here as well.

Allow the darker paint to bleed in naturally to create more texture.

For the very dark areas of the whale, use a lot of paint and only a little water for a highly concentrated mix.

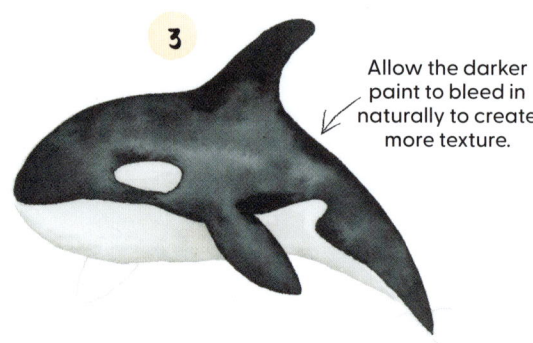

Add shading with fine pale lines.

Butterfly Fish

Burnt Umber

Ivory Black

Mix 1: Winsor Lemon and a little Permanent Rose

Mix 2: Winsor Lemon and Permanent Rose

STEPS

1. Draw the outline lightly in pencil.

2. Add pale Burnt Umber to the edges and blend inwards.

3. Once dry, paint the stripes and back fin using mix 1 (yellow orange) and then add mix 2 (orange) to the edges.

4. Once dry, paint the front fin and tail using the same process.

5. With Ivory Black, paint the eye and false eye spot with a thin ring around each. Paint a black stripe at the start of the tail and add very fine lines to the fins and end of the tail.

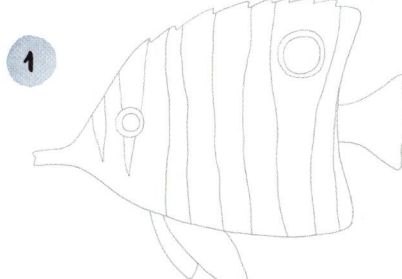

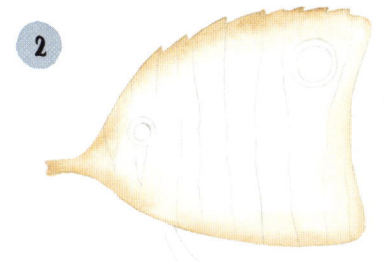

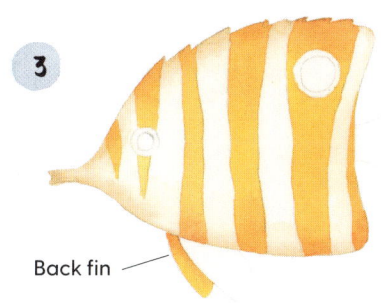

Back fin

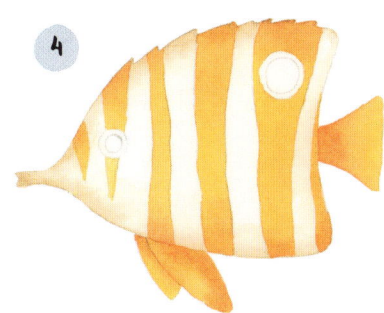

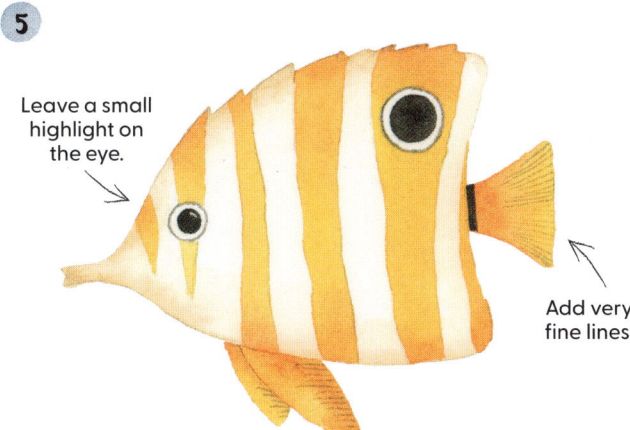

Leave a small highlight on the eye.

Add very fine lines.

Using a warmer color for the shading (brown instead of gray) complements the rest of the colors in this subject.

Home & Garden

It is easy to overlook objects that we see around us every day, but there is so much to be inspired by right at our fingertips. Take a wander around your home and start paying attention to the delicate details of objects: their patterns and textures, colors, highlights and shading. Even something that may at first seem a little uninspiring, like a lampshade, can be a really fun, quick project that you can use to experiment with different marks and shading, and practice your techniques while you learn.

Painting a stack of books, for example, allows you to practice painting harmoniously with different colors; painting a ball of yarn will help you to practice painting with values. I hope you will find these projects inspiring and helpful for building your watercolor skills!

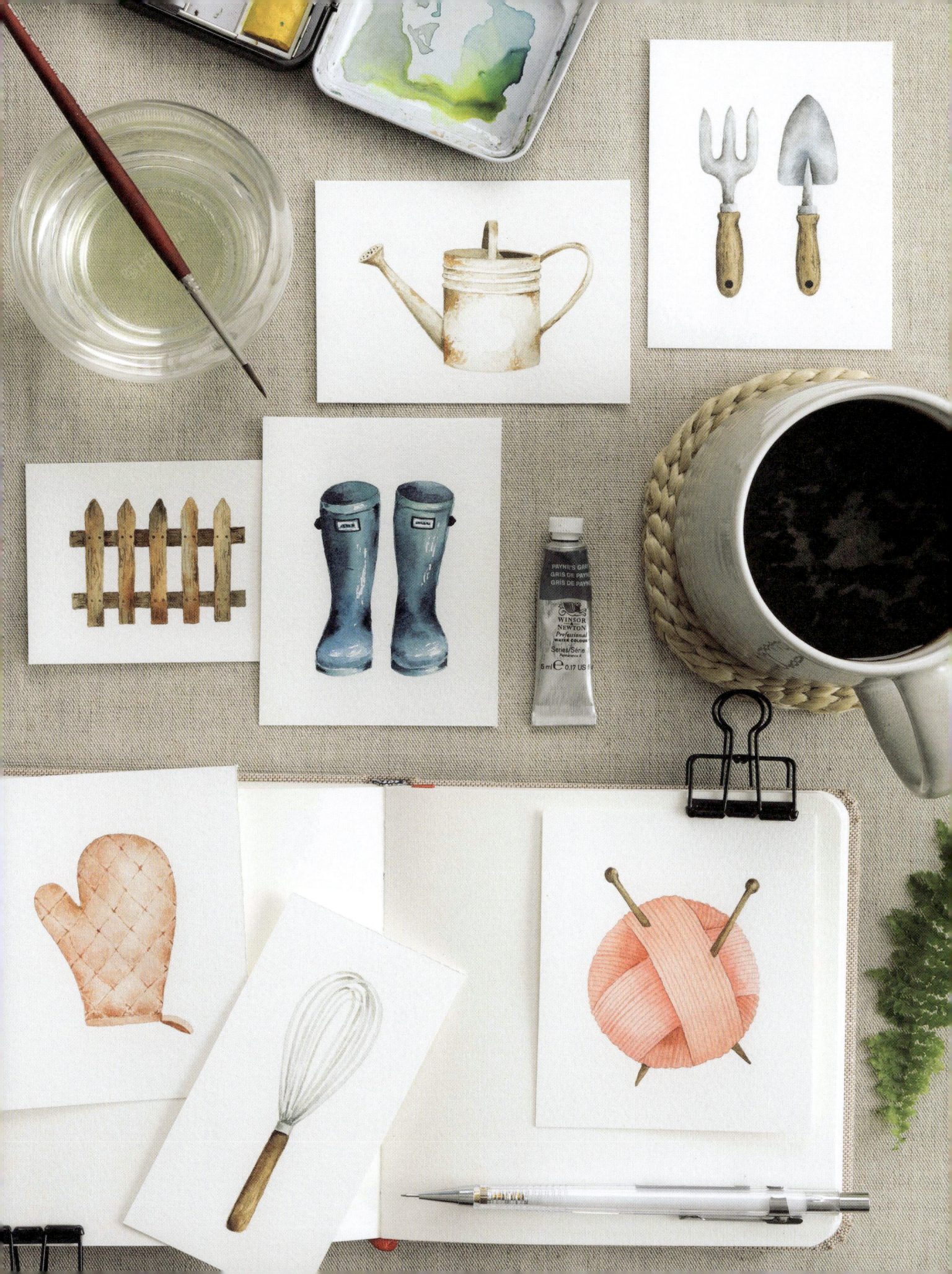

Burnt Umber

Payne's Gray

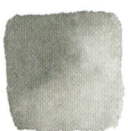

Mix 1: Payne's Gray and a little Burnt Umber

Mix 2: Burnt Umber and a little Payne's Gray

Books

STEPS

1. Draw the outline lightly in pencil.

2. For the book pages, wet the inside area and add pale Burnt Umber to the edges.

3. Once dry, use mix 1 (gray) to paint the second book and mix 2 (dark brown) for the fourth book. Once those are dry, paint the remaining book covers as shown.

4. With Burnt Umber, paint fine lines to define the pages.

5. With mix 2, add darker details to the pages. Finally, add details to the two spines with darker versions of the mixes as shown.

1

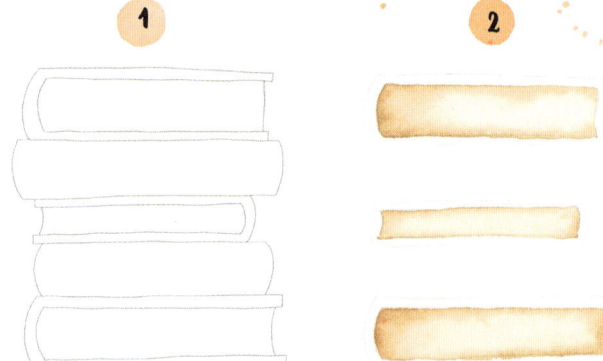

2

3

Burnt Umber —
Mix 1 (gray) —
Payne's Gray —
Mix 2 (dark brown) —
Payne's Gray (pale) —

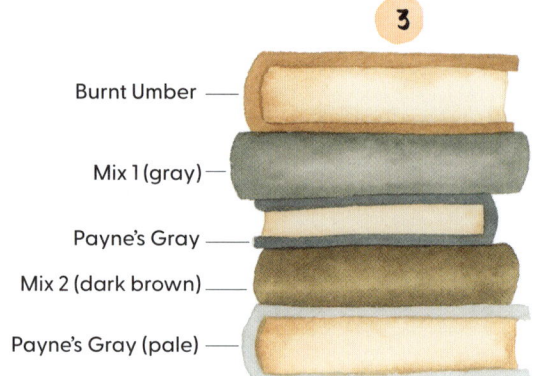

4

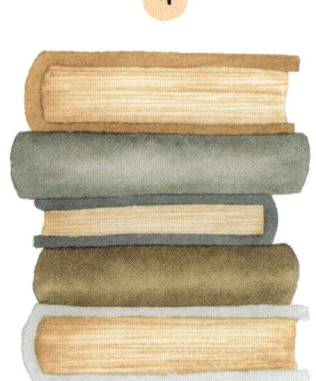

5

Darken near the spine and add darker, shorter lines for the pages.

Details in mix 1 —

Details in mix 2 —

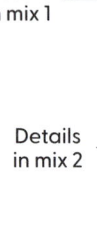

Lamp

Burnt Umber

Mix 1: Winsor Lemon and Permanent Rose

Mix 2: Burnt Umber and a little Indigo

STEPS

1. Draw the outline lightly in pencil.

2. Paint the lampshade with mix 1 (orange) and then add Burnt Umber to the side edges.

3. With mix 2 (dark brown), paint the stand, lifting a highlight on the right-hand side.

4. Once dry, paint the neck and add shading and detail to the stand with a darker mix 2.

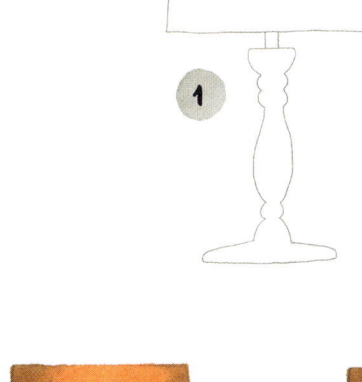

1

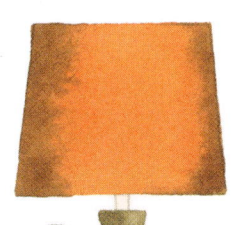

2

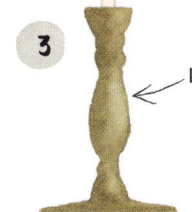

3

Lift highlight here.

4

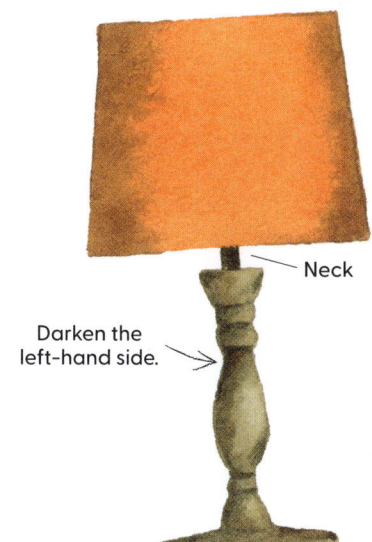

Neck

Darken the left-hand side.

Design your own lamps with different styles and colors!

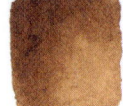

Burnt Umber

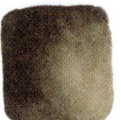

Mix 1: Burnt Umber and a little Indigo

Armchair

STEPS

1. Draw the outline lightly in pencil.

2. Paint the first two sections with mix 1 (dark brown).

3. Once dry, paint the next sections as shown with mix 1.

4. Once those are dry, paint the arm rests and front of the seat cushion with mix 1. Paint the legs with Burnt Umber.

5. With mix 1, paint the buttons with four fold lines coming out of each. Add shading to define the edges of the seat cushion and arm rests.

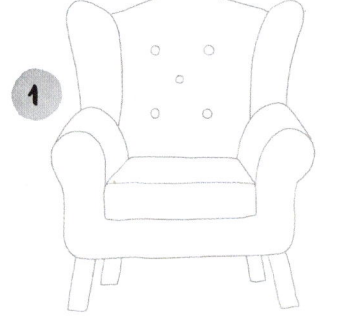

Paint with a pale mix first, then drop in darker paint so the cushions do not look flat.

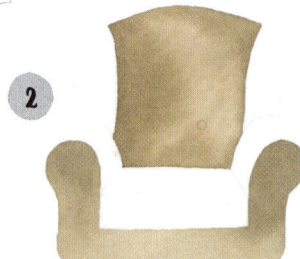

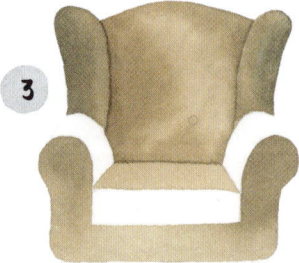

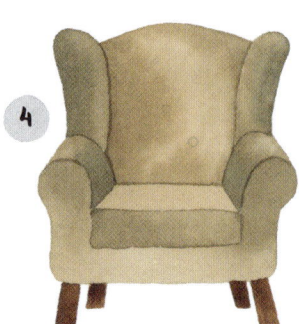

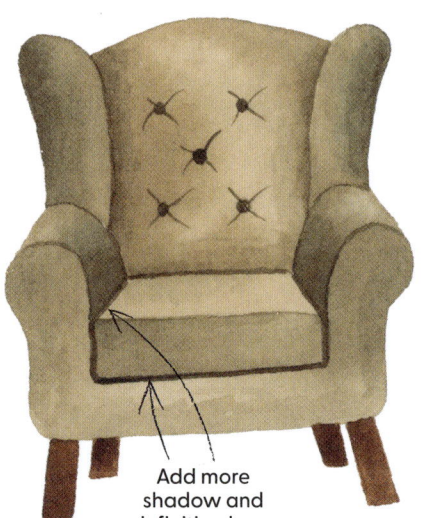

Add more shadow and definition here.

Rug

Payne's Gray

Mix 1: Payne's Gray and a little Burnt Umber

1

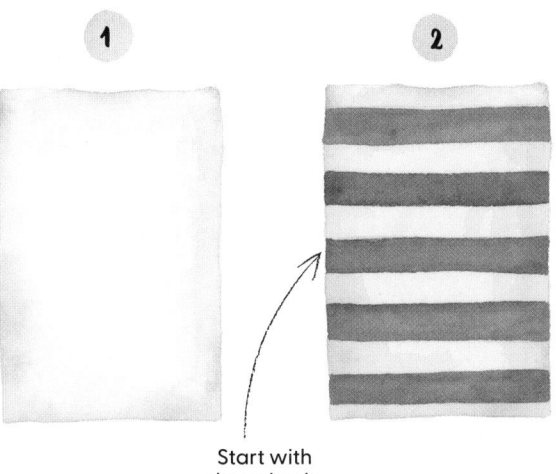

2

Start with the stripe in the center.

STEPS

1. Paint the edge of a rectangle with a very pale mix 1 (gray) and blend in towards the middle.

2. Once dry, use Payne's Gray to add thick stripes. To help space the stripes out evenly, start in the middle, then paint two at either side.

3. Paint thin stripes at either side of each thick stripe.

4. Add the tassels with pale Payne's Gray by painting small circles with a few lines coming out of each.

5. Once dry, add a little definition to the tassels with darker Payne's Gray.

3

4

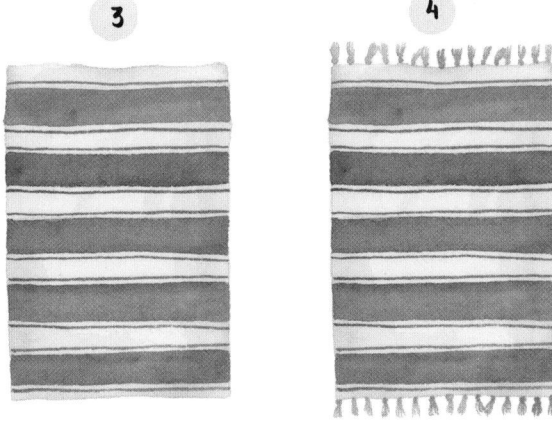

5

Darken the left-hand side of each circle and add a couple of darker lines.

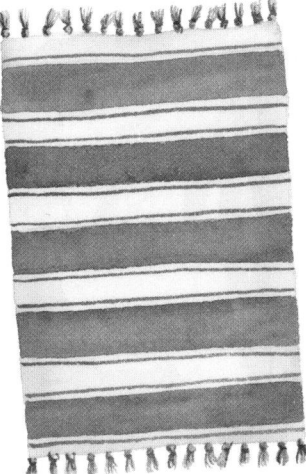

Play around with colors and patterns for endless designs!

Mix 1: Permanent Rose and a little Burnt Umber

Oven Mitt

STEPS

1. Draw the outline lightly in pencil.

2. With a pale mix 1 (pink), paint the glove, adding slightly darker paint around the edges.

3. Paint a pale horizontal line at the base and then slightly wavy diagonal lines crossing over each other over the main mitt.

4. Add darker dashes on the lines, especially where they cross over.

5. With a dry brush, add shading at the base of each diamond shape, around the edges of the mitt and in the darker area on the loop.

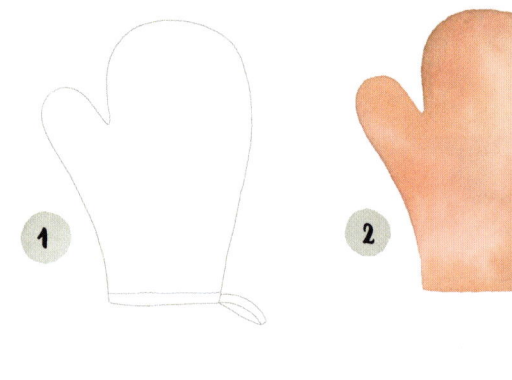

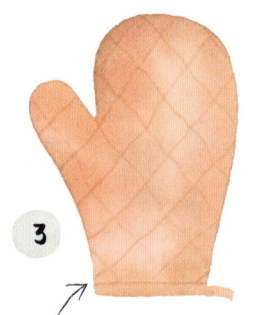

Paint a line here.

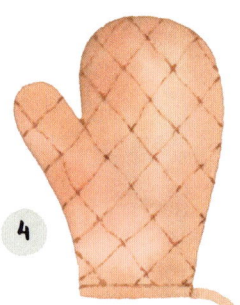

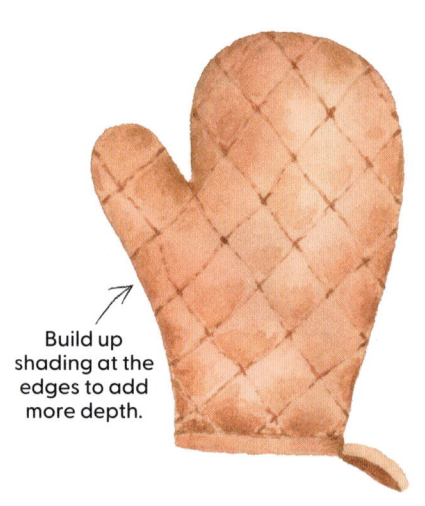

This is a great project to focus on practicing values as we are only using one color!

Build up shading at the edges to add more depth.

Whisk

Yellow Ochre

Burnt Umber

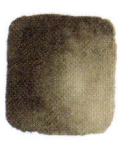
Mix 1: Payne's Gray and a little Burnt Umber

Mix 2: Burnt Umber and a little Indigo

STEPS

1. Draw a guide for the outline lightly in pencil.

2. With a pale mix 1 (gray), paint three loops in the middle that overlap each other. Paint the metal part at the top of the handle.

3. Once dry, paint three larger loops around the middle three, again overlapping each other.

4. Paint the handle with Yellow Ochre and then add Burnt Umber to the edges.

5. With a darker mix 1, add shading to the whisk where the loops overlap and where they meet the handle. With mix 2 (dark brown), add shading to the handle.

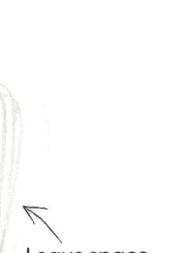

Leave space between these loops and the guideline.

1

2

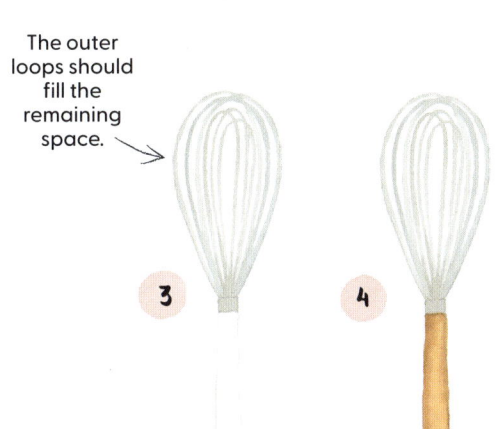

The outer loops should fill the remaining space.

3

4

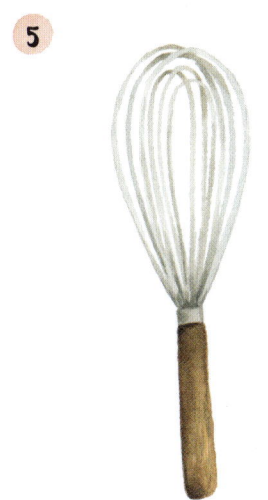

5

Have a look around your kitchen for more interesting subjects to paint!

Mix 1: Permanent
Sap Green,
Winsor Blue (Red
Shade) and a little
Permanent Rose

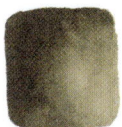

Mix 2: Burnt
Umber and a
little Indigo

Thread

STEPS

1. Draw the outline lightly in pencil.

2. Paint the base of the thread with a pale mix 1 (blue green), adding darker paint at the side edges.

3. With mix 2 (dark brown), paint the first two sections of the spool.

4. Once dry, paint the curved edges of the spool with a pale mix 2 and then darken the sides. With a darker mix 2, paint the hole at the top.

5. With mix 1, use very fine lines to add the first threads.

6. Fill in the gaps with slightly curved lines at a different angle. Add a wavy line for the end of the thread coming off to the side.

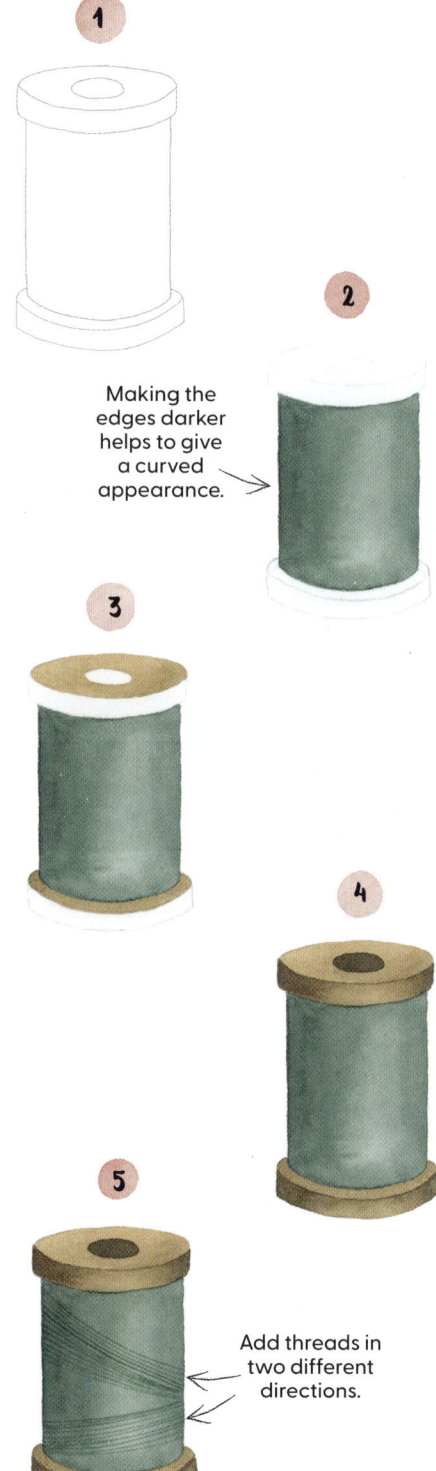

Making the edges darker helps to give a curved appearance.

Add threads in two different directions.

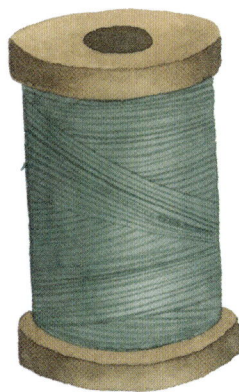

Buttons

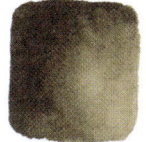

Mix 1: Burnt
Umber and a
little Indigo

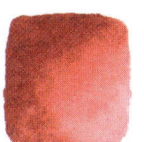

Mix 2: Permanent
Rose and Burnt
Umber

STEPS

1. Draw the outlines lightly in pencil.

2. Paint the center of each button with the color shown, leaving the holes unpainted.

3. Once dry, paint the surrounding circles, darkening the outer edges. Leave thin gaps for highlights.

4. Using darker mixes of each color, add shadow to the top left of each hole, the top left of the inner circle of each button and the bottom right of each outer circle.

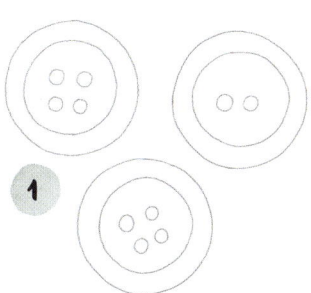

1

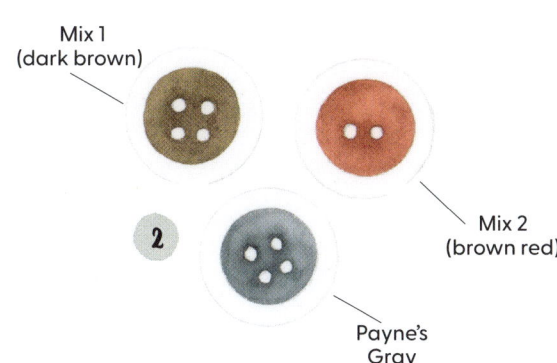

Mix 1
(dark brown)

Mix 2
(brown red)

2

Payne's
Gray

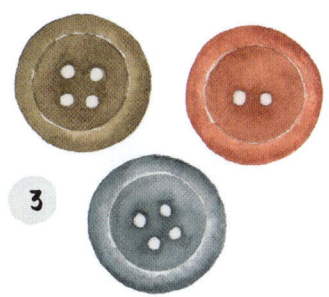

3

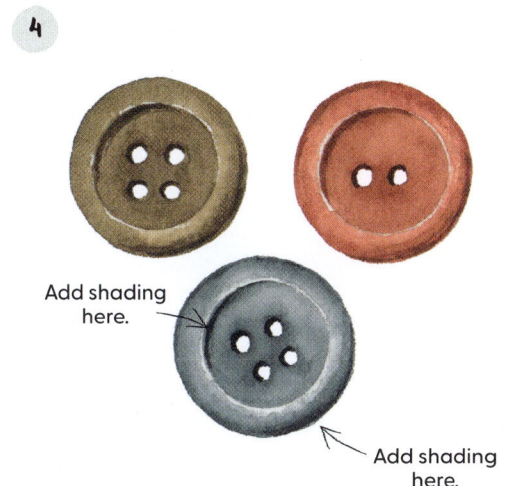

4

Add shading here.

Add shading here.

When adding shadows on subjects, choose the direction of your light source so you are consistent with where you place your shadows.

Mix 1: Permanent
Rose and a little
Burnt Umber

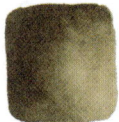

Mix 2: Burnt
Umber and a
little Indigo

Yarn

STEPS

1. Draw the outline lightly in pencil.

2. Paint the first strip with mix 1 (pink), making the outer edges slightly darker.

3. Once dry, paint the next strip, making it slightly darker at the edges than the previous strip.

4. Once dry, paint the final sections, making them slightly darker still.

5. With mix 2 (dark brown), paint the needles, lifting a highlight at the top of each.

6. With mix 1, paint curved lines across the yarn.

1

Make the edge bumpy.

2

3

4

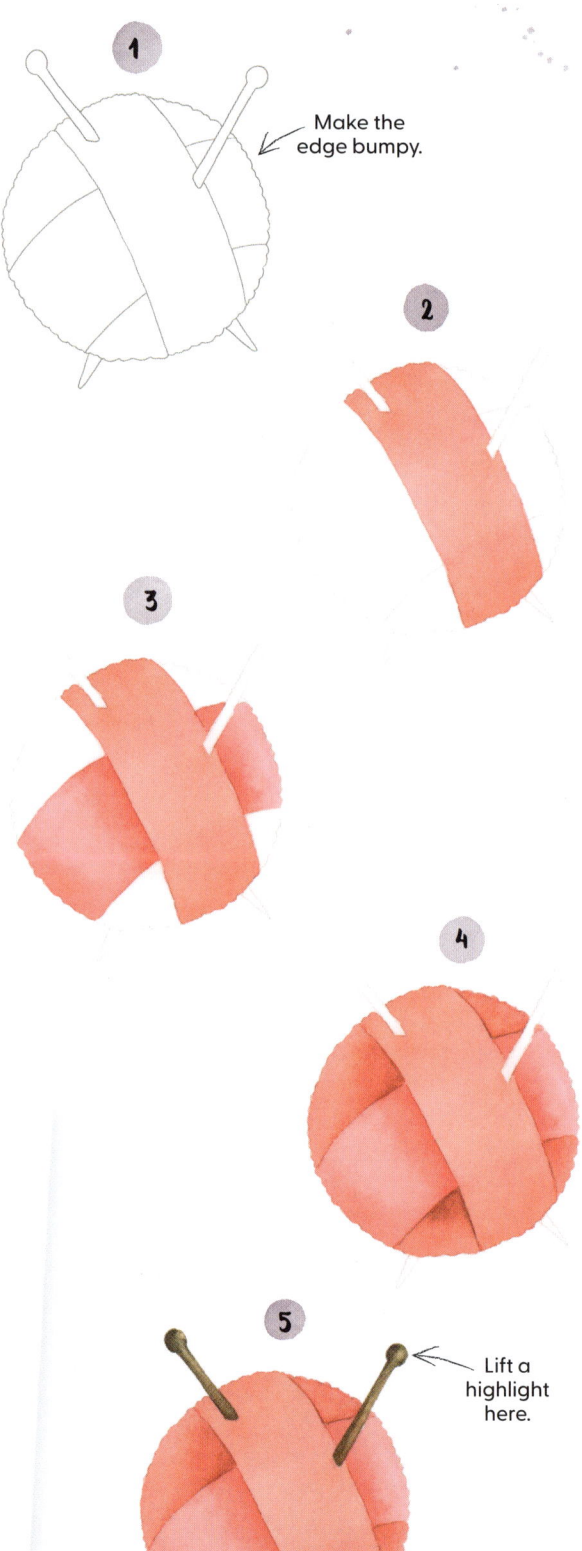

6

5

Lift a highlight here.

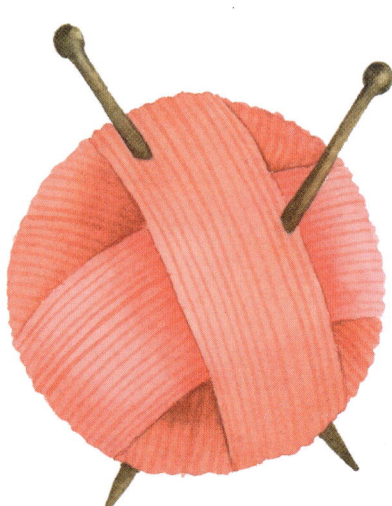

Paint Set

Payne's Gray

Mix 1: Payne's Gray and a little Burnt Umber

Plus various colors for the paint pans

STEPS

1. Draw the outline lightly in pencil.

2. With a pale mix 1 (gray), add shading as shown.

3. With Payne's Gray, paint a line around the outer edges, the hinges and the lines around the paint pans.

4. Fill in the containers with a variety of colors, leaving a gap around the edge and a small highlight on each.

5. Add messy splashes to the palette with a variety of colors.

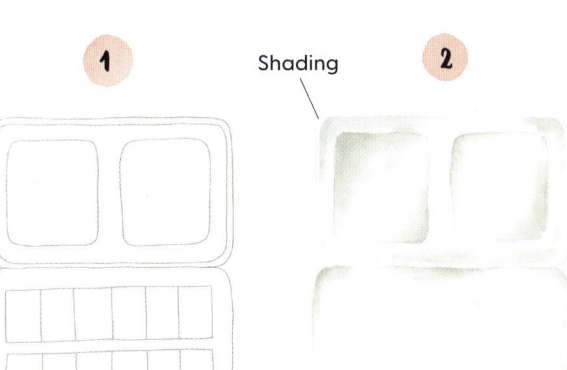

Shading

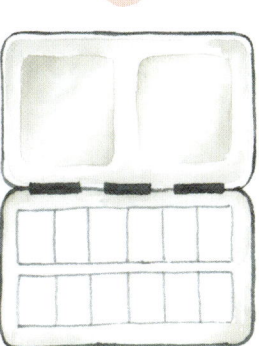
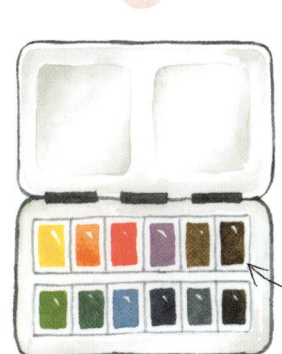

Leave space around each color.

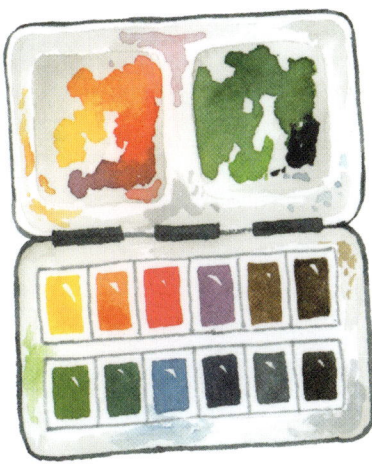

Choose your own colors to fill this paint set with!

Payne's Gray

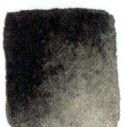

Ivory Black

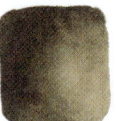

Mix 1: Burnt Umber and a little Indigo

Garden Tools

STEPS

1. Draw the outline lightly in pencil.

2. Paint the handles using mix 1 (dark brown), lifting a highlight on the right-hand side of each.

3. Once dry, paint the fork and the inner metal area of the spade using pale Payne's Gray. While still wet, add darker areas to some of the edges.

4. Once dry, paint the spade, adding darker paint at the edges and around the inner section.

5. With Ivory Black, add shading to the metal. With mix 1, add grain to the wood and a hole at the end of each handle.

1

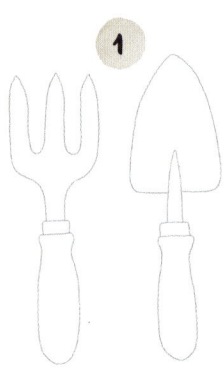

2

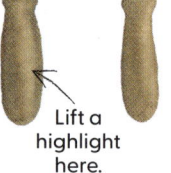

Lift a highlight here.

3

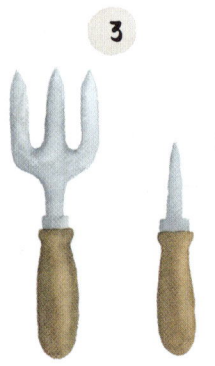

4

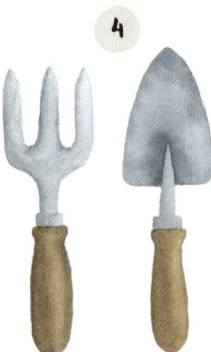

5

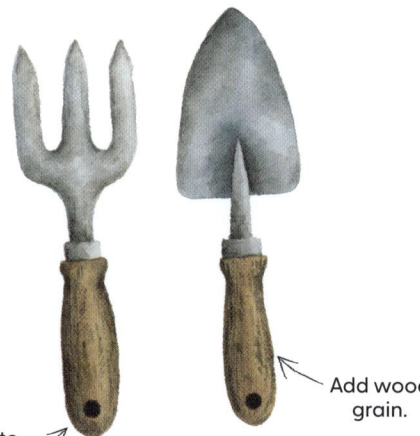

Add a hole to each handle.

Add wood grain.

Watering Can

Burnt Umber

Mix 1: Burnt Umber and a little Indigo

STEPS

1. Draw the outline lightly in pencil.

2. Paint the shadows on the front, top handle and end of the spout in mix 1 (dark brown).

3. Once dry, paint the shadows on the top, side handle and spout in mix 1.

4. Add more shadows with a darker mix 1, defining the ridges on the front.

5. Using a dark mix 1, paint the underside of the top handle, the hole at the top and the dots on the sprinkler.

6. With Burnt Umber and a dry brush, add some patchy areas of rust, especially around the edges.

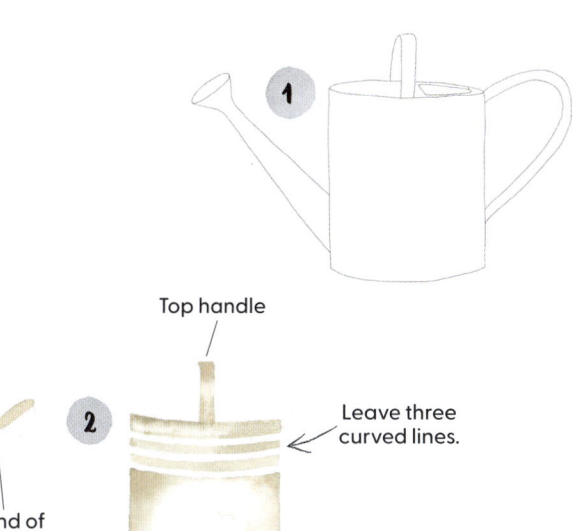

Top handle

Leave three curved lines.

End of spout

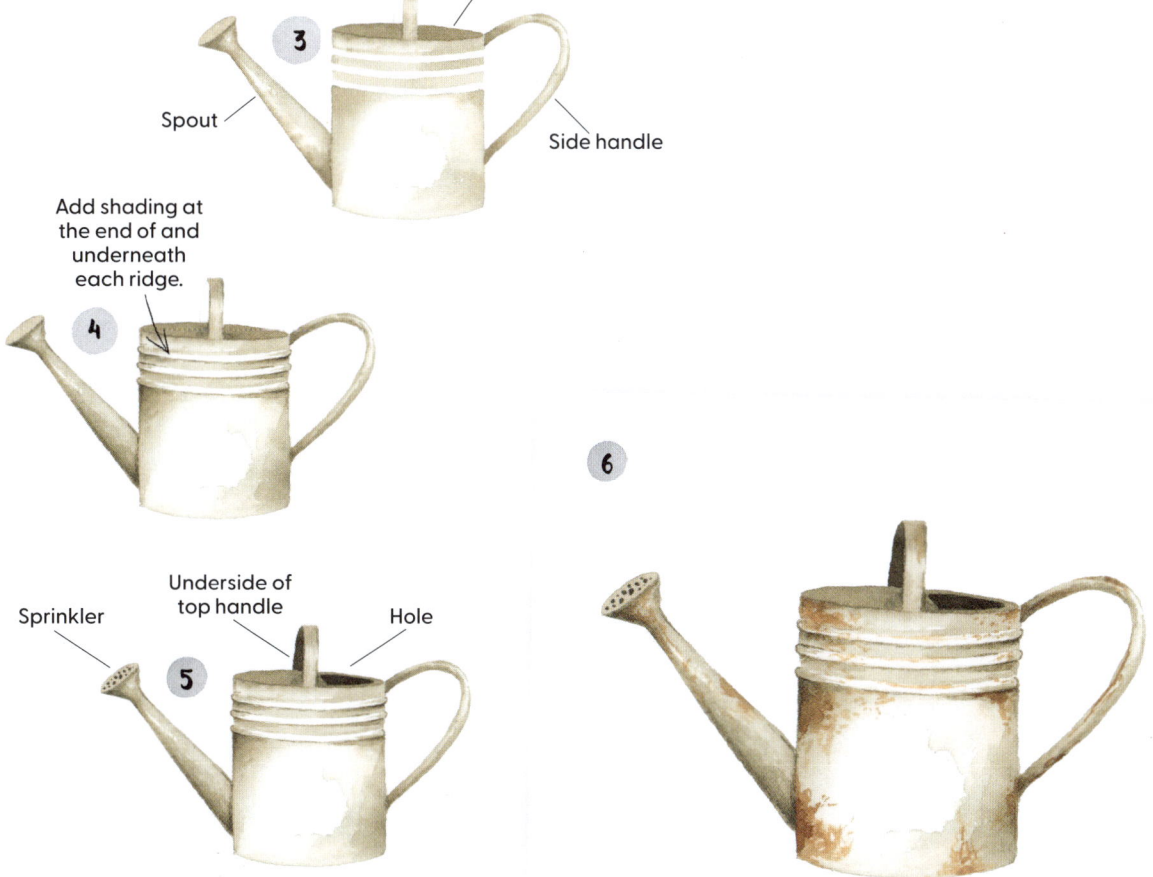

Top

Spout

Side handle

Add shading at the end of and underneath each ridge.

Sprinkler

Underside of top handle

Hole

Burnt Umber

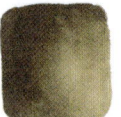

Mix 1: Burnt Umber and a little Indigo

Fence

STEPS

1. Draw the outline lightly in pencil.

2. With Burnt Umber and mix 1 (dark brown), paint the vertical fence panels.

3. Once dry, paint the horizontal wood with mix 1, making it slightly darker than the panels.

4. With mix 1, paint dots for nails.

5. With mix 1, paint grain on the wood with dashes and curves.

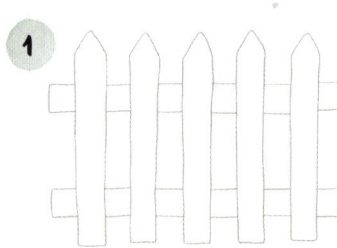

1

2

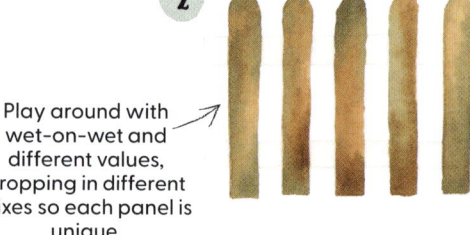

Play around with wet-on-wet and different values, dropping in different mixes so each panel is unique.

3

4

Paint dots for nails.

5

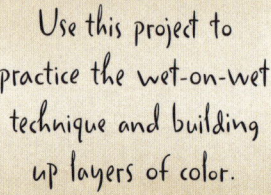

Use this project to practice the wet-on-wet technique and building up layers of color.

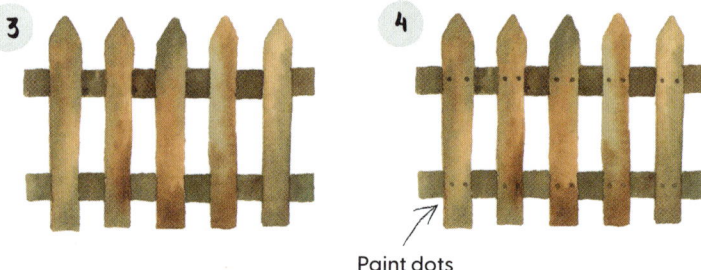

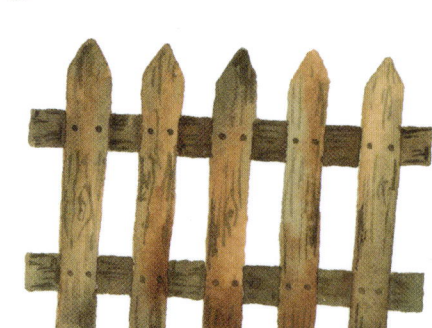

Rain Boots

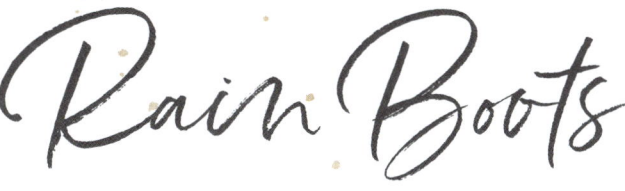

Indigo

Mix 1: Winsor Blue (Red Shade) and Winsor Lemon

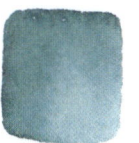
Mix 2: Winsor Blue (Red Shade) and a little Winsor Lemon

Plus opaque white

STEPS

1. Draw the outline lightly in pencil.

2. With mix 1 (blue green) and mix 2 (blue), paint the first layer for the main part of the boots, lifting lighter areas around the toes.

3. With both mixes, paint the soles, leaving a highlight on each. With mix 2 and Indigo, paint the inside of the boots.

4. Use Indigo to add a fine line at the top of each boot, then add shadows across the boots with a darker mix 2 and Indigo.

5. With more Indigo, paint the buckles. Add the logos, painting a rectangle with a squiggle inside on each, then fill in the space with an opaque white. Add highlights on the boots using opaque white.

Lift highlights here.

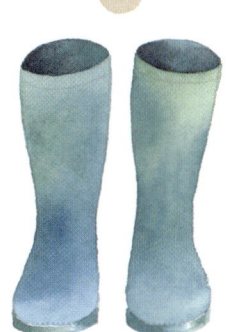

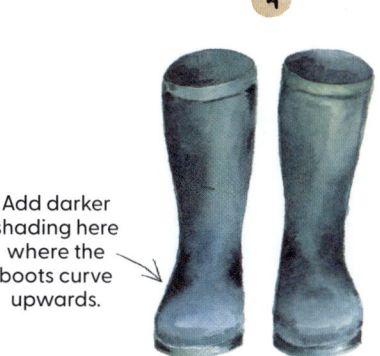

Add darker shading here where the boots curve upwards.

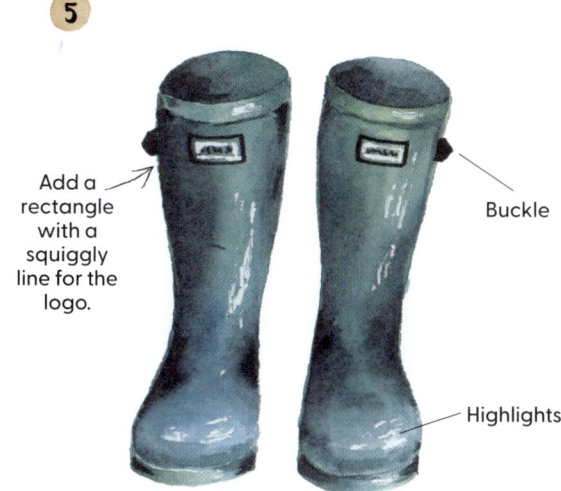

Add a rectangle with a squiggly line for the logo.

Buckle

Highlights

Around the World

Travel can give us the opportunity to visit buildings and things of interest all around the world that can be fun to paint, from a summery beach hut to a sailboat or hot-air balloon. These subjects are not as easily accessible in everyday life, so when I am out and about I love to take photos – or find pictures in magazines or online – of anything that may inspire me for a later painting session! Many of these projects have fine details like the brickwork on the windmill or the wood grain on the boat and signposts. Take as much time as you need to practice first using the Techniques section, and remember to keep your paper towel handy to take excess water out of your paintbrush. This will help you to achieve the delicate brushstrokes that you need.

Many of these projects are also subjects that you can make your own with different colors and patterns, from the hot-air balloon to the sails on the boat and the patterns on the tipi.

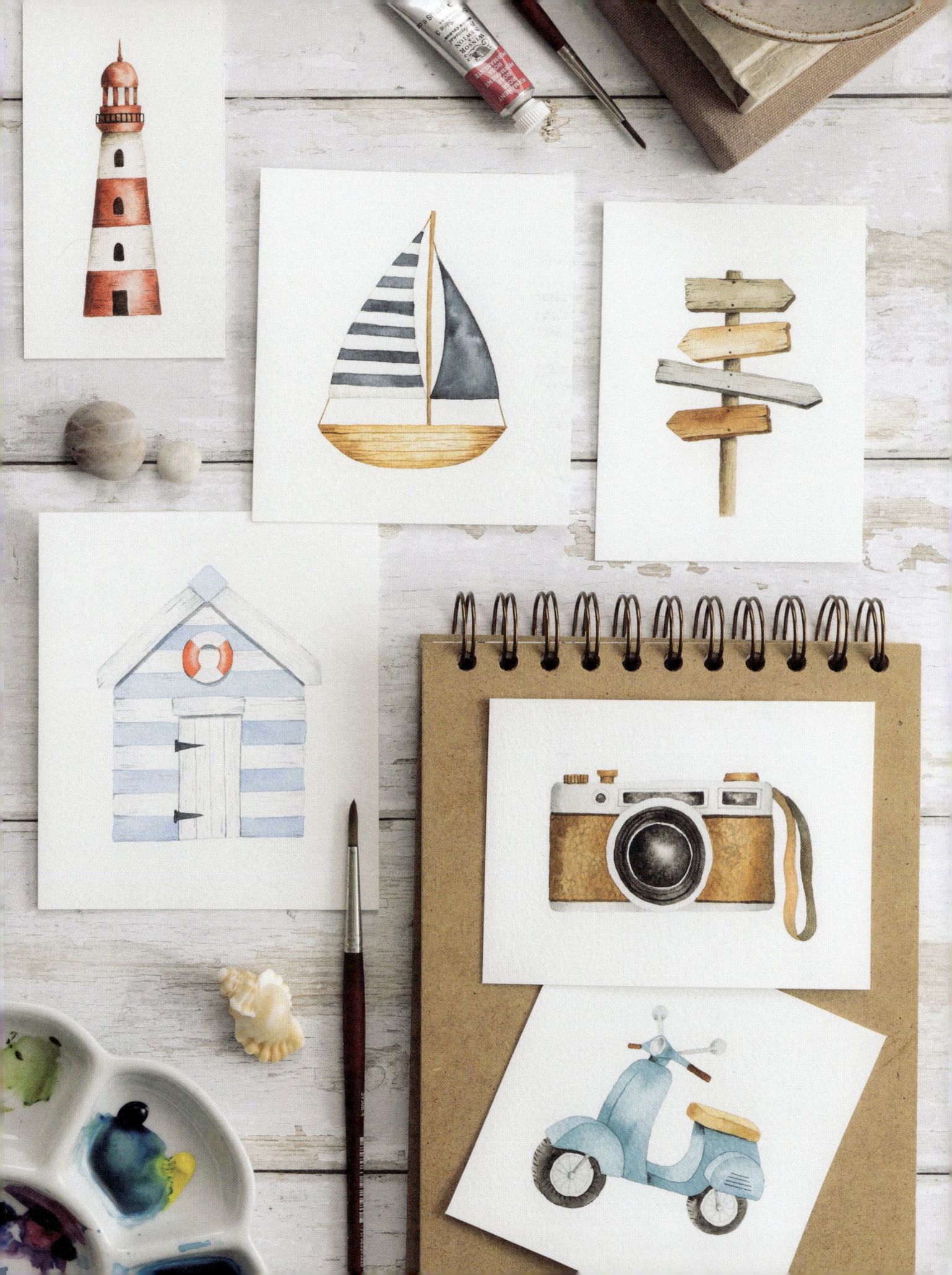

Yellow Ochre

Burnt Umber

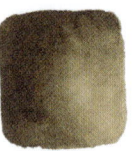
Mix 1: Burnt Umber
and a little Indigo

Plus opaque white

Suitcase

STEPS

1. Using Yellow Ochre, paint a rectangle with slightly curved corners. While it is still wet, add Burnt Umber to the edges.

2. With a mid-value mix 1 (dark brown), paint the straps, handle and corner patches, leaving three holes for studs in each.

3. With a darker mix 1, paint the buckles and details on the straps.

4. With more mix 1, add shading to the handle, the corner patches, the studs and around the straps.

5. Add highlights to the handle, buckle and studs with an opaque white.

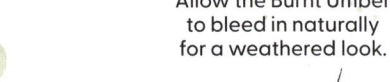
Allow the Burnt Umber to bleed in naturally for a weathered look.

1

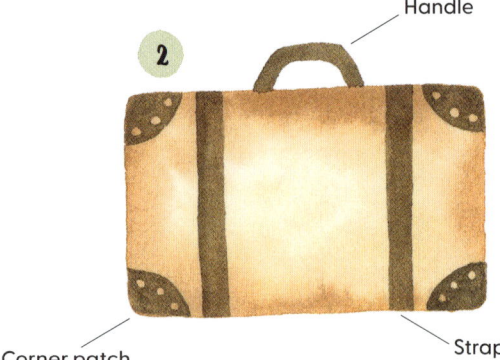
2

Handle

Corner patch

Strap

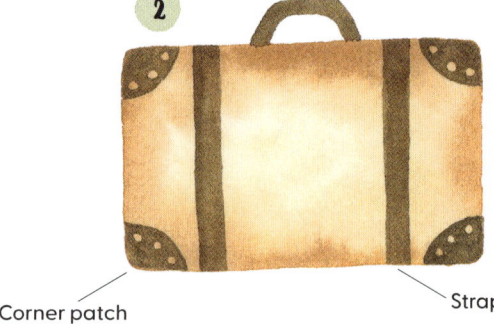

Darken the top of each strap here.

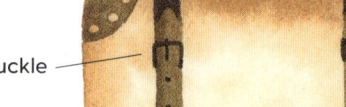
3

Buckle

Add dots on each strap for the holes.

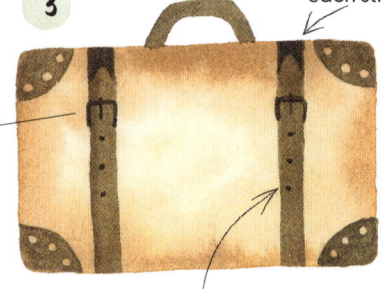

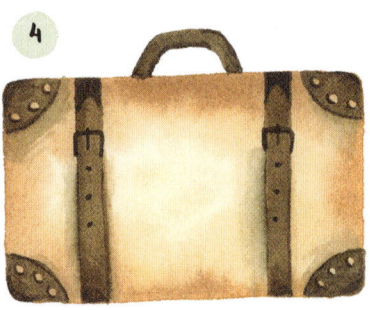
4

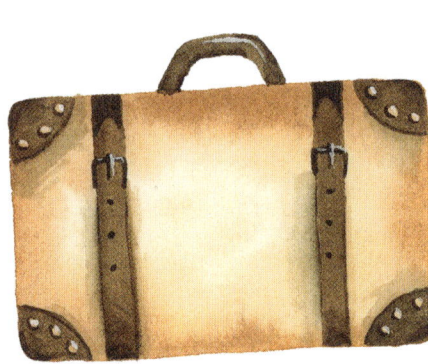
5

Globe

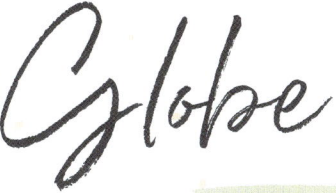

STEPS

1. Draw the outline lightly in pencil.

2. Wet the inside of the land areas and add mix 1 (neutral green) to the edges.

3. Once dry, wet the inside of the sea areas and add pale Indigo to the edges.

4. With Burnt Umber, paint the wooden stand.

5. With mix 2 (dark brown), add shading to the stand to define each section. Using a pale mix 3 (gray), paint curved lines horizontally and vertically across the globe.

Indigo

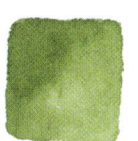

Burnt Umber

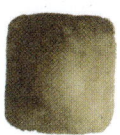

Mix 1: Permanent Sap Green and a little Permanent Rose

Mix 2: Burnt Umber and a little Indigo

Mix 3: Payne's Gray and a little Burnt Umber

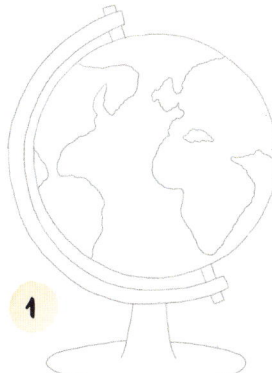

1

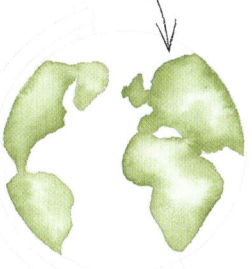

Allow the paint to bleed in from the edges.

2

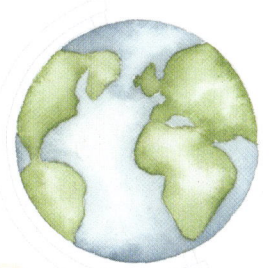

3

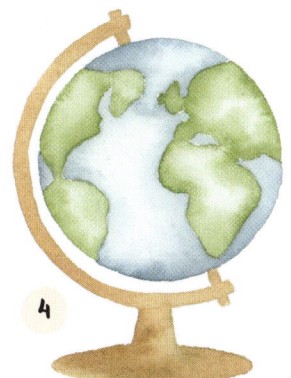

4

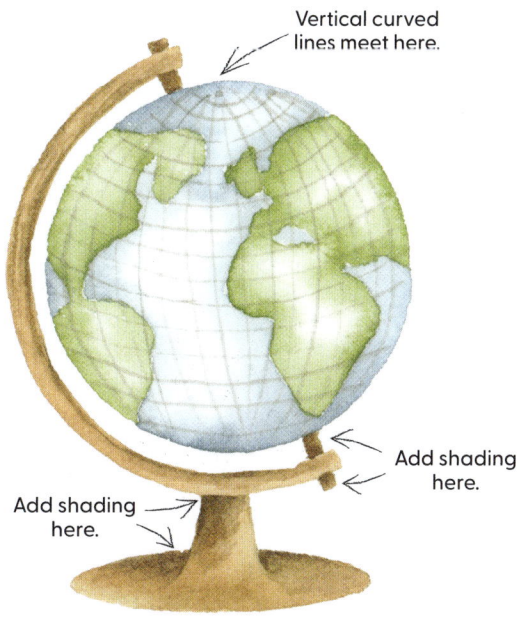

5

Vertical curved lines meet here.

Add shading here.

Add shading here.

Ivory Black

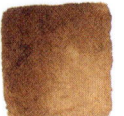

Burnt Umber

Mix 1: Payne's Gray and a little Burnt Umber

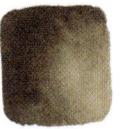

Mix 2: Burnt Umber and a little Indigo

Camera

STEPS

1. Draw the outline lightly in pencil.

2. With a pale mix 1 (gray), paint the gray sections, as shown.

3. Once dry, wet the inside of the black areas, then add Ivory Black around the edge of each, leaving highlights in the center. With Burnt Umber, paint the buttons on top, the first part of the strap and the main body of the camera. Add mix 2 (dark brown) to the edges to darken.

4. Once dry, paint the ring around the lens with Ivory Black, leaving a thin gap. Paint the inside of the strap with mix 2. Add shadow to the gray sections with mix 1.

5. With Ivory Black, paint three thin darker rings inside the ring painted in step 4. With mix 1, paint the lines surrounding the rectangles and circle in the top section. With mix 2, add detail to the buttons, paint lines at the top and bottom of the main body of the camera and then add fine squiggly lines for texture on the main brown area.

1
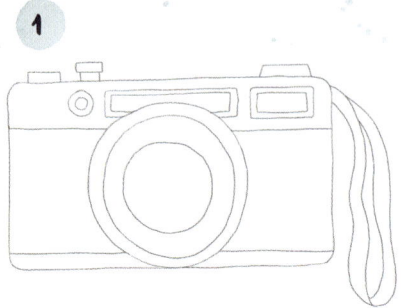

2

3
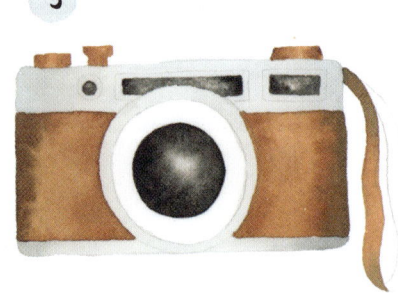

4
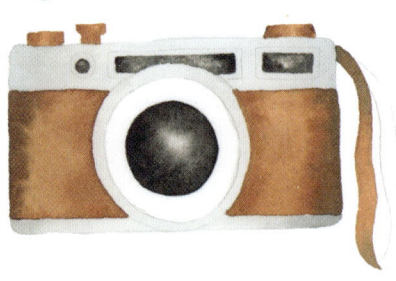

Add extra shadow here.

5
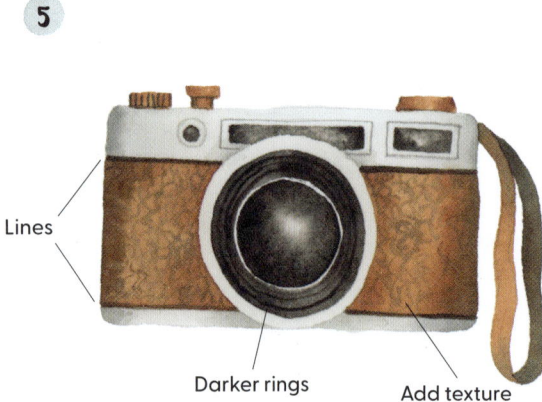

Lines

Darker rings

Add texture

Hot-Air Balloon

Burnt Umber

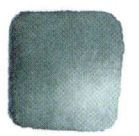
Mix 1: Winsor Blue (Red Shade) and a little Winsor Lemon

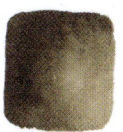
Mix 2: Burnt Umber and a little Indigo

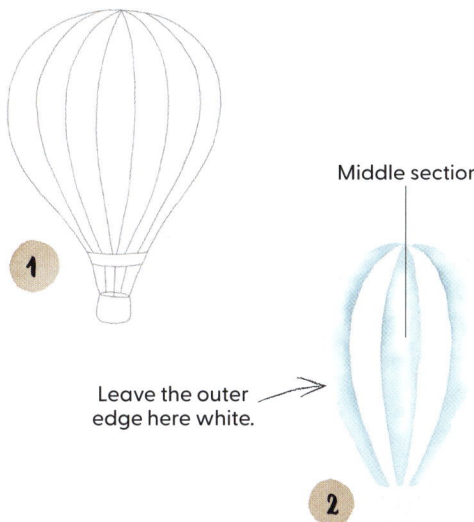

1

Middle section

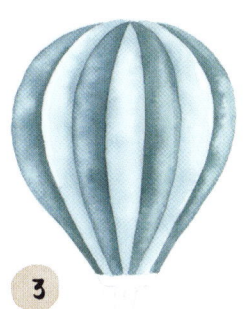

Leave the outer edge here white.

2

STEPS

1. Draw the outline lightly in pencil.

2. Wet the inside of the middle section and add pale mix 1 (green blue) to the edges. For the sections either side, add paint to the inner edges and blend outwards, leaving the outer edge white.

3. Once dry, paint the remaining sections with a darker mix 1, leaving or lifting highlights.

4. Paint the bottom rim of the balloon with mix 1. Paint the basket with Burnt Umber. Once dry, paint the inside of the basket with darker Burnt Umber.

5. With mix 2 (dark brown), paint the ropes and the pattern on the basket.

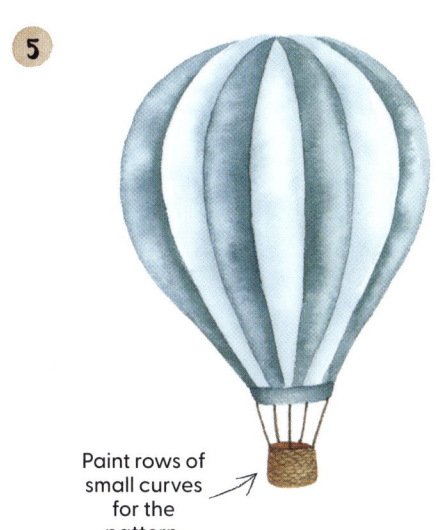

3

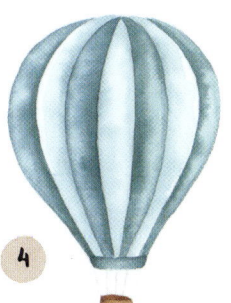

4

5

Paint rows of small curves for the pattern.

The highlights help make each section of the balloon look curved and inflated. Keep your paper towel close by for lifting paint.

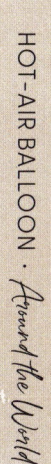

Winsor Blue
(Red Shade)

Payne's Gray

Mix 1: Permanent
Rose and a little
Winsor Lemon

Beach Hut

STEPS

1. Draw the outline lightly in pencil.

2. With Winsor Blue (Red Shade), paint the stripes and the diamond on the roof.

3. With very pale Payne's Gray, paint the outer edges of the white areas. With a slightly darker paint, add a shadow underneath the roof, the life ring and the door ledge.

4. With mix 1 (red), paint the two side sections of the life ring, lifting a highlight in each.

5. With dark Payne's Gray, add the door hinges, vertical lines on the door and grain (dashes) on all of the wood.

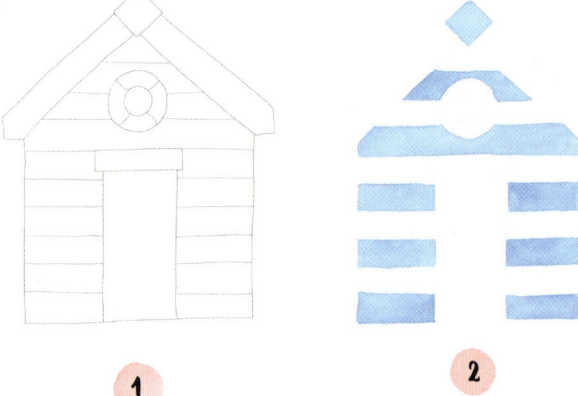

1

2

Follow the shape of the roof for the shadow.

3

4

5

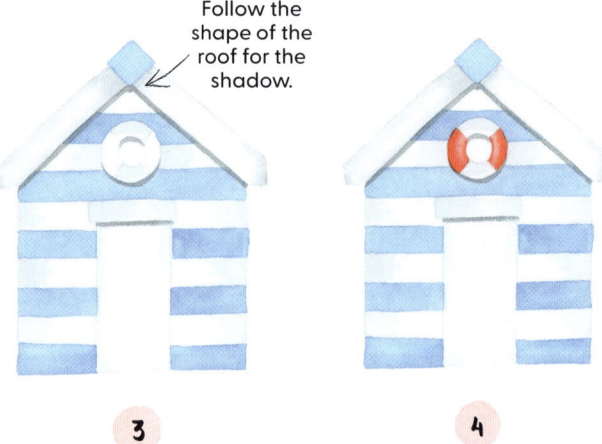

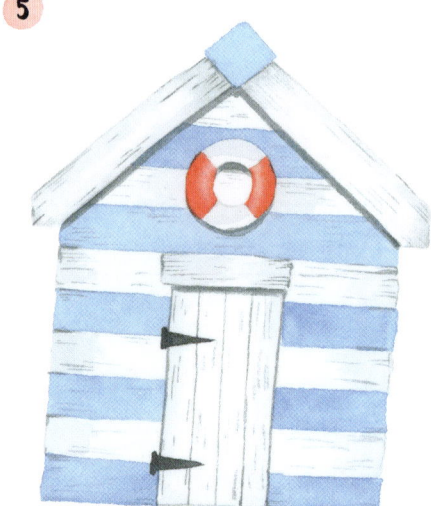

Try not to be too uniform with the grain. Paint lines close together and then leave patches of space.

Lighthouse

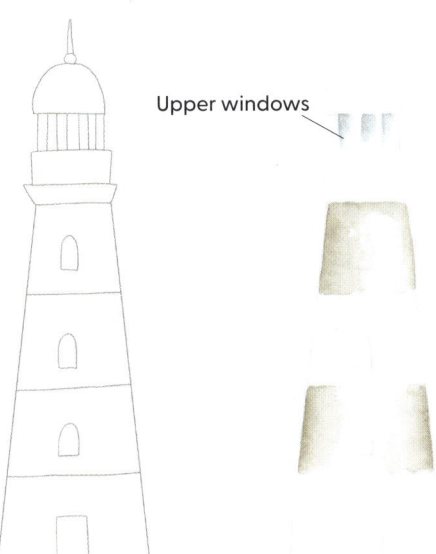

Upper windows

Payne's Gray

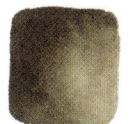

Mix 1: Burnt Umber and a little Indigo

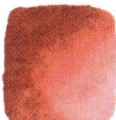

Mix 2: Permanent Rose and Burnt Umber

STEPS

1. Draw the outline lightly in pencil.

2. With a pale mix 1 (dark brown), add shadow to the edges of the white sections. Paint the upper windows with pale Payne's Gray.

3. With mix 2 (brown red), paint the remaining sections, making the edges darker.

4. With mix 1, add extra shading to the edges and to help define each section.

5. Paint the final details using a dark mix 1, including the windows, door and railing.

1

2

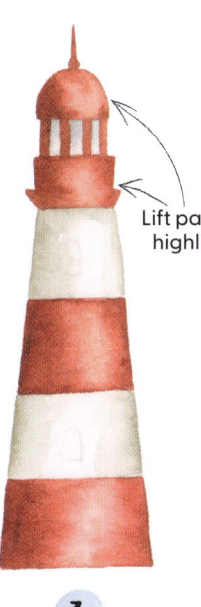

Lift paint for highlights

3

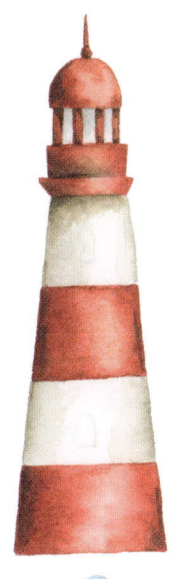

4

5

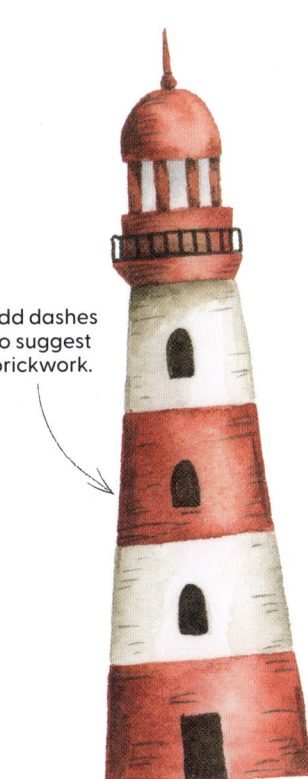

Add dashes to suggest brickwork.

Yellow Ochre

Burnt Umber

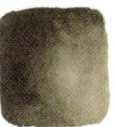

Mix 1: Burnt Umber and a little Indigo

Windmill

STEPS

1. Draw the outline lightly in pencil.

2. Paint the wall with Yellow Ochre, adding Burnt Umber to the edges.

3. Once dry, paint the roof with a pale mix 1 (dark brown) and then darken the edges.

4. With mix 1, paint four squares in each window. Add detail to the door and brick lines on the wall. Add a little shadow under the roof, under the windows and around the door.

5. With mix 1, paint two thick lines crossing each other for the sails.

6. Once dry, add a small circle to join the sails together and some shading to where the lines cross. Add criss-crossing lines to the sails.

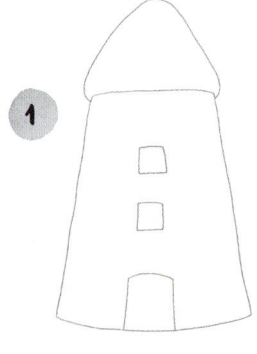

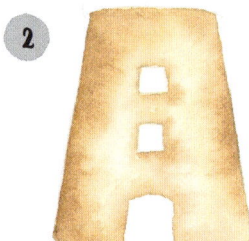

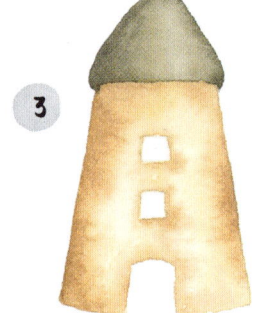

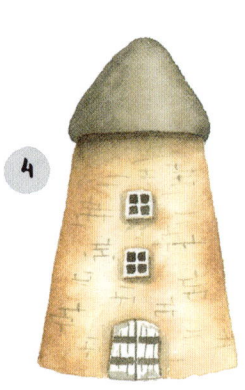

For the doors, paint fine vertical lines, then add thicker horizontal lines. Shade around the edge.

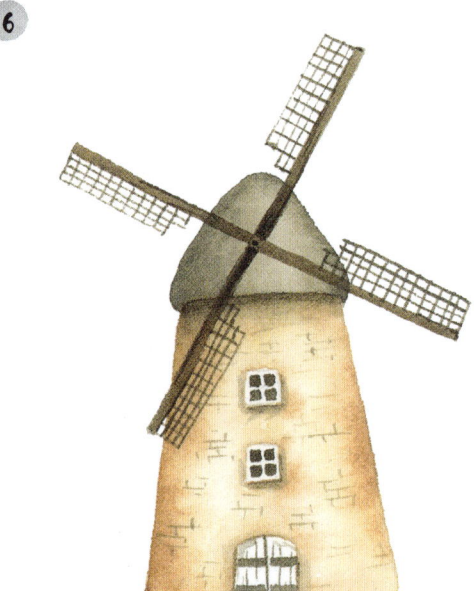

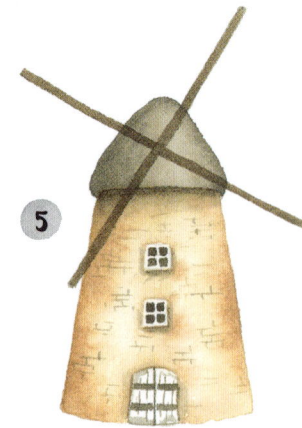

Boat

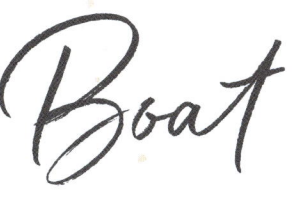

Payne's Gray

Yellow Ochre

Burnt Umber

Mix 1: Payne's Gray and a little Burnt Umber

STEPS

1. Draw the outline lightly in pencil.

2. Wet the inside of the left-hand sail and add a pale mix 1 (gray) to the edges. Paint the sail on the right with Payne's Gray and then darken the edges.

3. Paint the boat with Yellow Ochre, then add Burnt Umber at the edges. Paint the mast with Burnt Umber.

4. Paint stripes on the left-hand sail with Payne's Gray.

5. With Burnt Umber, paint the ropes and add detail to the boat.

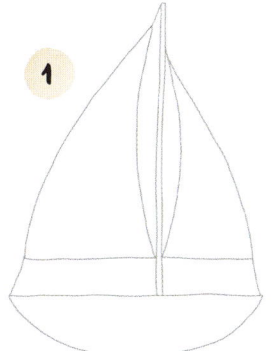

1

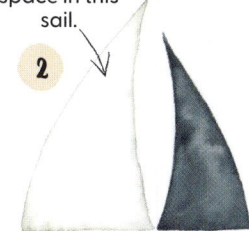

Leave plenty of white space in this sail.

2

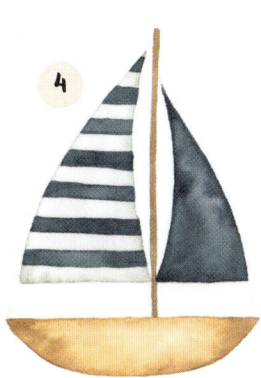

3

4

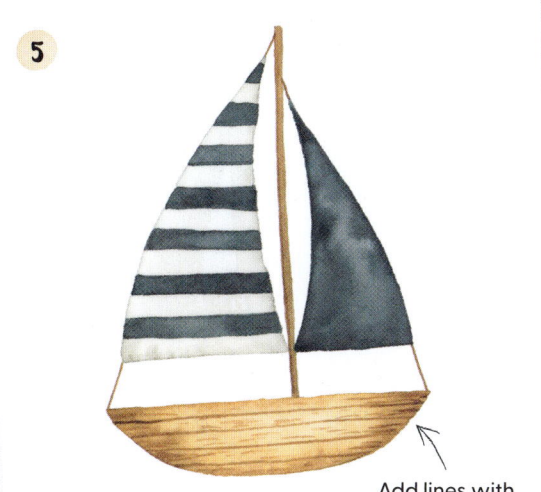

5

Add lines with dashes in between.

Have fun experimenting with different colors and patterns for the sails!

Burnt Umber

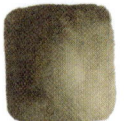

Mix 1: Burnt Umber and a little Indigo

Mix 2: Payne's Gray and a little Burnt Umber

Signpost

STEPS

1. Draw the outline lightly in pencil.

2. Paint the front of each sign with a variety of brown or gray mixes as shown.

3. With mix 1 (dark brown), paint the pole, lifting a highlight on the right-hand side.

4. Once dry, paint the edge of each sign with a darker version of the color used for the front.

5. With mix 1, add dots for nails, grain (dashes) on the wood and shadow on the pole under each sign.

1

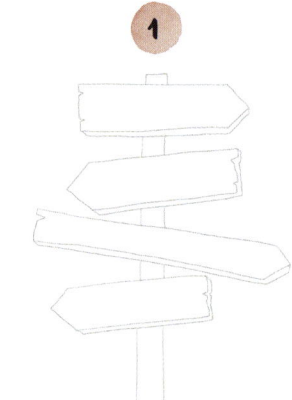

2

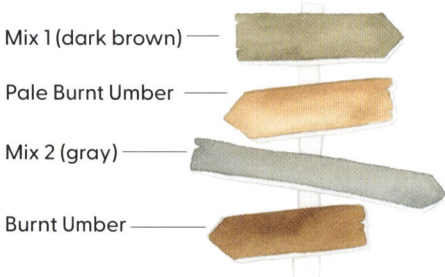

Mix 1 (dark brown)

Pale Burnt Umber

Mix 2 (gray)

Burnt Umber

3

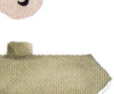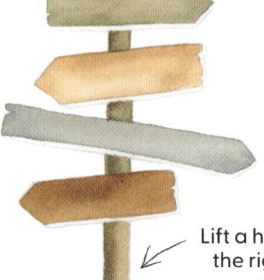

Lift a highlight on the right-hand side.

4

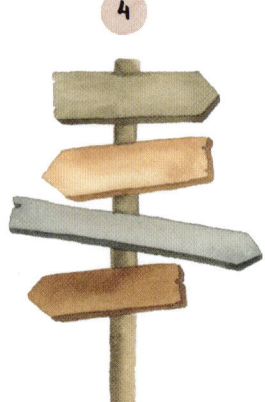

5

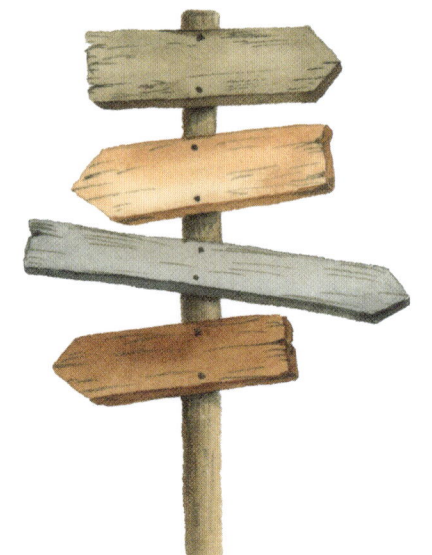

Tipi

STEPS

1. Draw the outline lightly in pencil.

2. Wet the outer fabric of the tent and then paint the edges with a pale mix 1 (dark brown).

3. Once dry, paint the tent poles with Burnt Umber.

4. With mix 1, add shading to the tent and the poles.

5. With a darker mix 1, paint the inside of the tent. Paint the ropes on the tent and on the poles.

6. With mix 2 (brown red), add patterns to the tent and to the trim at the top and bottom.

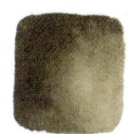

Burnt Umber

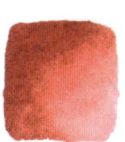

Mix 1: Burnt Umber and a little Indigo

Mix 2: Permanent Rose and Burnt Umber

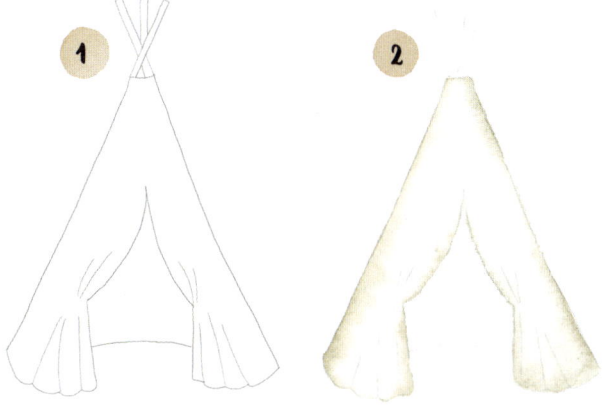

1

2

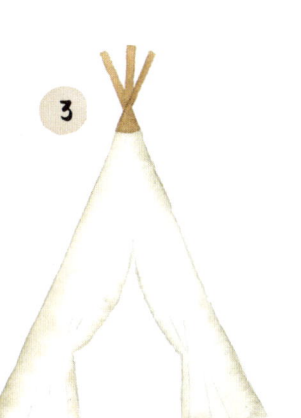

3

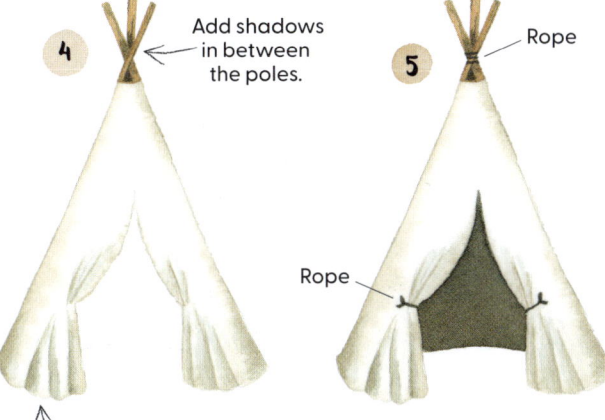

4

Add shadows in between the poles.

Add shading to the folds in the fabric.

5

Rope

Rope

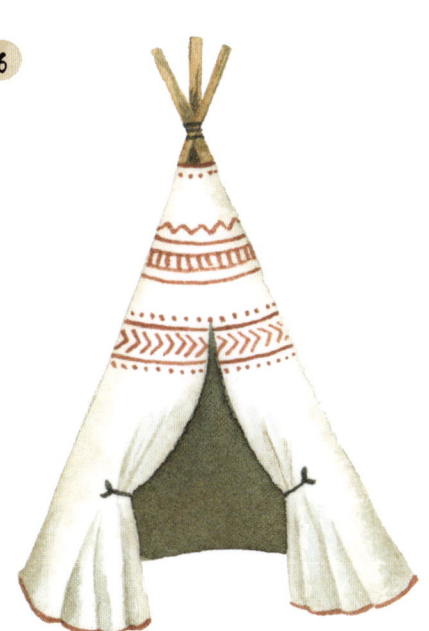

6

Yellow Ochre

Burnt Umber

Mix 1: Burnt Umber and a little Indigo

Mix 2: Payne's Gray and a little Burnt Umber

Plus opaque white

Castle Door

STEPS

1. Draw the outline lightly in pencil.

2. Paint the middle of the door with Yellow Ochre and then add in Burnt Umber and mix 1 (dark brown) around the edges. Darken the top and left-hand edges for a bit of shadow from the archway.

3. Once dry, paint the cobblestones, alternating between Yellow Ochre, Burnt Umber, mix 1 and mix 2 (gray), allowing the paints to bleed into each other.

4. With mix 1, paint a line down the center of the door, followed by slightly lighter lines either side. Add a bit of shading to each cobblestone, using a slightly darker mix of each color.

5. With a dark mix 1, paint the door handles, hinges and nails along the door and add the cement between the cobblestones. Add some extra markings to each cobblestone with mix 1 and an opaque white.

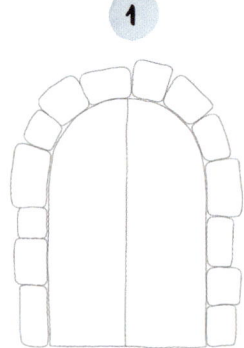

1

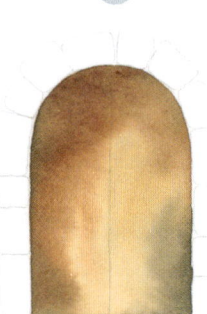

2

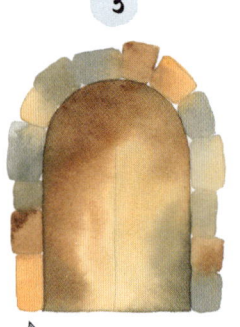

3

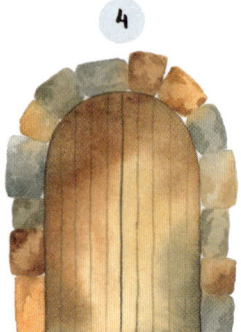

4

Start at the bottom left, and work up, around and down to the bottom right.

5

Each cobblestone is painted while the previous one is still wet so they bleed into each other and create a lovely natural aged affect.

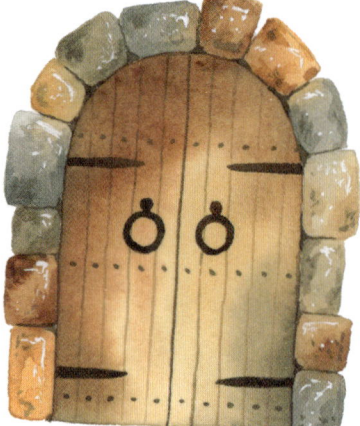

Scooter

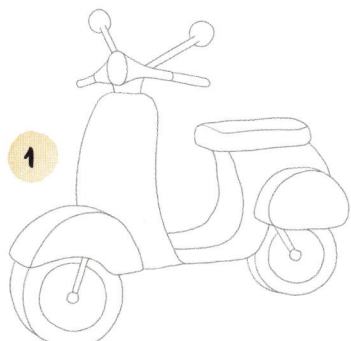

1

 Yellow Ochre

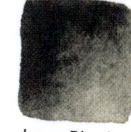 Ivory Black

 Burnt Umber

 Payne's Gray

 Mix 1: Payne's Gray and a little Burnt Umber

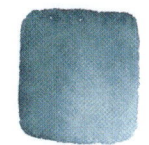 Mix 2: Winsor Blue (Red Shade) and a little Winsor Lemon

STEPS

1. Draw the outline lightly in pencil.

2. Paint the gray sections with mix 1 (gray) and the seat with Yellow Ochre. Once dry, paint the first blue sections as shown with mix 2 (blue).

3. Once dry, paint the remaining blue sections. With mix 1, paint shadows onto the wing mirrors and the light. Paint shadow and details onto the wheels.

4. With Ivory Black, paint the tyres, lifting a highlight on the left-hand edge of each. Paint the handles with Burnt Umber.

5. With mix 2 and Payne's Gray, darken any blue areas of the scooter as needed for more definition. With Burnt Umber, darken the edge of the seat. Add details on the wheels with Ivory Black.

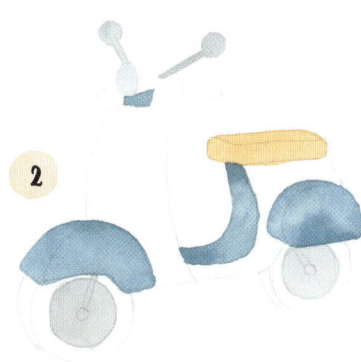

2

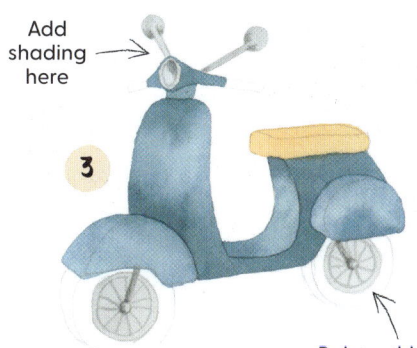

3

Add shading here →

Paint a thin circle around the edge and then add lines coming out from the center.

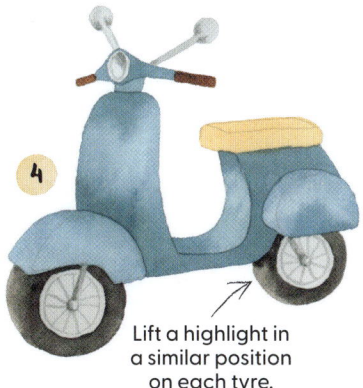

4

Lift a highlight in a similar position on each tyre.

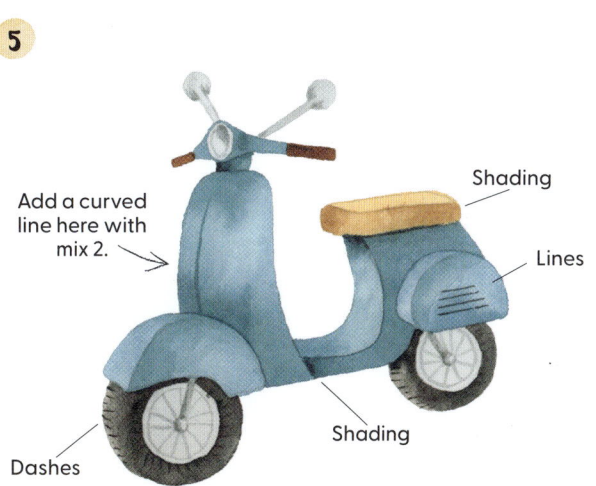

5

Add a curved line here with mix 2.

Shading

Lines

Shading

Dashes

Final Words

I hope this book has filled you with inspiration for painting throughout the year! Now, why not try some of the projects with different colors or patterns. You can use your paintings to create decorations for celebrations or events, or they will make beautiful gifts for loved ones. Bookmarks, gift tags and greeting cards are my favorite to make, but you can also make larger pieces to frame for wall art or cut pieces out to add to your journal.

Keep looking out for other subjects that inspire you as well, observing the shapes, colors and patterns. Remember to keep it simple, starting with an initial sketch and then working on the base layers with some beautiful wet-on-wet bleeds. Gradually build up the layers with more concentrated mixes and finer details. Experiment and explore and, most importantly, relax and have fun!

Try changing the flavor of the Donut, Smoothie or Ice Cream. For this chocolate icing, I used the dark brown mix made with Burnt Umber and a little Indigo.

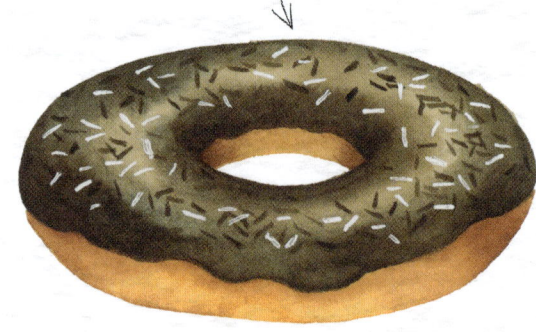

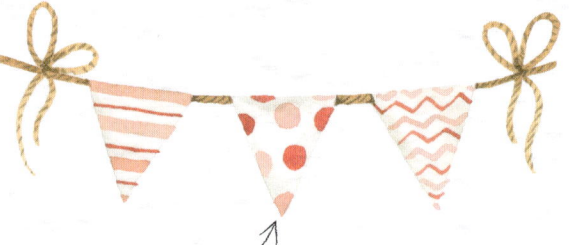

The Bunting project in the Celebrations section is easy to adapt for different events and color schemes.

There are many projects where you can play with the patterns and colors, such as the Flip-Flops, Presents, Rug and Boat.

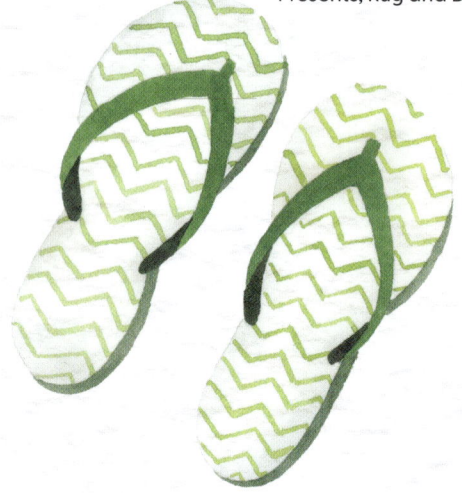

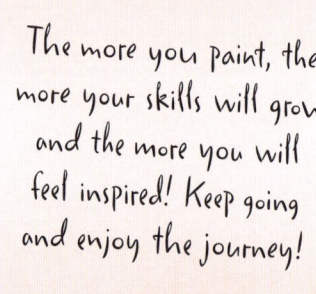

The more you paint, the more your skills will grow and the more you will feel inspired! Keep going and enjoy the journey!

ABOUT THE AUTHOR

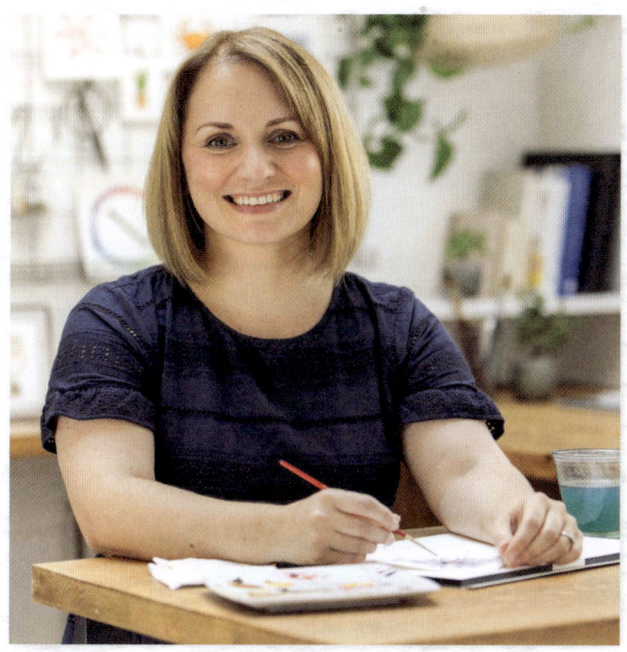

Sharone Stevens is a self-taught watercolor artist who has built a successful online business, teaching aspiring artists across the world how to paint. Using art as a form of therapy and self-care, she loves to share her passion for painting by inspiring, motivating and educating others on how it can be used for relaxation. She is a 'Top Teacher' on Skillshare and the author of the bestseller *Watercolor for the Soul*, published in March 2022. She lives just outside London with her husband, two children and two cats.

Website: sharonestevensdesign.co.uk

Instagram: @sharonestevensdesign

Sharone would love to see the paintings you create using this book!

Tag them on social media using #howtopaintit

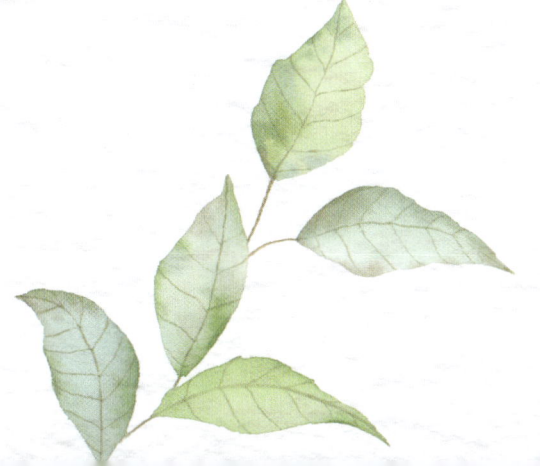

Acknowledgments

I am so grateful for the success of my first book, *Watercolor for the Soul*, and for the opportunity to create this second book, which has been such fun. Once again, I thank my husband, my biggest supporter, who always gives me advice and encouragement. I made my first book when my eldest was only little and now, a few years later, it has been lovely to involve him more in the process and discuss project ideas with him. To my youngest, born amid discussions about the book, thank you for being so good with your daytime naps and allowing me to work! I am also grateful for my wider family and friends who have supported and encouraged me throughout this journey. Finally, thank you to Ame and the team at David and Charles who have continued to believe in me and helped to turn my ideas into another book of which I am so proud.

A DAVID AND CHARLES BOOK
© David and Charles, Ltd 2025

David and Charles is an imprint of David and Charles, Ltd
Suite A, Tourism House, Pynes Hill, Exeter, EX2 5WS

Text and artwork © Sharone Stevens 2025
Layout and photography © David and Charles, Ltd 2025

First published in the UK and USA in 2025

Sharone Stevens has asserted her right to be identified
as author of this work in accordance with the Copyright,
Designs and Patents Act, 1988.

A catalogue record for this book is available from the
British Library.

ISBN-13: 9781446313770 paperback
ISBN-13: 9781446313794 EPUB

This book has been printed on paper from
approved suppliers and made from pulp
from sustainable sources.

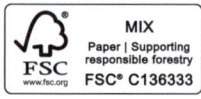

FSC MIX
Paper | Supporting responsible forestry
FSC® C136333

Printed in China through Asia Pacific Offset for:
David and Charles, Ltd
Suite A, Tourism House,
Pynes Hill, Exeter, EX2 5WS

10 9 8 7 6 5 4 3 2

Publishing Director: Ame Verso
Publishing Manager: Jeni Chown
Editor: Victoria Allen
Project Editor: Claire Coakley
Lead Designer: Sam Staddon
Designer: Anna Wade
Pre-press Designer: Sue Reansbury
Illustrations: Sharone Stevens
Art Direction: Sarah Rowntree
Photography: Jason Jenkins
Production Manager: Beverley Richardson

Full-size printable versions of the outlines are
available to download free from
www.bookmarkedhub.com. Search for this
book by the title or ISBN: the files can be
found under 'Book Extras'. Membership of
the Bookmarked online community is free.

David and Charles publishes high-quality
books on a wide range of subjects. For more
information visit www.davidandcharles.com.

Share your art with us on social media using
#dandcbooks and follow us on Facebook
and Instagram by searching for
@dandcbooks.

Layout of the digital edition of this book may
vary depending on reader hardware and
display settings.